The Dental Evidence Manual

How to Work, Document, and Defend

CUSTOMED

SERIES EDITORS

Dr. Ravinder Singh Channey

Ph.D. D. Sc. (Med. Journalism)

Ripudaman Singh Channey

B. Pharm., M.B.A. (Pharma Marketing)

The Dental Evidence Manual

How to Work, Document, and Defend

First Edition 2025.

For the use only of a Registered Medical Practionar or a Hospital, or a Laboratory.

Printed and Published by

CUSTOMED

D-71, Hauz Khas, New Delhi-110 016, India.

customedgroup.com

info@customedgroup.com

ISBN: 978-81-998476-9-9

DISCLAIMER

The editors, publisher, and printer of "***The Dental Evidence Manual: How to Work, Document, and Defend***" have made every effort to ensure that the information presented in this book is accurate, up-to-date, and in line with current medical and legal standards at the time of publication. However, the field of pain management and medico-legal issues is constantly evolving, and new developments may occur that are not reflected in this book.

This book is intended for educational and informational purposes only. It is not a substitute for professional medical advice, diagnosis, or treatment. The techniques and approaches discussed in this book should only be performed by licensed healthcare professionals in accordance with local, regional, and national laws, guidelines, and best practices. It is the responsibility of each reader to ensure compliance with all applicable legal, ethical, and professional standards within their jurisdiction before applying any of the techniques described herein.

Neither the authors, publisher, nor printer can be held liable for any direct, indirect, incidental, or consequential damages, including but not limited to injury, malpractice claims, legal actions, or any other legal disputes arising from the use or misuse of the information contained in this book. Readers are strongly advised to consult with appropriate legal and medical professionals for personalized guidance related to their specific circumstances.

By using this book, readers acknowledge and agree that the authors, publisher, and printer assume no responsibility or liability for any outcomes associated with the use of the material presented.

This disclaimer is applicable internationally and covers all legal jurisdictions.

The Dental Evidence Manual

How to Work, Document, and Defend

CUSTOMED

Dedication

To every student who has ever trembled

holding a dental elevator for the first time,

to every young surgeon

who stayed late to rewrite a case note,

and to every teacher

who insisted that ethics is not theory but habit -

this book is for you.

For the unseen hours spent sterilizing, documenting, explaining,

for the patients who trusted even when afraid,

and for the profession that demands steadiness over brilliance.

May this work remind you that diligence outlasts talent..

Dr. Ravinder Singh Channey

Ripudaman Singh Channey

Series Editors

Preface

Dentistry has never been only about enamel and instruments. It is a practice of judgment - hundreds of small decisions made every day under the quiet pressure of responsibility. Each local anesthetic, radiograph, or suture carries not just clinical consequence but legal weight.

This book was written to bring those two worlds together - science and accountability - into one usable volume. It is not another procedural manual or a collection of laws. It is a bridge: every clinical step explained with the same seriousness it deserves when questioned in retrospect.

The goal is clarity. For students, it turns scattered lessons into structured pathways. For practitioners, it restores discipline to habits that time has blurred. For institutions, it serves as a record of how defensible dentistry can be taught and practiced.

Every chapter follows one pattern - procedure, red flags, legal view, case learning, and references. That rhythm allows the reader to act safely in the clinic and to stand calmly in any inquiry. The language is straightforward, the tone unpretentious, and the intention transparent: to preserve both tissue and trust.

This work owes its depth to the many clinicians, teachers, and legal experts who have shown that excellence without documentation is luck - and luck is not a defense.

Dr. Ravinder Singh Channey

Ripudaman Singh Channey

Series Editors

CONTENTS

Every safe procedure begins long before the first incision. Sterilization, ergonomics, consent, and emergency readiness form the unseen architecture of dentistry. This opening section sets that foundation - the discipline of order, hygiene, and accountability that supports everything that follows.

After the inner tissues come the supporting ones. Periodontics demands consistency — prevention, charting, maintenance. It transforms daily observation into legal protection. This section links tooth survival to record survival, showing that what surrounds a tooth often decides its fate.

When disease or injury extends beyond routine care, surgery begins. This section expands the field from socket to skeleton - fractures, flaps, infections, and reconstruction - all carried out with traceable precision. It connects tissue handling with procedural accountability, merging operative skill and legal foresight.

- ***Section 7: Prosthodontics, Forensics, and Ethical Governance***

Every act of treatment ends in reconstruction or reflection. This final section unites prosthetic restoration, forensic responsibility, and ethical governance - closing the loop between clinical performance and professional conduct. It anchors the clinician's legacy in documented honesty and defensible practice.

SECTION 1

Foundations and Clinical Setup

Dentistry may appear to begin with the tooth, but it truly begins with order. A sterile instrument, a stable posture, a complete consent form - these are not administrative tasks; they are the unseen procedures that make every clinical act possible. Foundations define professionalism, and this section restores that forgotten truth.

Here the reader revisits what most rush past during training: how sterility cycles are validated, how operator posture saves a career, how every local anesthetic injection should be planned with both physiology and liability in mind. It moves from the tangible - the sterilizer log, the chair position - to the intangible but equally binding: how to document a patient's risk factors, or how to prove that consent was truly informed.

Each chapter functions like a calibration drill. The first ensures asepsis isn't just practiced but proven. The next trains ergonomics into muscle memory so fatigue never blunts precision. Others teach how to manage anesthesia failures safely, how to plan analgesia rationally, and how to turn documentation from a burden into protection.

By the end of this section, a dentist can run a clinic that is physically efficient, legally defensible, and ethically grounded. These early pages demand discipline, not creativity - the kind of discipline that later allows creativity to thrive safely in every treatment you perform..

CHAPTER 1

Principles of Sterilization and Infection Control

Cleanliness is not decoration in dentistry; it is discipline. Every postoperative infection, unexplained fever, or wound breakdown draws one question - was sterilization complete and documented? This chapter transforms that routine task into a clear, stepwise science that protects both patient and practitioner.

Purpose and Indications

Sterilization eliminates all microorganisms including spores from instruments and surfaces that contact oral tissues. Infection control prevents transmission between patients, operator, and environment. It applies universally, regardless of the complexity of the procedure [1].

Preparation and Zoning

Every dental clinic must function through three fixed zones.

1. **Contaminated zone** - where used instruments are collected and cleaned.

2. **Clean zone** - where instruments are packed and sterilized.

3. **Sterile zone** - where processed instruments are stored.

Movement must always be one-way. Any crossover or backflow between zones breaks the aseptic chain and is indefensible during inspection [2].

- ***Step 1: Decontamination and Cleaning***

Rinse used instruments under running water to remove visible debris. Immerse them in an ultrasonic cleaner with enzymatic detergent for 10 minutes. Manual scrubbing is avoided to prevent puncture injuries.

Red flag: Hand scrubbing of scalers or files causes sharps injury and spreads hepatitis B or C among staff. Ultrasonic cleaning must never be skipped.

- ***Step 2: Drying and Inspection***

Dry all instruments with lint-free cloth or compressed air. Examine under bright light for stains, cracks, or rust. Discard defective items.

Red flag: Moist instruments trap steam, leading to incomplete sterilization. Cracked handles harbor debris that resists autoclaving.

- ***Step 3: Packaging***

Arrange instruments in sterilization pouches with both internal and external indicators. Label each pouch with date, cycle number, and initials. Do not overfill or fold edges.

Red flag: Overfilled pouches and loosely sealed corners cause cold zones inside the autoclave. Any pouch that emerges wet or torn must be reprocessed.

- ***Step 4: Sterilization***

Load the autoclave properly, allowing steam circulation. Run at 121°C for 30 minutes or 134°C for 3 - 5 minutes depending on the load. Verify pressure and temperature before each cycle.

Red flag: Mixing wrapped and unwrapped loads or early door opening breaks sterility. Skipping the warm-up phase often leaves internal cold spots [3][4].

- ***Step 5: Monitoring***

Use three checks for every cycle - mechanical (gauges), chemical (color strips), and biological (weekly spore test). Record all results in the sterilization logbook.

Red flag: A failed spore test ignored or repeated without correction is professional negligence. Elective care must stop until sterility is reconfirmed.

- ***Step 6: Storage and Handling***

Allow packs to cool before storage. Keep them in closed, dry cabinets away from sinks or sunlight. Use a first-in, first-out system.

Red flag: Handling pouches with contaminated gloves or storing near moisture sources leads to recontamination. Even intact pouches lose sterility if stored for more than three months.

- ***Step 7: Record Keeping***

Record the date, cycle parameters, operator, indicator results, and corrective actions. Retain records for a minimum of two years.

Red flag: Incomplete or missing logs turn a single infection into a defenseless lawsuit. Proper documentation proves diligence even when infection occurs from unrelated causes [5].

- ***Step 8: Surface and Environmental Decontamination***

Clean all contact surfaces with intermediate-level disinfectant before and after each patient. Flush chair waterlines for two minutes each morning and thirty seconds between patients.

Red flag: Neglecting waterline flushing allows biofilm growth and bacterial aerosols. This failure is easy to prove during any audit [7].

- ***Step 9: Waste Disposal and Sharps Management***

Segregate biomedical waste correctly - red bag for disposables, blue or white container for glass and metal, yellow for tissue and extracted teeth, puncture-proof container for sharps. Never recap needles with both hands.

Red flag: Improper segregation violates Biomedical Waste Rules 2016 and invites prosecution. Every needlestick must be logged and managed under hepatitis B and HIV protocol [8].

- ***Step 10: Post-Exposure Protocol***

Step 10a: Wash the site immediately with soap and water.

Red flag: Use of alcohol or antiseptic solutions delays wound healing and interferes with testing.

Step 10b: Encourage mild bleeding but avoid squeezing the wound.

Red flag: Squeezing spreads contamination deeper into tissue.

Step 10c: Report within one hour. Baseline test operator and patient, and begin prophylaxis as per national guidelines.

Red flag: Delay beyond 24 hours nullifies prophylaxis benefit and constitutes negligence [9].

Defensibility and Documentation Anchors

Sterilization failures are classified as institutional negligence. Maintain autoclave validation reports, spore-test results, biomedical waste records, and staff vaccination files. Display a written infection control policy. Photograph sterilization areas monthly for internal documentation. These records convert a possible accusation into a defensible case [10].

Case Study

A 34-year-old patient developed postoperative cellulitis following a routine third molar extraction. Investigation revealed that the elevator used had been autoclaved without proper drying, leaving residual moisture inside the joint. Cultures showed spore-forming bacilli. The patient filed a negligence claim citing cross-infection. The clinic had no sterilization log or biological indicator records for that week. The claim was settled against the practitioner, and the license was suspended for three months.

Case Learnings

1. Incomplete drying before autoclaving causes sterilization failure even when temperature and time are correct.
2. Every cycle must have written or electronic proof of parameters and indicator results.
3. Sterilization logs are legal documents; their absence equates to presumed guilt.
4. Cross-infection can arise from a single unrecorded breach; only documentation proves intent and diligence.
5. Periodic audits and staff training prevent complacency that often leads to such events.

Quick Checklist

- Instrument flow only one direction
- Cycle data recorded each time
- Weekly spore test done and filed
- All pouches dry, sealed, and dated
- Disposable items never reused
- Protective barriers replaced between patients
- Surfaces disinfected before each patient

- Waterlines flushed regularly
- Biomedical waste segregated properly
- Exposure incidents documented and followed up

References

1. *Centers for Disease Control and Prevention. Guidelines for Infection Control in Dental Health-Care Settings. MMWR 2003;52(RR-17):1 - 61.*
2. *World Health Organization. Infection Prevention and Control in Health Care. Geneva: WHO; 2018.*
3. *Miller CH, Palenik CJ. Infection Control and Management of Hazardous Materials for the Dental Team. 6th ed. Elsevier; 2018.*
4. *Harte JA. Standard and Transmission-Based Precautions: Infection Prevention for Dental Health Care Personnel. J Am Dent Assoc. 2010;141(5):572 - 581.*
5. *Occupational Safety and Health Administration. Bloodborne Pathogens and Needlestick Prevention. OSHA; 2020.*
6. *Kohn WG et al. CDC Guidelines for Infection Control in Dental Health-Care Settings. 2003.*
7. *Pankhurst CL, Coulter W. Do contaminated dental unit waterlines pose a risk of infection? Br Dent J. 2007;203(9):557 - 562.*
8. *Government of India. Biomedical Waste Management Rules. Ministry of Environment, Forest and Climate Change; 2016.*
9. *Centers for Disease Control and Prevention. Updated U.S. Public Health Service Guidelines for the Management of Occupational Exposures to HIV and Recommendations for Postexposure Prophylaxis. 2013.*
10. *Dental Council of India. Clinical Establishment and Infection Control Standards. 2022.*

CHAPTER 2

Clinical Ergonomics and Operator Positioning

In dentistry, fatigue is a silent thief. It steals precision, comfort, and professionalism. Wrong posture and poor ergonomics don't just hurt the operator's back; they shorten careers, reduce concentration, and increase procedural errors. This chapter teaches how to work longer, safer, and smarter - protecting both your spine and your license.

Purpose and Indications

Clinical ergonomics ensures efficient posture, balanced operator-assistant movement, and optimal visibility without strain. The aim is to prevent musculoskeletal disorders, maintain procedural control, and guarantee patient comfort throughout treatment [1].

Preparation and Zoning

Every dental operatory should have clearly defined work zones.

1. **Operator zone** - the area in which the dentist performs all active procedures.

2. **Assistant zone** - the field for four-handed dentistry, suction, and instrument transfer.

3. **Static zone** - the location of heavy or rarely moved equipment such as curing lights.

4. **Transfer zone** - the safe path for passing instruments.

Red flag: Overlapping zones between operator and assistant cause accidental instrument drops, needle sticks, and tray contamination [2].

- ***Step 1: Operator Posture and Seating***

Sit upright with the spine in its natural S-curve. Keep shoulders relaxed, elbows close to the body, and forearms parallel to the floor. Adjust stool height so that thighs are parallel and feet flat.

Red flag: Forward bending more than 20 degrees or twisted neck posture leads to chronic cervical strain. Repeated violation of ergonomic posture during procedures can be traced to operator fatigue and recorded as contributory negligence in injury claims.

- ***Step 2: Patient Positioning***

Adjust the patient chair so the mouth is at the level of the operator's elbow. For maxillary work, recline the chair until the occlusal plane is about 60 - 70 degrees to the floor. For mandibular work, keep the chair more upright.

Red flag: Improper headrest adjustment or excessive neck extension can cause transient syncope or cervical discomfort in patients. Any incident of fainting during position change must be recorded with vital signs and reported [3].

- ***Step 3: Operator Clock Positions***

For a right-handed operator, use the 8 o'clock to 12 o'clock positions depending on the quadrant being treated. For a left-handed operator, use 12 o'clock to 4 o'clock.

Red flag: Working constantly from one clock position (for convenience) increases back asymmetry and shoulder imbalance, leading to early musculoskeletal disorders.

- ***Step 4: Four-Handed Dentistry and Instrument Transfer***

The assistant should sit 4 - 6 inches higher than the operator for clear visibility. Instruments are passed below the patient's chin with a smooth rolling motion, never over the patient's face.

Red flag: Passing sharp instruments over the patient's face or chest can lead to accidental injury. Failure to train assistants properly is a preventable and legally traceable risk [4].

- ***Step 5: Lighting and Field Visibility***

Position the dental light directly above the patient's mouth for maxillary work and angled slightly down for mandibular work. The operator's line of sight should align with the beam without glare. Use magnification loupes for better posture.

Red flag: Poor illumination causes the operator to lean forward repeatedly, leading to neck fatigue and decreased precision. Inadequate lighting is also cited as a contributing factor in procedural errors [5].

- ***Step 6: Instrument Layout and Accessibility***

Arrange instruments in the order of use from left to right (for right-handed operators). Keep the most frequently used tools within the primary reach zone of 20 inches.

Redflag: Searching for instruments during a procedure breaks aseptic flow and increases contamination risk. Cluttered trays are often photographed during audits as evidence of non-standard infection control [6].

- ***Step 7: Microbreaks and Stretching***

Schedule brief pauses every 40 - 45 minutes. Stretch neck, shoulders, and wrists. Perform gentle back extensions between patients.

Red flag: Ignoring microbreaks accumulates static muscle load, leading to long-term disability claims and decreased procedural consistency.

- ***Step 8: Documentation and Record Keeping***

For every staff member, maintain an ergonomics checklist, posture audit forms, and record of training in four-handed dentistry. These records prove workplace safety compliance.

Red flag: Lack of ergonomic compliance records can be cited under occupational health violation in case of staff injury or compensation claims [7].

Defensibility and Documentation Anchors

Ergonomic compliance is part of occupational safety law. Maintain records of chair adjustments, stool types, and assistant training sessions. In case of injury to staff or patient due to equipment positioning, these documents establish that due diligence was followed [8].

Case Study

A 42-year-old dentist complained of chronic shoulder and wrist pain after years of practicing endodontics without ergonomic aids. He routinely worked from the 9 o'clock position for all quadrants. Over time, he developed cervical spondylosis and carpal tunnel syndrome, rendering him unfit for clinical practice for several months. A labor inspection revealed absence of ergonomic risk assessments and no documentation of staff training. The clinic faced occupational health penalties and insurance denial due to lack of preventive measures.

Case Learnings

1. Consistent posture errors accumulate into irreversible musculoskeletal damage.
2. Ergonomic checklists and staff training are legal requirements, not optional extras.
3. Periodic audits of chair, stool, and light position prevent chronic strain.
4. Proper assistant positioning reduces operator fatigue and improves procedural safety.
5. Ergonomics is preventive medicine for the operator; neglect of it harms both health and reputation.

Quick Checklist

- Spine upright and neutral
- Elbows close, shoulders relaxed
- Patient chair adjusted to elbow level
- Lighting centered, glare-free
- Assistant higher by 4 - 6 inches
- Instrument tray within easy reach
- Microbreaks every 45 minutes
- All ergonomic training documented

References

1. *Valachi B, Valachi K. Mechanisms leading to musculoskeletal disorders in dentistry. J Am Dent Assoc. 2003;134(10):1344 - 1350.*
2. *Gupta A, Ankola AV, Hebbal M. Dental ergonomics to combat musculoskeletal disorders: a review. Int J Occup Saf Ergon. 2013;19(4):561 - 571.*
3. *Rundcrantz BL, Johnsson B, Moritz U. Cervical pain and discomfort among dentists. Swed Dent J. 1991;15(3):105 - 112.*
4. *Finkbeiner BL. Four-handed dentistry revisited. J Contemp Dent Pract. 2000;1(4):1 - 16.*
5. *Morse T, Bruneau H, Dussetschleger J. Musculoskeletal disorders of the neck and shoulder in dental practitioners. Appl Ergon. 2010;41(3):444 - 450.*
6. *Rucker LM, Sunell S. Ergonomic risk factors associated with clinical dentistry. J Calif Dent Assoc. 2002;30(2):139 - 148.*
7. *Occupational Safety and Health Administration. Ergonomics: Prevention of Musculoskeletal*

Disorders in Dental Practice. OSHA; 2020.

8. *Dental Council of India. Occupational Safety Standards in Dental Clinics. 2022.*

CHAPTER 3

Instrumentation, Maintenance, and Turnover Protocols

A well-maintained instrument tray is the true measure of a disciplined dental clinic. Instruments are the extension of the clinician's skill, and their cleanliness, sharpness, and readiness directly affect accuracy, speed, and infection control. Neglected maintenance or poorly organized turnover creates clinical delays, operator fatigue, and medico-legal exposure. This chapter builds the method to manage instruments as critical assets, not disposable tools.

Purpose and Indications

Instrumentation protocols ensure that every instrument used in dental practice remains functional, safe, and traceable. The goal is to minimize procedural interruptions, ensure asepsis, and maintain accountability for every instrument used in patient care [1].

Preparation and Zoning

Divide the clinic into three areas:

1. **Procedure zone** - where sterilized instruments are used during treatment.

2. **Cleaning and maintenance zone** - where decontamination and sharpening are performed.

3. **Storage zone** - where sterilized and categorized instruments are kept for future use.

Red flag: Mixing sterilized and contaminated instruments in the same tray or workspace nullifies the sterilization process and violates infection control standards [2].

- ***Step 1: Instrument Classification and Identification***

Categorize instruments into critical, semi-critical, and non-critical items.

Mark each with color codes or laser-etched identification numbers for traceability. Maintain a master inventory sheet.

Red flag: Unlabeled or indistinguishable instruments make sterilization validation and loss tracking impossible. Missing instruments after a procedure raise suspicion of foreign-body retention or negligence.

- ***Step 2: Pre-Use Inspection***

Before every procedure, check for corrosion, misalignment, loose joints, or dull edges. Confirm function and integrity of locking mechanisms in surgical instruments.

Red flag: Using worn or damaged instruments increases tissue trauma, prolongs surgery, and risks breakage inside the mouth. Breakage incidents are legally indefensible if prior inspection is undocumented [3].

- ***Step 3: Sharpening and Maintenance***

Perform sharpening of scalers, curettes, elevators, and chisels on a weekly schedule using Arkansas or ceramic stones. Use magnification to confirm bevel symmetry. Apply light lubricant film after cleaning to prevent corrosion.

Red flag: Excessive sharpening changes instrument angulation and cutting efficiency. Poorly maintained instruments reduce tactile control and increase operator fatigue, directly impacting procedural outcomes [4].

- ***Step 4: Organization and Tray Setup***

Arrange instruments in procedural sequence - examination, preparation, operative, and finishing tools. Maintain separate trays for restorative, surgical, and endodontic setups. Each tray should include a checklist for quick verification before sterilization and before procedure start.

Red flag: Missing instruments discovered mid-procedure break concentration and prolong chair time. Such errors reflect poor turnover management and can be cited as contributory negligence if patient harm follows [5].

- ***Step 5: Instrument Turnover During Procedures***

Use four-handed technique for efficient turnover. The assistant should pass instruments below the patient's chin and retrieve used ones immediately. All used instruments must go into a designated receptacle for post-use cleaning.

Red flag: Piling instruments on the bracket table during procedures increases contamination risk. Accidental needle or bur injuries occur most often during unorganized turnover.

- ***Step 6: Post-Procedure Processing***

Immediately after completion, remove debris under running water and immerse used instruments in enzymatic detergent. Avoid drying of blood residues. Record used tray identification in the logbook.

Red flag: Allowing debris to dry on instruments within 30 minutes of use makes cleaning difficult and incomplete, resulting in sterilization failure [6].

- ***Step 7: Storage and Stock Rotation***

After sterilization, store instruments in labeled drawers or sealed cassettes. Maintain a first-in, first-out rotation to prevent long-term storage beyond sterility validity. Conduct monthly inventory audits.

Red flag: Unsealed or open storage invites airborne contamination and rusting. Absence of stock rotation leads to expired sterilization dates and missing documentation in audits [7].

- ***Step 8: Record Keeping and Traceability***

Maintain an electronic or manual log of each tray: date of use, operator name, sterilization cycle number, and any maintenance performed. Use barcoding or QR tagging systems for traceability.

Red flag: Failure to track instruments individually breaks the chain of accountability. In any cross-infection or retained-instrument claim, missing trace records shift the liability entirely onto the clinician [8].

Defensibility and Documentation Anchors

All instrument maintenance and sterilization cycles must be traceable through dated records. Maintain service reports for autoclaves, ultrasonic cleaners, and handpiece sterilizers. Keep a log of instrument purchases, repairs, and disposals. During medico-legal investigation, these documents demonstrate compliance with national infection control and biomedical waste regulations [9].

Case Study

A 55-year-old patient underwent flap surgery for chronic periodontitis. Two days later, swelling and suppuration appeared at the surgical site. Culture identified contamination with non-tuberculous mycobacteria. Investigation revealed that the surgical curette used had micro-pitting and rusting due to skipped weekly maintenance. The instrument had not been inspected for over six months, and the clinic had no maintenance records. The infection spread to adjacent tissues, requiring hospitalization. The case resulted in compensation due to proven negligence in equipment upkeep.

Case Learnings

1. Every instrument requires scheduled inspection and maintenance; age of use must be tracked.
2. Documentation of maintenance and sterilization records is the only legal defense against contamination claims.
3. Visual inspection and sharpening logs must form part of the sterilization protocol.
4. Instruments with visible corrosion should be replaced immediately; repair logs cannot excuse unsafe use.
5. Routine audits prevent cumulative negligence that often remains unnoticed until complications arise.

Quick Checklist

- All instruments categorized and labeled
- Pre-use inspection documented
- Sharpening performed weekly
- Trays arranged by procedural sequence
- Assistant turnover practiced and safe
- Used instruments cleaned within 30 minutes
- Sterilized instruments stored sealed and dated
- Inventory rotation followed monthly

- Maintenance and sterilization logs updated daily
- Traceability records available on request

References

1. *Miller CH, Palenik CJ. Infection Control and Management of Hazardous Materials for the Dental Team. 6th ed. Elsevier; 2018.*
2. *World Health Organization. Infection Prevention and Control in Health Care. Geneva: WHO; 2018.*
3. *Rutala WA, Weber DJ. Disinfection, sterilization, and antisepsis: An overview. Am J Infect Control. 2019;47A:S2 - S9.*
4. *Zarra T, Lambrianidis T. Maintenance and care of dental instruments and equipment. Dent Clin North Am. 2017;61(4):809 - 825.*
5. *Rucker LM, Sunell S. Ergonomic risk factors associated with clinical dentistry. J Calif Dent Assoc. 2002;30(2):139 - 148.*
6. *Harte JA. Standard and Transmission-Based Precautions in Dental Infection Control. J Am Dent Assoc. 2010;141(5):572 - 581.*
7. *Centers for Disease Control and Prevention. Guidelines for Infection Control in Dental Health-Care Settings. MMWR 2003;52(RR-17):1 - 61.*
8. *Government of India. Biomedical Waste Management Rules. Ministry of Environment, Forest and Climate Change; 2016.*
9. *Dental Council of India. Clinical Establishment and Infection Control Standards. 2022.*

CHAPTER 4

Local Anesthesia - Pharmacology, Techniques, and Failures

Local anesthesia is the most frequently performed procedure in dentistry and the most underestimated. Its success determines patient cooperation; its failure exposes the operator to panic, injury, or legal complaint. A technically perfect extraction or restoration means little if pain control is inadequate. This chapter outlines how to achieve predictable anesthesia, prevent complications, and document defensible practice.

Purpose and Indications

Local anesthesia aims to create reversible loss of pain sensation in a defined area without altering consciousness. It is indicated for virtually all operative and surgical dental procedures requiring painless field control. Its safe administration relies on accurate anatomy, dosage calculation, aspiration technique, and vigilant observation [1].

Preparation and Pre-Anesthetic Assessment

Review medical history, allergies, systemic diseases, and medications. Evaluate for hepatic or renal impairment, pregnancy, bleeding disorders, and cardiovascular conditions. Record baseline vitals. Confirm consent and explain expected duration of numbness.

Red flag: Failure to elicit drug allergy or medical history before injection can result in anaphylaxis or drug interaction - legally indefensible as a "preventable event" [2].

- ***Step 1: Selection of Anesthetic Agent***

Choose agent based on procedure length and patient profile. Lidocaine

2% with 1:100,000 adrenaline remains standard; alternatives include articaine, mepivacaine, and bupivacaine for longer duration.

Red flag: Using vasoconstrictor-containing agents in uncontrolled cardiac or hyperthyroid patients without physician clearance can cause hypertensive crises or arrhythmias. Always note agent name, concentration, and vasoconstrictor ratio in records [3].

- ***Step 2: Calculation of Maximum Dose***

Determine safe dosage by weight. For lidocaine, maximum is 4.4 mg/kg (adult average 7 carpules). Always aspirate before injecting.

Red flag: Exceeding maximum dose or failing to aspirate leads to systemic toxicity. Documentation of aspiration is mandatory; its absence shifts liability completely to the operator [4].

- ***Step 3: Armamentarium Check***

Inspect syringe, cartridge, and needle integrity before use. Discard expired or cloudy solutions. Confirm free needle flow and ensure sharpness.

Red flag: Cracked cartridges or blunt needles cause tissue trauma, hematoma, and injection failure. Reuse of needles or cartridges is indefensible under infection control standards [5].

- ***Step 4: Injection Technique and Landmark Identification***

Position patient semi-reclined, with mouth and head aligned for access. Identify anatomical landmarks before penetration. For infiltration, insert at mucobuccal fold; for block, target the foramen or nerve trunk.

Red flag: Blind insertion or uncertain landmark identification causes anesthesia failure or nerve injury. Nerve damage during blind injection without anatomical verification constitutes negligent practice [6].

- ***Step 5: Aspiration and Slow Injection***

Aspirate in two planes before every 0.2 - 0.3 ml deposit. Inject slowly, 1 ml per 60 seconds. Observe patient response.

Red flag: Rapid injection or ignoring aspiration results in intravascular administration, dizziness, or cardiovascular collapse. Any sudden systemic reaction requires immediate emergency response and event documentation [7].

- ***Step 6: Observation During Latency***

Wait 2 - 5 minutes for onset. Check for tissue blanching and soft tissue numbness before proceeding.

Red flag: Proceeding before full onset increases likelihood of pain and sudden movement, leading to injury from rotating instruments. Continuing despite patient distress can be considered assault under medicolegal review [8].

- ***Step 7: Management of Failed Anesthesia***

Reassess landmarks, raise injection point by 3 - 5 mm, or switch to alternative techniques such as intraligamentary or intraosseous injections. For inflamed tissue, use articaine infiltration if not contraindicated.

Red flag: Repeated blind reinjection without diagnostic reassessment risks nerve trauma and hematoma formation. Document every repeat attempt and the patient's tolerance [9].

- ***Step 8: Management of Complications***

If systemic toxicity occurs (tinnitus, dizziness, tremors, or seizure), stop immediately, position patient supine, maintain airway, administer oxygen, and prepare for emergency management.

Red flag: Delayed recognition of systemic toxicity or failure to initiate oxygen therapy worsens prognosis. Absence of resuscitation equipment is a punishable safety lapse [10].

- ***Step 9: Postoperative Advice***

Warn patients not to bite or chew until numbness resolves. Avoid hot foods. Record total volume administered and onset duration.

Red flag: Failure to advise patients on self-inflicted injury precautions (lip or cheek biting in children) may lead to preventable tissue trauma and complaint of negligence [11].

Defensibility and Documentation Anchors

Each injection must have traceable documentation: agent name, concentration, volume, needle size, site, aspiration confirmation, onset, and any adverse events. Keep an emergency log of every complication. Photograph and record injection sites for teaching or incident review. Maintain crash cart records and training logs for emergency preparedness [12].

Case Study

A 37-year-old hypertensive patient underwent multiple restorations under local anesthesia. The operator administered two carpules of lidocaine with adrenaline without checking blood pressure or consulting the patient's physician. During injection, the patient developed palpitations and chest discomfort, requiring emergency hospital transfer. The subsequent inquiry confirmed omission of medical history documentation and absence of recorded vitals. The case was judged as negligence due to avoidable adverse reaction.

Case Learnings

1. Pre-anesthetic evaluation and documentation of vitals are as critical as the injection itself.
2. Vasoconstrictor use in high-risk patients requires medical clearance and explicit documentation.
3. Every syringe must be aspirated and injection given slowly; no exceptions.
4. Absence of written anesthesia records equates to presumed negligence.
5. A well-maintained emergency log and trained staff can convert a crisis into a defended event.

Quick Checklist

- Medical history and vitals recorded
- Agent and dose calculated
- Cartridge and needle checked
- Landmarks identified and visualized
- Aspiration confirmed before deposit
- Injection given slowly and observed
- Onset verified before procedure
- Complications managed and recorded

- Postoperative advice provided
- Anesthesia record signed and stored

References

1. *Malamed SF. Handbook of Local Anesthesia. 7th ed. St. Louis: Elsevier; 2019.*
2. *Becker DE, Reed KL. Local anesthetics: review of pharmacological considerations. Anesth Prog. 2012;59(2):90 - 101.*
3. *Yagiela JA. Adverse drug interactions in dental practice: interactions associated with vasoconstrictors. J Am Dent Assoc. 1999;130(5):701 - 709.*
4. *Council on Scientific Affairs, American Dental Association. Recommendations for safe use of local anesthesia. ADA; 2021.*
5. *Harte JA. Infection prevention in dental anesthesia delivery. J Am Dent Assoc. 2010;141(5):572 - 581.*
6. *Pogrel MA. Permanent nerve involvement resulting from inferior alveolar nerve blocks. J Am Dent Assoc. 2010;141(7):836 - 844.*
7. *Neal JM et al. ASRA practice advisory on local anesthetic systemic toxicity. Reg Anesth Pain Med. 2018;43(2):113 - 123.*
8. *Bennett CR. Monheim's Local Anesthesia and Pain Control in Dental Practice. 7th ed. Elsevier; 2018.*
9. *Rosenberg PA et al. Supplemental anesthesia techniques for endodontic pain. Endod Topics. 2002;3:14 - 25.*
10. *Becker DE. Pharmacodynamic considerations for dental local anesthetics. Anesth Prog. 2017;64(4):207 - 218.*
11. *Jastak JT, Yagiela JA, Donaldson D. Local Anesthesia of the Oral Cavity. Philadelphia: WB Saunders; 1995.*
12. *Dental Council of India. Clinical Establishment and Safety Protocols for Dental Practice. 2022.*

CHAPTER 5

Pain Pathways and Analgesic Planning

Pain is the language of tissue distress. In dentistry, its control defines patient trust and operator confidence. Mismanaged pain does more than harm comfort - it signals inadequate diagnosis, poor pharmacologic planning, or unsafe drug use. Every pain episode that follows a dental procedure can become a complaint, and every complaint can become a case. This chapter explains how to interpret pain physiology, plan analgesia wisely, and avoid medicolegal pitfalls.

Purpose and Indications

Analgesic planning aims to prevent, reduce, and control dental pain through correct drug selection, timing, and dosage. Understanding pain pathways helps identify whether discomfort arises from inflammation, nerve injury, or anxiety. This foundation converts reactive prescribing into preventive management [1].

Preparation and Assessment

Assess pain intensity, origin, and timing. Distinguish inflammatory pain from neuropathic or referred pain. Review medical history for hepatic, renal, gastrointestinal, or cardiac disorders. Document allergy, drug history, and prior adverse reactions.

Red flag: Prescribing NSAIDs or paracetamol without checking for hepatic or renal impairment is a common legal error. Documenting contraindications protects both clinician and patient [2].

- ***Step 1: Understanding Pain Pathways***

Pain perception follows three stages - transduction at the peripheral nerve ending, transmission through trigeminal pathways, and modulation within the central nervous system. Dental pain originates mainly from pulpal inflammation and periodontal tissue pressure.

Red flag: Treating every pain as inflammatory without recognizing neuropathic patterns leads to repeated extractions or overtreatment. Failure to differentiate pain types is a diagnostic error [3].

- ***Step 2: Selection of Analgesic Class***

For mild to moderate pain, use NSAIDs such as ibuprofen 400 - 600 mg every 6 hours. For moderate to severe pain, combine NSAID with paracetamol 500 mg. In cases of severe acute pain, short-term opioids (tramadol 50 mg or codeine 30 mg) may be used with caution.

Red flag: Prescribing fixed-dose combinations containing both NSAIDs and opioids without understanding cumulative dosing causes overdose and adverse events. Each drug and its total daily dose must be clearly recorded in the case sheet [4].

- ***Step 3: Timing of Administration***

For procedural pain, preemptive analgesia 30 minutes before treatment provides better control. Continue postoperative analgesia for 24 - 48 hours as per severity.

Red flag: Delaying first analgesic dose until pain peaks increases total drug requirement and patient dissatisfaction. Lack of written postoperative instructions becomes evidence of negligence in pain mismanagement claims [5].

- ***Step 4: Gastroprotection and Risk Mitigation***

In patients with history of gastritis or peptic ulcer, prescribe proton pump inhibitors (pantoprazole 40 mg) along with NSAIDs. For cardiac patients on antiplatelet drugs, use paracetamol as first-line analgesic.

Red flag: Ignoring drug interactions with warfarin, antiplatelets, or antihypertensives can lead to bleeding, renal injury, or cardiac complications. Such preventable events are legally indefensible [6].

- ***Step 5: Pediatric Analgesic Planning***

Use weight-based dosing: ibuprofen 10 mg/kg every 6 - 8 hours or paracetamol 15 mg/kg every 6 hours. Avoid aspirin in children under 12 years due to risk of Reye's syndrome.

Red flag: Off-label adult dosing in children without documentation of calculation is malpractice. Always record child's weight and dose calculation in the treatment note [7].

- ***Step 6: Geriatric and Medically Compromised Patients***

Use lowest effective dose for shortest duration. Prefer paracetamol or selective COX-2 inhibitors where renal or gastric tolerance is poor.

Red flag: Chronic use of NSAIDs in elderly patients without renal or hepatic monitoring causes predictable toxicity. In absence of recorded monitoring, practitioner bears full responsibility [8].

- ***Step 7: Emergency Analgesic Protocols***

For severe postoperative pain unrelieved by routine medication, reassess cause - retained infection, dry socket, or nerve injury. Provide supplemental local anesthesia or nerve block rather than escalating systemic opioids.

Red flag: Repeated prescription of opioids without re-evaluation risks dependency and legal scrutiny under the Narcotic Drugs and Psychotropic Substances Act [9].

- ***Step 8: Documentation and Patient Instructions***

Record exact drug, dose, timing, and duration in treatment notes and prescriptions. Provide written postoperative instructions specifying when to take each dose and when to report worsening pain.

Red flag: Vague or verbal pain-control advice creates confusion and exposes clinician to claims of inadequate follow-up care. Signed patient acknowledgement of medication advice is the simplest legal protection [10].

Defensibility and Documentation Anchors

All analgesic prescriptions must be legible, justified by diagnosis, and traceable to clinical records. Prescribing controlled drugs without entry in narcotic register violates law. Mention drug allergies and contraindications on both prescription and consent form. Keep record of written postoperative instructions in case file [11].

Case Study

A 45-year-old male with known gastritis underwent multiple extractions. He was prescribed ibuprofen 600 mg three times daily without gastroprotection. On the third day, he presented with upper abdominal pain and hematemesis, requiring hospitalization. The hospital traced the cause to NSAID-induced gastric bleeding. During inquiry, the dental notes showed no documentation of medical history, no mention of drug selection rationale, and no postoperative instruction sheet. The case was ruled as professional negligence due to preventable prescribing error.

Case Learnings

1. Pain control is pharmacologic precision, not reflex prescribing.
2. Every prescription must follow individualized risk assessment - age, comorbidity, and concurrent drugs.
3. Absence of written instructions equals absence of proof of communication.
4. Co-prescribing gastroprotection when indicated prevents both harm and litigation.
5. Pain records should form part of postoperative documentation to demonstrate continued care.

Quick Checklist

- Pain source assessed and documented
- Medical history and allergies reviewed
- Drug class and dose selected appropriately
- Preemptive analgesia given when indicated
- Gastroprotection prescribed where needed
- Weight-based pediatric dosing followed
- Elderly dose reduced and monitored
- Opioid use justified and recorded
- Written instructions given and signed
- Prescription copy filed with case record

References

1. *McQuay HJ, Moore RA. An evidence-based resource for pain relief. Oxford University Press; 1998.*
2. *Ong CK, Lirk P, Seymour RA, Jenkins BJ. The efficacy of preemptive analgesia for acute postoperative dental pain. Anesth Analg. 2005;100(3):757 - 773.*
3. *Hargreaves KM, Berman LH. Cohen's Pathways of the Pulp. 12th ed. St. Louis: Elsevier;*

2022.

4. *Moore PA, Hersh EV. Combining ibuprofen and acetaminophen for acute dental pain. J Am Dent Assoc. 2013;144(8):898 - 908.*
5. *Becker DE. Pain management: Part 1 - Managing acute and postoperative dental pain. Anesth Prog. 2010;57(2):67 - 79.*
6. *Hersh EV, Pinto A, Moore PA. Adverse drug interactions in dental practice: Analgesics, antibiotics, and antifungal agents. J Am Dent Assoc. 2011;142(12):1482 - 1496.*
7. *American Academy of Pediatric Dentistry. Guideline on Pain Management in Pediatric Dental Patients. 2021.*
8. *Gagliese L, et al. Pain management in the elderly: clinical and legal implications. Pain Res Manag. 2015;20(1):45 - 50.*
9. *Government of India. Narcotic Drugs and Psychotropic Substances Act. 1985 (as amended).*
10. *General Dental Council (UK). Standards for the Dental Team: Prescribing and Record Keeping. 2013.*
11. *Dental Council of India. Safe Prescribing and Medication Record Guidelines for Dental Practice. 2022.*

CHAPTER 6

Medical History, Risk Stratification, and Consent Essentials

The safest procedure can become fatal in a medically fragile patient if history is ignored or consent is vague. A few extra minutes spent questioning and documenting can prevent cardiac arrests, allergic reactions, and courtroom summons. This chapter converts patient assessment and consent from formality into clinical armor.

Purpose and Indications

The goal is to identify systemic risks before any dental procedure, modify treatment accordingly, and ensure that every patient understands, accepts, and signs for proposed care. Proper documentation of history and consent transforms medical awareness into legal protection [1].

Preparation and Environment

Conduct history-taking in a calm, private setting where patients can disclose honestly. Have standard medical history forms covering cardiovascular, respiratory, endocrine, hematologic, renal, hepatic, and allergic conditions. Keep updated drug reference lists for verification.

Red flag: Rushing history at the chairside while instruments are laid out discourages disclosure. Incomplete medical forms without clinician signature are inadmissible as evidence of diligence [2].

- ***Step 1: Personal and Demographic Details***

Record full name, age, gender, contact details, occupation, and identification number. Include emergency contact and primary physician details.

Red flag: Missing demographic or physician information delays emergency response and communication in case of adverse events. Failure to record identity verification can complicate medico-legal correspondence.

- ***Step 2: Systemic and Medical History***

Ask targeted questions about cardiovascular disease, hypertension, diabetes, asthma, bleeding disorders, epilepsy, tuberculosis, and thyroid conditions. Confirm last medical review and current medications.

Red flag: Performing extractions or giving adrenaline-based anesthesia in uncontrolled hypertensives or diabetics without clearance leads to avoidable morbidity. Documenting "patient denies systemic illness" without supportive questioning is a weak legal defense [3].

- ***Step 3: Drug History and Allergies***

List all prescription, over-the-counter, and herbal medicines. Specifically ask about anticoagulants, antiplatelets, steroids, and previous allergic reactions to anesthetics, antibiotics, or latex.

Red flag: Ignoring drug interactions with warfarin or antidiabetic drugs can cause bleeding or hypoglycemia. Absence of documented allergy inquiry is viewed as negligence in any reaction claim [4].

- ***Step 4: Social and Family History***

Ask about smoking, alcohol, recreational drugs, or radiation exposure. Record hereditary bleeding or cardiac disorders.

Red flag: Missing social history omits important anesthetic and healing implications. Smoker's delayed healing and unrecorded substance abuse are recurring causes of post-operative failure and patient disputes [5].

- ***Step 5: Physical Examination and Vital Signs***

Record blood pressure, pulse, temperature, oxygen saturation, and blood sugar where indicated. For high-risk or medically compromised patients, repeat vitals before major procedures.

Red flag: Proceeding without baseline vitals invalidates any claim of preoperative stability. A patient collapse during procedure without recorded vitals is automatically classed as procedural negligence [6].

- ***Step 6: Risk Stratification and Treatment Modification***

Classify patients as ASA I (healthy), ASA II (mild systemic disease), ASA III (severe disease), or ASA IV (life-threatening condition). Modify appointment length, chair position, and anesthetic dose accordingly.

Red flag: Failing to stratify risk means no documented evidence that risk-benefit judgment was exercised. Courts view this as lack of clinical reasoning, not just documentation failure [7].

- ***Step 7: Investigations and Specialist Clearance***

Request laboratory or physician consultation when systemic instability is suspected. Keep copies of correspondence and clearance letters.

Red flag: Verbal physician approvals without written proof are worthless in inquiries. Proceeding with invasive procedures in absence of clearance is indefensible when complications arise [8].

- ***Step 8: Informed Consent Discussion***

Explain diagnosis, proposed treatment, possible risks, alternatives, costs, and expected outcomes in the language the patient understands. Encourage questions and obtain signed consent before treatment.

Red flag: Generic "consent to treatment" forms without procedure-specific details or patient signatures are invalid. Consent obtained under distress or after sedation holds no legal weight [9].

- ***Step 9: Written Consent Documentation***

Record date, time, procedure name, and names of witnesses. For minors, obtain consent from parent or guardian with proof of relationship.

Red flag: Absence of guardian consent in pediatric or mentally challenged patients constitutes battery under law. Altered or predated consent forms are prosecutable offenses [10].

- ***Step 10: Updating and Storage***

Update medical history at every visit. Store consent and risk forms securely for a minimum of five years after treatment completion.

Red flag: Reusing old records without review fails the continuity-of-care requirement. Missing storage or unauthorized access to records violates data protection regulations [11].

Defensibility and Documentation Anchors

Maintain standardized medical history and consent templates approved by the clinic. Ensure all entries are dated, signed, and updated periodically. Cross-reference anesthetic and prescription records. In any adverse event, these documents serve as primary evidence of due diligence, communication, and patient autonomy [12].

Case Study

A 58-year-old diabetic patient underwent flap surgery after giving verbal consent. No written consent or updated medical history was recorded. During the procedure, he developed hypoglycemia and fainted, leading to minor trauma and hospitalization. The patient's family filed a negligence claim citing lack of information and monitoring. Investigation confirmed that neither recent blood sugar levels nor drug details were documented. The dentist was held liable for failure to assess risk and obtain valid informed consent.

Case Learnings

1. Every procedure, no matter how minor, needs documented written consent.
2. Medical history must be refreshed at every appointment; systemic stability can change daily.
3. Risk stratification and clearance letters are proof of clinical judgment.
4. Informed consent is communication, not paperwork; comprehension must be documented.
5. Absence of signed consent and updated history eliminates all defenses in adverse events.

Quick Checklist

- Demographics and physician details recorded
- Full systemic and drug history obtained
- Allergies clearly documented
- Social and family history taken
- Baseline vitals recorded and filed
- Patient classified by ASA status
- Medical clearance letters attached
- Diagnosis and risks explained
- Written, signed consent secured
- History updated at each visit and safely stored

References

1. *Little JW, Falace DA, Miller CS, Rhodus NL. Dental Management of the Medically Compromised Patient. 9th ed. St. Louis: Elsevier; 2023.*
2. *Scully C, Cawson RA. Medical Problems in Dentistry. 8th ed. Elsevier; 2022.*
3. *Malamed SF. Medical Emergencies in the Dental Office. 8th ed. Elsevier; 2020.*
4. *Becker DE. Drug interactions in dental practice. Anesth Prog. 2011;58(3):109 - 119.*
5. *Glick M. Clinical implications of medical risk assessment in dentistry. J Am Dent Assoc. 2019;150(6):436 - 444.*
6. *American Society of Anesthesiologists. ASA Physical Status Classification System. 2020.*
7. *Jeske AH. Risk assessment in dental care of medically compromised patients. Compend Contin Educ Dent. 2010;31(4):274 - 282.*
8. *Dental Council of India. Clinical Establishment and Safety Standards for Dental Practice. 2022.*
9. *General Dental Council (UK). Standards for the Dental Team: Consent. 2013.*
10. *Indian Medical Council. Informed Consent in Clinical Practice - Legal Advisory. 2021.*
11. *Government of India. Personal Data Protection Bill. 2021.*
12. *Ministry of Health and Family Welfare. National Guidelines on Medical Record Maintenance. 2018.*

CHAPTER 7

Emergency Drugs, Crash Cart Setup, and Basic Life Support

A medical emergency inside a dental clinic turns routine into crisis within seconds. The difference between an incident and a fatality is not luck - it is preparedness. Every dental professional must be trained, equipped, and documented to handle collapse, allergy, or arrest before help arrives. This chapter establishes the protocol for readiness that saves lives and sustains legal defense.

Purpose and Indications

Emergency preparedness ensures the immediate recognition and management of life-threatening events during dental care. It involves availability of essential drugs, functional equipment, trained staff, and a clear chain of action until medical help arrives [1].

Preparation and Readiness Check

Inspect the crash cart at the start of each clinic day. Verify drug expiry dates, oxygen cylinder pressure, and presence of all emergency equipment. Maintain a laminated emergency contact list near every operatory.

Red flag: Missing or expired emergency drugs or empty oxygen cylinders are direct evidence of negligence in an adverse event. Readiness logs are mandatory for defensibility [2].

- ***Step 1: Composition of Emergency Drug Kit***

The crash cart must include these minimum drugs:

Adrenaline (1:1000 ampoules) - anaphylaxis and cardiac arrest

Nitroglycerin spray - angina

Aspirin 300 mg tablets - suspected myocardial infarction

Antihistamines (chlorpheniramine or diphenhydramine) -

allergic reactions

Salbutamol inhaler - bronchospasm or asthma

Glucose (oral gel and 25% IV) - hypoglycemia

Hydrocortisone injection - severe allergic reaction

Midazolam or diazepam - seizures

Atropine - bradycardia

Normal saline and Ringer's lactate - IV access fluids

Red flag: Absence of any critical drug or failure to know its location during emergency nullifies response time. The entire staff must know exact contents and location of the crash cart [3].

- ***Step 2: Emergency Equipment Setup***

The cart must contain:

- Portable oxygen cylinder with regulator and masks
- Suction apparatus with sterile tubing
- Blood pressure monitor and stethoscope
- Pulse oximeter
- Syringes, needles, IV sets, and tourniquet
- Automated External Defibrillator (AED) where feasible

Red flag: Equipment malfunction during crisis due to lack of periodic testing is legally equal to absence of equipment. Monthly service logs are compulsory [4].

- ***Step 3: Recognition of Common Dental Emergencies***

Most dental emergencies fall into five groups - vasovagal syncope, anaphylaxis, hypoglycemia, asthma attack, and cardiac arrest. Each must have a standard management sequence displayed in operatory.

Red flag: Failure to recognize early signs (pallor, sweating, confusion, wheeze) delays action. In every recorded death during dental treatment, recognition delay has been the first proven error [5].

- ***Step 4: Management of Vasovagal Syncope***

Step 4a: Stop procedure immediately; place patient supine with legs elevated; ensure airway patency.

Red flag: Sitting an unconscious patient upright worsens cerebral hypoxia and can lead to cardiac arrest.

Step 4b: Loosen tight clothing, maintain airway, and use ammonia vapor if available. Monitor pulse and breathing.

Red flag: Failure to document vital signs post-episode can be treated as concealment in subsequent inquiries.

- ***Step 5: Management of Anaphylaxis***

Step 5a: Administer adrenaline 0.5 mg (0.5 ml of 1:1000) intramuscularly into mid-thigh; repeat every 5 minutes if required.

Red flag: Delay beyond two minutes in administering adrenaline drastically increases mortality. Oral antihistamines alone are inadequate in true anaphylaxis.

Step 5b: Call emergency services, start oxygen, and monitor vitals continuously.

Red flag: Lack of written record of administered dose, time, and route violates standard emergency protocol documentation [6].

- ***Step 6: Management of Hypoglycemia***

Step 6a: If conscious, give oral glucose gel or sweetened drink.

Red flag: Giving oral glucose to an unconscious patient risks aspiration.

Step 6b: If unconscious, administer 25 ml of 25% glucose intravenously or 1 mg glucagon intramuscularly.

Red flag: Not checking blood sugar in diabetic patients pre-procedure negates preventive care and can lead to malpractice charge [7].

- ***Step 7: Management of Asthma Attack***

Step 7a: Stop procedure, seat patient upright, and administer two puffs of salbutamol inhaler.

Red flag: Forcing patient into supine position worsens breathing distress.

Step 7b: Provide oxygen and monitor pulse oximetry.

Red flag: Absence of pulse oximeter reading during documentation weakens legal defense in case of deterioration [8].

- ***Step 8: Management of Cardiac Arrest***

Step 8a: Confirm unresponsiveness, call for help, and begin chest compressions at 100 - 120/minute with depth of 5 cm.

Red flag: Delayed CPR beyond 3 minutes from collapse significantly reduces survival.

Step 8b: Attach AED as soon as available and follow prompts. Continue compressions until medical team arrives.

Red flag: Performing CPR without training can cause rib fractures and airway injury; however, not attempting CPR at all is legally and ethically indefensible [9].

- ***Step 9: Documentation and Post-Emergency Reporting***

After stabilization or transfer, record complete sequence - time of onset, symptoms, drugs administered, vital signs, staff involved, and ambulance details.

Red flag: Incomplete documentation post-emergency is often treated as tampering or concealment. Every line must be time-stamped and signed [10].

- ***Step 10: Training and Periodic Drills***

Conduct mock drills every three months. Record staff participation and retraining schedules for Basic Life Support (BLS) certification.

Red flag: Absence of BLS certification among clinic staff disqualifies the claim of preparedness during legal review [11].

Defensibility and Documentation Anchors

Maintain an updated crash cart checklist signed daily. Keep annual calibration and service certificates for oxygen cylinders, suction units, and AEDs. Retain staff BLS training certificates and mock drill attendance logs. In a medico-legal situation, these documents serve as primary proof of readiness and compliance with clinical establishment norms [12].

Case Study

A 52-year-old patient with a known history of hypertension and mild asthma developed breathlessness and collapse following administration of local anesthesia with adrenaline. The dental team had no oxygen cylinder in working order, and no adrenaline ampoule could be located. The patient suffered cardiac arrest before paramedics arrived and could not be revived. Post-investigation, the clinic was found without an emergency drug kit or maintenance log. The dentist was charged with culpable negligence leading to death.

Case Learnings

1. The first rule of emergencies is preparedness - not improvisation.
2. Emergency drug kits must be present, updated, and known to every staff member.
3. Delay in adrenaline use during anaphylaxis or cardiac collapse is fatal both medically and legally.
4. Equipment logs, drug inventories, and BLS certification are non-negotiable defenses.
5. Emergencies demand training, not bravery; every action must follow a documented protocol.

Quick Checklist

- Crash cart stocked and checked daily
- All emergency drugs within expiry
- Oxygen supply and suction functional
- AED accessible and charged
- Staff trained and certified in BLS
- Mock drills conducted quarterly
- Emergency contact list displayed
- Vital signs monitored and recorded
- Post-event documentation completed and signed
- Copies of all reports stored securely

References

1. *Malamed SF. Medical Emergencies in the Dental Office. 8th ed. Elsevier; 2020.*
2. *American Heart Association. Basic Life Support Guidelines. 2020.*
3. *British Dental Association. Management of Medical Emergencies in the Dental Practice. 2022.*
4. *Resuscitation Council (UK). Emergency Treatment of Anaphylactic Reactions: Guidelines for Healthcare Providers. 2021.*

5. *Haas DA. Preparing dental offices for medical emergencies. J Am Dent Assoc. 2010;141(Suppl 1):14S - 19S.*

6. *Govindarajan P, et al. Dental management of anaphylaxis: clinical review. Indian J Dent Res. 2018;29(2):190 - 195.*

7. *Little JW, Falace DA, Miller CS, Rhodus NL. Dental Management of the Medically Compromised Patient. 9th ed. Elsevier; 2023.*

8. *ADA Council on Scientific Affairs. Recommendations for oxygen and emergency equipment in dental settings. ADA; 2021.*

9. *Perkins GD et al. European Resuscitation Council Guidelines for Resuscitation. Resuscitation. 2021;161:1 - 60.*

10. *Ministry of Health and Family Welfare, India. National Emergency Preparedness Standards for Dental Clinics. 2022.*

11. *Occupational Safety and Health Administration. Emergency Preparedness and Response in Dental Practices. OSHA; 2020.*

12. *Dental Council of India. Clinical Establishment and Safety Compliance for Dental Practice. 2022.*

CHAPTER 8

Documentation, Photography, and Record Retention

In dentistry, memory fades but records speak forever. A well-documented case can defend an honest error; an undocumented one can condemn flawless work. This chapter lays out how to create clinical records that communicate, protect, and endure.

Purpose and Indications

Documentation preserves the chronology of care - diagnosis, treatment, progress, and consent - as legal proof of diligence. Photographic and radiographic records strengthen evidence and continuity. Record retention ensures traceability long after treatment is completed [1].

Preparation and Documentation Setup

Prepare standardized forms for medical history, consent, treatment plans, progress notes, prescriptions, and billing. Maintain separate folders for each patient, physical or digital, with date and clinician signature.

Red flag: Using random sheets or scattered digital files breaks continuity. Missing dates or unsigned entries render the entire record legally inadmissible [2].

- ***Step 1: Patient Registration and Identification***

Record full name, age, gender, contact details, and unique ID. Link every form and image with this ID. Verify identity at every visit.

Red flag: Mislabelled or unverified files can lead to mix-ups between patients, creating serious data-protection and medico-legal violations [3].

- ***Step 2: Clinical Examination and Diagnosis Recording***

Note presenting complaint in patient's own words. Record clinical findings, investigations, and provisional diagnosis. Write legibly or use typed notes.

Red flag: Copy-paste templates without individual details show lack of clinical judgment. Inconsistent handwriting or missing initials suggests tampering during audit [4].

- ***Step 3: Treatment Planning and Consent Integration***

Attach treatment plan with diagnosis, risk explanation, and patient signature. Note alternative options and reasons for selected procedure.

Red flag: Absence of documented risk-benefit discussion implies no informed consent even if verbal discussion occurred. Courts value written detail, not recollection [5].

- ***Step 4: Procedure Notes***

Record date, procedure, anesthesia used, instruments, materials, and complications. Write immediately after completion, not retrospectively.

Red flag: Delayed or back-dated entries raise suspicion of manipulation. Each note must bear time, initials, and witness where possible [6].

- ***Step 5: Photographic and Radiographic Records***

Capture pre-operative, intra-operative, and post-operative photographs. Use digital cameras or intraoral scanners with date-stamp enabled. Obtain written consent for photography, especially if used for education or marketing.

Red flag: Using patient images for social media without documented consent violates data-protection and privacy laws. Courts treat this as breach of confidentiality [7].

- ***Step 6: Storage and Backup***

Maintain dual storage - primary (physical file or hard drive) and secondary (cloud or encrypted backup). Index all images and reports under patient ID and date.

Red flag: Sole reliance on unsecured personal devices leads to data loss and privacy breaches. Every backup system must comply with data-protection laws [8].

- ***Step 7: Record Retention Period***

Keep adult patient records for at least five years after last visit; pediatric and medico-legal cases for ten years or until patient reaches adulthood, whichever is longer. Maintain imaging and lab reports alongside treatment notes.

Red flag: Destroying or discarding records before legal retention period may be treated as deliberate suppression of evidence [9].

- ***Step 8: Corrections and Additions***

For any correction, strike once through the error, write the correct entry, date, and sign. Avoid erasure, overwriting, or deletion. For electronic records, maintain audit trail.

Red flag: Illegible corrections or deleted entries invalidate authenticity of entire file. Electronic edits without timestamp compromise legal credibility [10].

- ***Step 9: Confidentiality and Access Control***

Allow patient access to their own records upon written request. Restrict third-party disclosure to authorized agencies or insurers with consent.

Red flag: Sharing case images or data with pharmaceutical or educational bodies without written permission breaches confidentiality and data-protection statutes [11].

- ***Step 10: Regular Audits and Review***

Conduct record audits every six months to verify completeness, signatures, and storage safety. Document audit findings and corrective actions.

Red flag: Clinics with no audit trail appear administratively negligent. In investigations, absence of internal checks implies systemic failure [12].

Defensibility and Documentation Anchors

Every patient file must contain: identity details, medical history, consent forms, treatment notes, radiographs, prescriptions, billing records, and follow-up communications. Entries should be chronological, dated, and signed. Maintain access logs for digital systems and file retention certificates when archiving or disposing. These form the backbone of legal defense in malpractice claims [13].

Case Study

A 39-year-old woman complained of nerve pain following endodontic treatment. She alleged wrong-tooth procedure and lack of consent. The dentist had no pre-operative photograph, no treatment note of working length, and no signed consent form. The only evidence was a bill mentioning "RCT upper premolar." Radiographs were missing. The case concluded against the clinician; the court noted "absence of proper documentation implies absence of due care."

Case Learnings

1. Documentation is not memory support; it is the clinical record of accountability.
2. Each photograph, radiograph, and form is part of a single legal story.
3. Electronic backups must mirror physical records with equal security.
4. Consent and treatment notes together prove intention and competence.
5. Good records cannot prevent complications but can prevent conviction.

Quick Checklist

- Standardized patient file used
- Identity and demographics verified
- Clinical findings and diagnosis recorded
- Treatment plan signed by patient
- Procedure notes written same day
- Photographs and radiographs stored with ID
- Dual storage and regular backup maintained
- Retention period tracked and logged
- Corrections dated and signed
- Confidentiality maintained and audit done

References

1. *General Dental Council (UK). Standards for the Dental Team: Record Keeping. 2013.*
2. *Ministry of Health and Family Welfare, India. National Guidelines on Medical Record Maintenance. 2018.*
3. *World Health Organization. Guidance on Health Record Management and Confidentiality. 2021.*
4. *Indian Medical Council. Legal Documentation and Clinical Records Advisory. 2021.*
5. *Dental Council of India. Clinical Establishment and Record Maintenance Standards. 2022.*

6. *Bhatia V. Legal documentation and risk management in dental practice. J Indian Dent Assoc. 2020;14(3):118 - 123.*

7. *Government of India. Personal Data Protection Bill. 2021.*

8. *American Dental Association. HIPAA Privacy and Security Rules for Dental Practices. 2020.*

9. *Medical Council of India. Minimum Retention Period for Medical Records. 2010.*

10. *Health Information Technology Act, India. Electronic Records and Audit Trails. 2019.*

11. *National Dental Association. Patient Confidentiality and Data Sharing Guidelines. 2022.*

12. *Occupational Safety and Health Administration. Clinical Documentation and Audit Requirements. 2020.*

13. *World Dental Federation (FDI). Global Principles of Dental Record Keeping. 2022.*

SECTION 2

Exodontia and Minor Oral Surgery

There are few moments in dentistry as decisive as an extraction. It is the procedure most patients remember — for relief or regret. To the clinician, it is anatomy, technique, and timing. To the law, it is consent, judgment, and record. This section bridges those three worlds, turning routine extractions into deliberate, defendable surgery.

Exodontia begins long before forceps touch enamel. Each case starts with indication and ends with documentation. Here, the clinician learns how to plan an extraction scientifically — reading roots, bone, and systemic health before committing. The chapters move from principles of case selection to the choreography of simple and surgical removal, flap elevation, bone contouring, and suturing.

*Every technical step carries a **Red flag:** a socket that bleeds too long, a fracture that wasn't disclosed, a nerve proximity that wasn't recorded. Each flag becomes a teaching moment — not to instill fear, but foresight. The goal is not just to extract teeth cleanly, but to extract risk from the equation.*

From managing impacted third molars to recognizing when to refer, these chapters stress a rhythm: anticipate, act, and annotate. Post-extraction care and communication are treated as extensions of surgery, not afterthoughts. The section closes by translating surgical duty into legal language — what constitutes informed consent, how to record complications, and how to handle disclosure when things go wrong.

By the end of this section, the reader should stand able to perform exodontia that heals predictably and withstands scrutiny. Technique may define success in the mouth, but documentation defines it everywhere else.

CHAPTER 9

Principles of Exodontia - Indications, Contraindications, and Planning

Tooth extraction is not an act of removal but of controlled detachment - separating what must go while preserving what must remain. This chapter builds the clinical reasoning behind every extraction, the red flags that prevent disaster, and the documentation that protects the operator.

Purpose and Indications

Extraction removes teeth that are non-restorable, pathologic, or detrimental to oral or systemic health. Common indications include gross decay, periodontal destruction, failed endodontic therapy, orthodontic requirements, impaction, and prosthetic planning [1].

Preparation and Preoperative Evaluation

Take detailed medical and dental history. Review for bleeding disorders, hypertension, diabetes, anticoagulant use, or previous surgical complications. Record blood pressure and blood sugar if indicated. Obtain radiograph to assess root morphology and proximity to vital structures.

Red flag: Proceeding without radiographic evaluation risks root or bone fracture and nerve injury. Operating on a medically compromised patient without clearance is indefensible [2].

- ***Step 1: Case Selection and Treatment Planning***

Assess indication, difficulty, and systemic suitability. Classify as simple or surgical extraction. Modify plan according to access, bone density, and medical risks.

Red flag: Undertaking complex impactions in a general setup without surgical support violates standard of care. Referring late after complication is worse than referring early [3].

- ***Step 2: Preoperative Preparation***

Verify patient identity, tooth number, and side. Explain procedure, risks, and alternatives. Obtain written consent. Prepare instruments, sterile field, and anesthesia plan.

Red flag: Wrong-site extraction due to skipped verification is one of the most common and indefensible dental errors. A signed consent does not protect against wrong-tooth negligence [4].

- ***Step 3: Local Anesthesia and Soft-Tissue Reflection***

Administer local anesthesia appropriate to site and duration. Confirm numbness. Reflect soft tissue gently with periosteal elevator for surgical access.

Red flag: Forcing reflection before full anesthesia leads to patient movement and soft-tissue tearing. Proceeding despite pain violates patient autonomy and constitutes procedural assault [5].

- ***Step 4: Tooth Luxation and Elevation***

Apply elevators along the long axis, using controlled rotational pressure to expand socket. Maintain firm finger rest to control force.

Red flag: Excessive force or lack of counter-support causes alveolar fracture or displacement of tooth into sinus or soft tissue. Failure to record such accidents compounds liability [6].

- ***Step 5: Tooth Delivery and Socket Inspection***

Use forceps following path of withdrawal, maintaining constant pressure until periodontal ligament gives way. Inspect socket for remaining roots, granulation, or bone spicules.

Red flag: Ignoring broken root tips or leaving sharp bone edges results in infection or delayed healing. Any retained fragment must be documented and explained to patient [7].

- ***Step 6: Hemostasis and Wound Care***

Apply pressure pack for 30 minutes. Curette socket only if infected debris is visible. Avoid overzealous curettage. Suture when indicated.

Red flag: Uncontrolled bleeding or failure to check clot formation before discharge may lead to secondary hemorrhage. Every bleeding incident must be recorded with vital signs [8].

- ***Step 7: Postoperative Instructions and Follow-Up***

Advise patient to bite on gauze for 30 minutes, avoid spitting, smoking, or rinsing for 24 hours, and maintain soft diet. Prescribe analgesics or antibiotics only when indicated.

Red flag: Failure to provide written postoperative instructions can result in preventable complications such as dry socket or infection, for which dentist bears partial responsibility [9].

- ***Step 8: Documentation and Record Keeping***

Record indication, tooth number, anesthesia used, instruments, complications, and postoperative advice. Keep radiographs before and after procedure in patient file.

Red flag: Missing radiograph or absence of written consent eliminates defense in fracture or paresthesia cases [10].

Defensibility and Documentation Anchors

Maintain pre- and postoperative radiographs, consent forms, and procedure notes with time, site, and anesthetic details. Record every intraoperative event, even if managed successfully. Documentation of consent and complication management is vital evidence of diligence.

Case Study

A 43-year-old male presented with a decayed mandibular molar for extraction. The procedure was performed without preoperative radiograph or medical history. During elevation, excessive force fractured the lingual cortical plate, and the root tip displaced into the submandibular space. The patient developed infection and paresthesia. Legal review found no record of preoperative assessment or informed consent. The case was ruled as negligence due to failure in procedural planning and documentation.

Case Learnings

1. Radiographic evaluation and medical clearance are non-negotiable steps in exodontia.

2. Every extraction must have documented indication, plan, and consent.
3. Controlled force is skill; excessive force is carelessness.
4. Complications must be managed and recorded transparently.
5. Proper planning converts even difficult extractions into defensible procedures.

Quick Checklist

- Radiograph reviewed and diagnosis confirmed
- Medical and drug history verified
- Written consent signed and filed
- Anesthesia achieved and confirmed
- Force applied along tooth axis only
- Socket inspected for remnants and clot
- Hemostasis achieved before discharge
- Postoperative instructions given in writing
- All findings recorded and radiographs stored

References

1. *Peterson LJ, Ellis E, Hupp JR, Tucker MR. Contemporary Oral and Maxillofacial Surgery. 7th ed. Elsevier; 2019.*
2. *Kruger GO. Textbook of Oral and Maxillofacial Surgery. 6th ed. CBS Publishers; 2021.*
3. *Malamed SF. Medical Emergencies in the Dental Office. 8th ed. Elsevier; 2020.*
4. *Dental Defence Union (UK). Wrong-Tooth Extraction Advisory. 2021.*
5. *Pogrel MA, Boyd JB. Complications of tooth extraction. Oral Maxillofac Surg Clin North Am. 2011;23(3):379 - 388.*
6. *Blondeau F, Daniel NG. Extraction of impacted mandibular third molars: postoperative complications and their risk factors. J Can Dent Assoc. 2007;73(4):325.*
7. *Howe GL. Minor Oral Surgery. 4th ed. Butterworth-Heinemann; 1995.*
8. *Stanley HR. Postextraction complications and their management. Dent Clin North Am. 1979;23(1):77 - 90.*
9. *Coulthard P et al. Management of post-extraction bleeding. Br Dent J. 2014;217(3):123 - 128.*
10. *Dental Council of India. Clinical Documentation and Consent Protocols. 2022.*

CHAPTER 10

Simple Extraction - Stepwise Technique and Red Flags

Extraction is simple only when it is respected. Every uncomplicated tooth removal is a test of control - anatomical, mechanical, and emotional. What separates a seasoned operator from a hurried one is restraint: pressure in the right direction, not power in the wrong. This chapter walks through the sequence that turns a potentially traumatic act into a predictable, defensible procedure.

Purpose and Indications

Simple extraction refers to the removal of a tooth that is visible in the mouth and can be mobilized without raising a flap or sectioning bone. It is indicated for carious, mobile, or non-restorable teeth with accessible crowns and favorable root anatomy [1].

Preparation and Preoperative Evaluation

Review medical and dental history. Confirm radiographic evaluation for root form, curvature, periapical pathology, and proximity to sinus or nerve. Verify tooth number and obtain written consent. Prepare sterile tray with appropriate forceps, elevators, and suction.

Red flag: Proceeding without a radiograph or using improper instruments (e.g., wrong forceps design) is a setup for fracture or nerve injury. Absence of documentation of consent and preoperative findings is indefensible [2].

- ***Step 1: Anesthesia and Field Preparation***

Administer appropriate local anesthesia and wait for full effect. Test tissue response before incision or elevation. Use suction to maintain a clear field.

Red flag: Inadequate anesthesia leads to sudden patient movement and soft-tissue tears. Continuing despite pain violates consent and can constitute assault [3].

- ***Step 2: Patient and Operator Positioning***

Seat patient with occlusal plane 15 - 20 degrees below operator's elbow level. Operator stands at correct clock position - 8 to 9 o'clock for right-handed, 3 to 4 o'clock for left-handed operator.

Red flag: Poor positioning causes loss of control, instrument slippage, and injury to lips or soft tissues. Improper ergonomics leading to operator fatigue compromises judgment during emergencies [4].

- ***Step 3: Grasp and Application of Forceps***

Select correct forceps and grasp the tooth as apically as possible. Apply gentle pressure along the long axis of the tooth. Support alveolus with non-dominant hand to absorb force.

Red flag: Grasping too high on the crown risks fracture. Lack of alveolar support transmits force to adjacent teeth, causing accidental mobility or fracture of neighboring restorations [5].

- ***Step 4: Luxation and Initial Mobility***

Use a straight elevator to expand the periodontal ligament space. Apply controlled, rotational movements, increasing amplitude gradually. Wait for ligament fibers to yield before delivering tooth.

Red flag: Jerky or uncontrolled movement can fracture alveolar bone or displace root into sinus or soft tissue. Excessive leverage without finger rest endangers nearby structures [6].

- ***Step 5: Tooth Delivery***

Once mobility is sufficient, apply steady, continuous traction along the path of withdrawal. Rotate or buccal-lingual rock as anatomy allows. Deliver the tooth smoothly.

Red flag: Sudden twisting or lateral jerking breaks root tips or alveolus. Forcing a stubborn tooth without reassessing causes preventable fracture. All fractures must be documented immediately [7].

- ***Step 6: Socket Inspection and Debridement***

Inspect socket for residual roots, bone spicules, or pathology. Irrigate gently with saline; avoid aggressive curettage.

Red flag: Failure to inspect socket results in retained fragments or debris, causing infection and delayed healing. Curetting vital bone excessively causes unnecessary postoperative pain [8].

- ***Step 7: Hemostasis and Postoperative Packing***

Apply sterile gauze pressure for 30 minutes. Ensure clot formation before discharge. For patients on anticoagulants, use local hemostatic agents if needed.

Red flag: Ignoring oozing or discharging patients before stable clot formation invites secondary hemorrhage. Discharge notes must include bleeding precautions [9].

- ***Step 8: Postoperative Instructions and Follow-Up***

Provide written and verbal instructions: no spitting, rinsing, smoking, or using straws for 24 hours; maintain soft diet and oral hygiene; report persistent bleeding or swelling.

Red flag: Verbal-only instructions are easily denied by patients during disputes. Written postoperative sheet with patient signature is crucial documentation [10].

- ***Step 9: Documentation and Legal Record***

Record anesthesia type, forceps used, tooth number, complications, and advice given. Preserve pre- and postoperative radiographs in patient file.

Red flag: Absence of documented technique or postoperative advice makes any complication appear as negligence, even if management was adequate [11].

Defensibility and Documentation Anchors

For every extraction, maintain: preoperative radiograph, written consent, anesthesia record, procedure note, and postoperative instruction sheet signed by the patient. These create a complete legal chain from planning to aftercare. Record any deviation or complication transparently with corrective action taken.

Case Study

A 29-year-old woman underwent simple extraction of an upper premolar. The operator did not review radiographs and used excessive buccal force, fracturing the thin alveolar wall. The fragment tore the mucosa, leaving bone exposure. The patient complained of prolonged pain and facial swelling. Legal review noted absence of radiographs, written consent, or postoperative advice in her records. The case was settled against the dentist due to inadequate documentation and preventable trauma.

Case Learnings

1. Every "simple" extraction needs full assessment and documentation.
2. Force without anatomical understanding causes more harm than disease.
3. Radiographs are mandatory for every extraction, even if tooth appears straightforward.
4. Written postoperative instructions prove that patient education was given.
5. Controlled movement and record keeping turn a manual task into a defensible procedure.

Quick Checklist

1. Radiograph reviewed and indication confirmed
2. Consent form signed and filed
3. Anesthesia tested before procedure
4. Patient and operator properly positioned
5. Forceps applied with alveolar support
6. Socket inspected and irrigated
7. Hemostasis achieved and recorded
8. Postoperative advice given in writing
9. Complications documented immediately
10. All notes signed and dated

References

1. *Kruger GO. Textbook of Oral and Maxillofacial Surgery. 6th ed. CBS Publishers; 2021.*
2. *Peterson LJ, Ellis E, Hupp JR, Tucker MR. Contemporary Oral and Maxillofacial Surgery. 7th ed. Elsevier; 2019.*
3. *Malamed SF. Handbook of Local Anesthesia. 7th ed. Elsevier; 2019.*
4. *Valachi B, Valachi K. Ergonomic principles in clinical dentistry. J Am Dent Assoc. 2003;134(12):1604 - 1612.*

5. *Howe GL. Minor Oral Surgery. 4th ed. Butterworth-Heinemann; 1995.*

6. *Pogrel MA, Boyd JB. Complications of tooth extraction. Oral Maxillofac Surg Clin North Am. 2011;23(3):379 - 388.*

7. *Blondeau F, Daniel NG. Extraction of impacted mandibular third molars: postoperative complications and risk factors. J Can Dent Assoc. 2007;73(4):325.*

8. *Stanley HR. Postextraction complications and management. Dent Clin North Am. 1979;23(1):77 - 90.*

9. *Coulthard P, Esposito M, Worthington HV. Interventions for preventing dry socket. Cochrane Database Syst Rev. 2014;(4):CD006968.*

10. *Dental Protection Limited. Guidelines on Postoperative Communication and Record Keeping. 2022.*

11. *Dental Council of India. Clinical Documentation and Consent Protocols. 2022.*

CHAPTER 11

Surgical Extraction and Flap Design

When simple extraction fails, surgical extraction begins - not as a rescue but as a planned transition. It is a test of patience, precision, and respect for anatomy. Bone removal and flap reflection demand foresight; rushing either leads to damage that even perfect sutures cannot undo. This chapter breaks surgical extraction into deliberate steps, showing how structure, sequence, and documentation keep both patient and clinician safe.

Purpose and Indications

Surgical extraction involves removal of a tooth or root that cannot be extracted by routine forceps technique. Indications include impacted or broken teeth, curved or divergent roots, dense bone, ankylosis, or hypercementosis [1].

Preparation and Preoperative Evaluation

Take detailed history and radiographs (periapical or CBCT if needed). Identify root shape, relation to sinus, mandibular canal, or adjacent structures. Prepare sterile surgical tray with elevators, retractors, handpiece, sutures, and hemostatic agents. Obtain written consent mentioning risk of nerve injury, sinus exposure, and fracture.

Red flag: Performing surgery without radiographic localization or risk explanation invalidates consent. Failure to mention possible nerve injury in written form makes even managed complications indefensible [2].

- ***Step 1: Anesthesia and Field Preparation***

Administer nerve block or infiltration as indicated. Confirm anesthesia before incision. Drape and disinfect the area using povidone-iodine and sterile gauze.

Red flag: Commencing incision without verifying anesthesia causes sudden patient movement, instrument slip, and tissue laceration. Always document anesthetic type, site, and dose [3].

- ***Step 2: Incision and Flap Design***

Design mucoperiosteal flap providing full access and minimal tension. Common designs include triangular and envelope flaps. Incision should be clean, made with a single stroke along sound bone, extending beyond lesion margins.

Red flag: Short, tentative, or poorly planned incisions cause tissue tearing and ischemia. Damaged flaps delay healing and are visible evidence of poor planning during post-op evaluation [4].

- ***Step 3: Flap Reflection***

Reflect mucoperiosteum gently with periosteal elevator in smooth strokes. Maintain constant contact with bone to avoid perforation. Keep flap moist with saline-soaked gauze.

Red flag: Forceful or blind reflection creates flap perforation and compromises blood supply. A dried or torn flap leads to wound dehiscence - preventable and legally indefensible [5].

- ***Step 4: Bone Removal (Osteotomy)***

Use round or fissure bur under copious sterile saline irrigation. Remove bone judiciously to expose tooth or root section. Maintain light, continuous motion without overheating.

Red flag: Dry cutting or excessive pressure burns bone and leads to osteonecrosis. Lack of irrigation documentation in operative notes indicates procedural negligence [6].

- ***Step 5: Tooth Sectioning***

Divide tooth into manageable parts along root morphology. Section crowns from roots or separate multi-rooted teeth along furcation lines.

Red flag: Sectioning without knowing root curvature can perforate sinus or nerve canal. Each section should be planned and recorded with radiographic reference [7].

- ***Step 6: Delivery of Tooth or Root Fragments***

Use elevators to dislodge sections along the path of least resistance. Avoid prying or levering against thin bony plates.

Red flag: Excessive force causes displacement of root fragments into sinus or soft tissue spaces. Attempting blind retrieval escalates injury -

record event and refer promptly if displacement occurs [8].

- ***Step 7: Socket Inspection and Debridement***

Inspect socket for remaining roots, debris, or bone spicules. Irrigate with saline; smooth sharp edges with bone file. Place hemostatic agent if required.

Red flag: Ignoring small retained fragments or untrimmed bone edges results in chronic pain or infection. Documentation of inspection and irrigation is part of operative proof [9].

- ***Step 8: Flap Repositioning and Suturing***

Reposition flap passively without tension. Use interrupted or horizontal mattress sutures with 3-0 silk or resorbable material. Ensure margins approximate without blanching.

Red flag: Over-tight sutures cause ischemia and sloughing. Gaps in closure permit food impaction and infection. Always record suture type and count [10].

- ***Step 9: Hemostasis and Postoperative Instructions***

Confirm bleeding control before discharge. Provide written instructions - avoid spitting, rinse gently after 24 hours, cold compress first 6 hours, and soft diet. Prescribe antibiotics and analgesics only if clinically indicated.

Red flag: Ignoring mild oozing or failing to instruct on bleeding management often leads to secondary hemorrhage and medicolegal blame for "incomplete procedure" [11].

- ***Step 10: Documentation and Review***

Document procedure date, anesthesia type, flap design, bone removal method, complications, and materials used. Schedule review within 48 hours to assess healing and remove sutures after 5 - 7 days.

Red flag: Missing operative note or absent follow-up entry implies incomplete care. Courts view absence of postoperative review as abandonment [12].

Defensibility and Documentation Anchors

Every surgical extraction must include radiographs, consent specifying possible nerve or sinus injury, operative note with flap type and bone removal details, and written postoperative instructions. Maintain photographs where feasible. Keep copies of all materials used. These records provide evidence of competence, communication, and continuity.

Case Study

A 36-year-old woman underwent surgical removal of an impacted mandibular third molar. No CBCT was obtained despite root proximity to the inferior alveolar canal. During sectioning, she developed paresthesia. There was no mention of nerve injury risk in her consent form or operative notes. The court held the dentist liable for negligence, citing lack of preoperative imaging and incomplete informed consent.

Case Learnings

1. Every surgical extraction must begin with imaging and a written risk explanation.
2. Consent without explicit mention of nerve or sinus injury is inadequate.
3. Documentation of flap design and irrigation confirms surgical prudence.
4. Forceful, unplanned sectioning is a preventable cause of nerve damage.
5. Follow-up visits and recordkeeping sustain legal defense when complications occur.

Quick Checklist

1. Radiograph and consent completed
2. Anesthesia verified and documented
3. Flap design marked and executed cleanly
4. Flap kept moist and intact
5. Bone removal with constant irrigation
6. Tooth sectioned along root morphology
7. Socket inspected and smoothed
8. Flap repositioned without tension
9. Hemostasis confirmed, sutures counted
10. Postoperative instructions written and signed

References

1. *Peterson LJ, Ellis E, Hupp JR, Tucker MR. Contemporary Oral and Maxillofacial Surgery. 7th ed. Elsevier; 2019.*
2. *Kruger GO. Textbook of Oral and Maxillofacial Surgery. 6th ed. CBS Publishers; 2021.*
3. *Malamed SF. Medical Emergencies in the Dental Office. 8th ed. Elsevier; 2020.*
4. *Howe GL. Minor Oral Surgery. 4th ed. Butterworth-Heinemann; 1995.*
5. *Rood JP. Flap design in oral surgery. Br Dent J. 1983;154(12):390 - 392.*
6. *Reeh ES, Messer HH. Bone temperature rise during implant site preparation. J Oral Maxillofac Surg. 1989;47(12):1342 - 1346.*
7. *Pogrel MA, Boyd JB. Complications of tooth extraction. Oral Maxillofac Surg Clin North Am. 2011;23(3):379 - 388.*
8. *Lustmann J, Schwartz-Arad D. Delayed response to displaced root fragments in the maxillary sinus. Int J Oral Maxillofac Surg. 1992;21(4):226 - 229.*
9. *Stanley HR. Postextraction complications and management. Dent Clin North Am. 1979;23(1):77 - 90.*
10. *Kahnberg KE. Flap design and suturing in oral surgery. Swed Dent J Suppl. 1980;6:1 - 59.*
11. *Coulthard P, Esposito M, Worthington HV. Interventions for preventing dry socket. Cochrane Database Syst Rev. 2014;(4):CD006968.*
12. *Dental Council of India. Clinical and Surgical Documentation Standards. 2022.*

CHAPTER 12

Management of Impacted Teeth - Assessment, Technique, and Complications

Impacted teeth sit quietly in bone until disturbed - then they test a clinician's anatomy, judgment, and composure. Surgical removal of impacted teeth, particularly third molars and canines, is among the most frequently litigated procedures in dentistry. The complication is rarely the impaction itself; it is the lack of assessment, consent, or controlled execution. This chapter builds the mindset and method that make impaction surgery safe, predictable, and defensible.

Purpose and Indications

Management of impacted teeth involves surgical exposure or removal of teeth that fail to erupt within expected time due to obstruction, malposition, or pathology. Indications include pain, pericoronitis, caries in adjacent teeth, cystic changes, resorption, and orthodontic or prosthetic planning [1].

Preparation and Preoperative Evaluation

Take complete medical and dental history. Obtain appropriate imaging - periapical, panoramic, or CBCT - to assess angulation, depth, relation to inferior alveolar nerve, and adjacent structures. Discuss all risks including paresthesia, sinus exposure, and fracture. Obtain written, procedure-specific consent.

Red flag: Proceeding with impaction removal without radiographic nerve mapping or failing to mention risk of nerve damage in written consent makes any postoperative numbness indefensible [2].

- ***Step 1: Classification and Case Selection***

Classify mandibular third molars by Pell and Gregory and Winter's systems. Evaluate space between ramus and distal second molar, angulation, and bone coverage. Select only cases within skill scope and facility capability.

Red flag: Attempting deep or distoangular impactions in a general dental setup without adequate surgical or anesthetic backup violates the principle of reasonable competence [3].

- ***Step 2: Preoperative Preparation***

Ensure sterile field, proper suction, good lighting, and instrument readiness - retractors, surgical handpiece, burs, elevators, and suture material. Mark incision lines mentally before anesthesia.

Red flag: Disorganized setup delays procedure and extends tissue trauma time. Lack of sterile readiness records weakens defense in postoperative infection claims [4].

- ***Step 3: Anesthesia and Positioning***

Administer inferior alveolar, lingual, and long buccal nerve blocks. Confirm full anesthesia before incision. Position patient with mandibular plane parallel to floor and operator at ergonomic clock position.

Red flag: Incomplete anesthesia leads to patient movement, instrument slippage, and soft-tissue damage. No mention of anesthesia verification in notes suggests procedural haste [5].

- ***Step 4: Flap Design and Reflection***

Plan a triangular or envelope flap for adequate exposure. Reflect full-thickness mucoperiosteal flap gently, keeping margins over sound bone. Protect lingual tissues with retractor where indicated.

Red flag: Lingual flap tearing or retractor absence during lower third molar surgery risks lingual nerve injury. Such injuries are always preventable and heavily litigated [6].

- ***Step 5: Bone Removal (Osteotomy)***

Remove bone covering crown using round bur under continuous irrigation. Create a gutter to expose tooth margins without excessive heat.

Red flag: Dry cutting or deep bur penetration injures nerve canal or sinus floor. Operative notes must mention irrigation and depth control to prove due care [7].

- ***Step 6: Tooth Sectioning***

Section crown from roots along lines of least resistance. For mesioangular impactions, divide tooth horizontally; for distoangular or vertical impactions, separate roots individually.

Red flag: Blind or deep sectioning may cause root displacement into sinus, infratemporal fossa, or submandibular space. Each section should be documented with reason and technique [8].

- ***Step 7: Delivery of Tooth or Root Segments***

Elevate sections gently, using minimal leverage. Support mandible externally to counteract force.

Red flag: Excessive buccal leverage fractures jaw in elderly or osteoporotic bone. Lack of external support documentation implies technical negligence [9].

- ***Step 8: Socket Debridement and Irrigation***

Inspect socket for remnants and irrigate thoroughly with saline. Smooth bone edges and confirm hemostasis.

Red flag: Retained follicle or cystic lining causes infection or delayed healing. Unrecorded inspection details in operative note imply incomplete surgery [10].

- ***Step 9: Flap Repositioning and Suturing***

Reposition flap tension-free and suture with interrupted or figure-of-eight technique. Apply gentle pressure to adapt tissue.

Red flag: Sutures too tight or under tension lead to sloughing. Absence of suture count or material record in notes raises questions of completeness [11].

- ***Step 10: Postoperative Instructions and Follow-Up***

Prescribe analgesics and antibiotics where indicated. Advise cold compresses for first 6 hours, soft diet, and gentle rinsing after 24 hours. Instruct patient to report swelling, bleeding, or persistent numbness.

Red flag: Failing to warn about transient paresthesia or dry socket causes patient panic and complaint escalation. Written instruction sheet with acknowledgment signature is essential [12].

Defensibility and Documentation Anchors

Maintain preoperative radiographs, classification details, consent specifying nerve or sinus injury risk, operative notes with irrigation and suture details, and postoperative photographs where appropriate. Schedule follow-up within 48 hours. These records create a verifiable chain of competence and communication.

Case Study

A 27-year-old male underwent surgical extraction of a horizontally impacted mandibular third molar. No CBCT was taken despite close proximity to the inferior alveolar canal on panoramic imaging. Postoperatively, he developed persistent numbness of the lower lip and chin. The consent form was generic and lacked mention of nerve injury risk. The dentist was held liable for negligence; the court observed that risk disclosure and radiographic mapping were both absent.

Case Learnings

1. Radiographic and written risk assessment are inseparable from surgical planning.
2. Informed consent must name specific nerves and structures at risk.
3. CBCT imaging should be obtained when panoramic film shows close nerve relation.
4. Precise documentation of irrigation, flap type, and suture placement demonstrates professional diligence.
5. Communication before and after surgery defines trust; silence breeds litigation.

Quick Checklist

- Radiograph and CBCT assessed
- Case classification documented
- Procedure-specific consent obtained
- Sterile setup verified and logged

- Anesthesia confirmed before incision
- Flap designed for full exposure
- Bone removal under irrigation
- Sectioning controlled and reasoned
- Socket inspected and smoothened
- Postoperative advice given and signed

References

1. *Peterson LJ, Ellis E, Hupp JR, Tucker MR. Contemporary Oral and Maxillofacial Surgery. 7th ed. Elsevier; 2019.*
2. *Kruger GO. Textbook of Oral and Maxillofacial Surgery. 6th ed. CBS Publishers; 2021.*
3. *Pell GJ, Gregory GT. Impacted mandibular third molars: classification and modified techniques for removal. Dent Digest. 1933;39:330 - 338.*
4. *Malamed SF. Medical Emergencies in the Dental Office. 8th ed. Elsevier; 2020.*
5. *Howe GL. Minor Oral Surgery. 4th ed. Butterworth-Heinemann; 1995.*
6. *Renton T, Yilmaz Z. Profiling of patients with post-surgical lingual and inferior alveolar nerve injuries. Br Dent J. 2012;213(11):E20.*
7. *Pogrel MA. Damage to the inferior alveolar nerve during third molar removal. Oral Maxillofac Surg Clin North Am. 2011;23(3):393 - 407.*
8. *Lustmann J, Schwartz-Arad D. Delayed response to displaced root fragments in the maxillary sinus. Int J Oral Maxillofac Surg. 1992;21(4):226 - 229.*
9. *Blondeau F, Daniel NG. Extraction of impacted mandibular third molars: postoperative complications and risk factors. J Can Dent Assoc. 2007;73(4):325.*
10. *Stanley HR. Postextraction complications and management. Dent Clin North Am. 1979;23(1):77 - 90.*
11. *Kahnberg KE. Flap design and suturing in oral surgery. Swed Dent J Suppl. 1980;6:1 - 59.*
12. *Dental Council of India. Clinical Establishment and Surgical Documentation Standards. 2022.*

CHAPTER 13

Post-Extraction Complications - Prevention and Management

No extraction ends when the tooth leaves the socket. Healing is the silent phase that tests how well the procedure was done, how clearly the patient was instructed, and how faithfully the documentation was kept. Most postoperative complaints arise not from rare mishaps but from predictable lapses - unrecorded bleeding, unmanaged pain, or poor communication. This chapter outlines the complications that follow extractions, how to prevent them, and how to respond when they occur.

Purpose and Indications

Post-extraction complication management ensures safe recovery and prevents morbidity after dental extractions. The objective is to anticipate, prevent, identify, and promptly treat complications while maintaining transparent communication and documentation [1].

Preparation and Early Assessment

Immediately after extraction, inspect the socket, verify clot formation, and review patient's medical history for bleeding or delayed-healing risks. Record baseline vital signs and brief the patient before discharge.

Red flag: Discharging a patient without verifying hemostasis or recording vital signs converts a preventable bleed into a medicolegal hazard [2].

- ***Step 1: Hemorrhage (Primary, Reactionary, or Secondary)***

Identify bleeding type - primary (intraoperative), reactionary (within 8 hours), or secondary (after 24 hours). Manage by pressure, suturing, hemostatic agents, or electrocautery. Investigate underlying coagulopathies or anticoagulant use.

Red flag: Assuming patient exaggeration and dismissing late bleeding complaints without examination is negligence. Every bleeding event must have a dated progress note and management record [3].

- ***Step 2: Dry Socket (Alveolar Osteitis)***

Typically occurs 2 - 3 days post-extraction with dull, radiating pain and empty socket. Prevent by gentle curettage, adequate irrigation, and avoiding traumatic extractions. Manage with saline irrigation, medicated dressing (eugenol or chlorhexidine), and analgesics.

Red flag: Excessive curettage or dislodging clot during irrigation causes secondary dry socket. Failure to document postoperative instructions about rinsing or smoking leads to partial liability [4].

- ***Step 3: Infection and Swelling***

Recognize early signs - pain, fever, purulent discharge, or restricted mouth opening. Manage with drainage, antibiotics, and supportive care. Maintain aseptic surgical protocols.

Red flag: Delayed recognition or blind antibiotic prescription without drainage worsens infection and risks spread to fascial spaces. Each infection episode must be entered in progress notes with antibiotic and culture record [5].

- ***Step 4: Trismus***

Usually results from prolonged mouth opening or injection trauma to medial pterygoid. Advise warm compresses, gentle mouth-opening exercises, and anti-inflammatory medication.

Red flag: Forcing mouth open during limited access surgery leads to muscle tear and prolonged disability. Lack of ergonomic breaks during long procedures is a preventable operator error [6].

- ***Step 5: Oroantral Communication***

Occurs during maxillary molar extractions with thin sinus floors. Suspect if air or fluid passes between socket and nose. Confirm with mirror fogging or Valsalva test. Close immediately with buccal advancement or palatal flap.

Red flag: Ignoring sinus communication or advising patient to "let it close naturally" results in chronic sinusitis and malpractice exposure. Consent must mention sinus exposure risk preoperatively [7].

- ***Step 6: Nerve Injury (Inferior Alveolar or Lingual Nerve)***

Recognize numbness, tingling, or burning after extraction or flap reflection. Reassess immediately, document findings, and refer for neurosensory evaluation.

Red flag: Failure to record onset time, area, and patient complaint makes nerve injury appear concealed. Proper documentation of CBCT findings and nerve proximity in consent form protects against liability [8].

- ***Step 7: Jaw Fracture or Alveolar Bone Loss***

Fractures result from excessive force or pathological bone. Detect by mobility, crepitus, or altered occlusion. Immobilize and refer for fixation.

Red flag: Attempting to realign or "stabilize" fracture without imaging or referral worsens damage. The event must be recorded and reported to patient and insurance immediately [9].

- ***Step 8: Soft-Tissue Tears and Lacerations***

Prevent by careful retraction and adequate visibility. Repair promptly with fine sutures and ensure tissue hydration.

Red flag: Ignoring torn mucosa or failing to record intraoperative repair invites future claims for scarring or disfigurement. Every intraoral tear deserves an entry in the operative note [10].

- ***Step 9: Delayed Healing and Bone Spicules***

Occurs in smokers, diabetics, or after traumatic extraction. Smooth spicules under local anesthesia and irrigate socket.

Red flag: Repeated trimming without addressing systemic factors prolongs recovery. Documentation must show patient was advised on systemic risk control [11].

- ***Step 10: Postoperative Communication and Follow-Up***

Call or message patient within 24 hours to assess pain, bleeding, or swelling. Schedule follow-up within 48 - 72 hours.

Red flag: Lack of follow-up or call record implies abandonment of care. Every postoperative contact must be logged with date, time, and outcome [12].

Defensibility and Documentation Anchors

Maintain preoperative consent detailing common complications. Document each postoperative complaint, visit, and advice with date and signature. Keep postoperative photographs for record. In court, a well-documented follow-up is stronger defense than even successful surgery.

Case Study

A 61-year-old patient on anticoagulants underwent molar extraction. The dentist neither consulted the physician nor noted INR levels. Postoperatively, secondary bleeding occurred after 36 hours, requiring hospital admission and transfusion. No consent or postoperative instruction record was found. The case was judged as negligent for failure to assess systemic status and poor postoperative follow-up documentation.

Case Learnings

1. Prevention starts with communication, not intervention.
2. Every postoperative event - even minor bleeding - deserves written entry.
3. Dry socket and bleeding remain the top two causes of legal complaints after extraction.
4. Written consent and postoperative instruction sheets protect against "non-disclosure" claims.
5. Follow-up logs are as critical as operative notes in proving continuity of care.

Quick Checklist

- Clot verified and bleeding controlled
- Dry socket prevention explained
- Antibiotic and analgesic plan documented
- Patient advised on smoking, spitting, rinsing
- Follow-up scheduled within 48 hours
- All complaints recorded with management

- Infection and nerve injury notes maintained
- Sinus and fracture cases referred promptly
- Photographs or radiographs taken when indicated
- All correspondence filed with patient record

References

1. *Kruger GO. Textbook of Oral and Maxillofacial Surgery. 6th ed. CBS Publishers; 2021.*
2. *Peterson LJ, Ellis E, Hupp JR, Tucker MR. Contemporary Oral and Maxillofacial Surgery. 7th ed. Elsevier; 2019.*
3. *Stanley HR. Postextraction complications and management. Dent Clin North Am. 1979;23(1):77 - 90.*
4. *Blum IR. Contemporary views on dry socket etiology and management. Br Dent J. 2002;193(5):275 - 282.*
5. *Malamed SF. Medical Emergencies in the Dental Office. 8th ed. Elsevier; 2020.*
6. *Rood JP, Murgatroyd J. Trismus and its management following oral surgery. Br Dent J. 1978;144(6):167 - 170.*
7. *Killey HC, Kay LW. An Analysis of 250 Cases of Oroantral Communication. Oral Surg Oral Med Oral Pathol. 1967;24(6):726 - 739.*
8. *Renton T, Yilmaz Z. Inferior alveolar nerve injury in mandibular third molar surgery. Br Dent J. 2012;213(11):E20.*
9. *Blondeau F, Daniel NG. Mandibular fractures following dental extractions. J Can Dent Assoc. 2007;73(4):325.*
10. *Howe GL. Minor Oral Surgery. 4th ed. Butterworth-Heinemann; 1995.*
11. *Coulthard P et al. Complications in oral surgery: prevention and management. Br Dent J. 2014;217(3):123 - 128.*
12. *Dental Council of India. Clinical Documentation and Postoperative Follow-Up Standards. 2022.*

CHAPTER 14

Medicolegal Aspects of Tooth Extraction - Documentation, Disclosure, and Defensibility

Every extraction carries two outcomes: a clinical one in the mouth and a legal one in the file. A well-managed tooth removal can still become a legal loss if the notes, consent, or communication falter. Medico-legal safety in oral surgery is not about avoiding complications - it is about proving diligence, foresight, and honesty. This chapter closes the circle of exodontia by connecting surgical technique with legal defensibility.

Purpose and Indications

This chapter aims to guide clinicians on documentation, consent, communication, and risk disclosure specific to extractions and minor oral surgery. It defines what must be written, what must be said, and what must never be assumed [1].

Preparation and Legal Awareness

Understand the basic legal expectations in dental procedures: duty of care, informed consent, competence, confidentiality, and documentation. Recognize that each extraction is a medical intervention governed by these principles.

Red flag: Believing that "routine" extractions require only verbal consent reflects ignorance of standard legal norms. Courts treat verbal-only consent as no consent at all [2].

- ***Step 1: Informed Consent and Risk Disclosure***

Consent must be written, dated, and procedure-specific. Include details of the tooth, anesthesia type, potential complications (bleeding, dry socket, sinus exposure, nerve injury, fracture), and post-treatment responsibilities. Use the patient's language, not medical jargon.

Red flag: Generic consent forms covering "any dental procedure" are invalid. Absence of mention of nerve or sinus injury is equivalent to nondisclosure in case of such outcomes [3].

- ***Step 2: Documentation of Assessment and Planning***

Attach preoperative radiographs, diagnosis, treatment plan, and risk evaluation. Note patient's medical conditions, allergies, and medication history.

Red flag: Missing radiographs or medical notes show lack of planning. Courts interpret missing records as "not performed." Each assessment must bear date and clinician's signature [4].

- ***Step 3: Procedure Note and Intraoperative Documentation***

Record tooth number, anesthesia type, instruments used, complications, and immediate management. Sign and date entries immediately after procedure.

Red flag: Rewriting or postdating notes once complications occur is document tampering - a criminal offense. Each page must be contemporaneous and initialed [5].

- ***Step 4: Communication During Complications***

If a mishap occurs (fracture, root displacement, nerve exposure), inform patient and document conversation in writing. Provide written referral if specialist management is needed.

Red flag: Concealment or delayed disclosure of complications transforms a manageable event into malpractice. Courts punish concealment more harshly than error itself [6].

- ***Step 5: Postoperative Advice and Written Instructions***

Provide written instructions regarding rest, diet, oral hygiene, and emergency contact. Obtain patient's signature acknowledging receipt.

Red flag: Verbal advice alone fails during litigation; patient's word outweighs the dentist's without a signed acknowledgment [7].

- ***Step 6: Follow-Up and Review Records***

Schedule and record postoperative visits. Enter findings, healing progress, and any patient complaint in progress notes.

Red flag: Lack of follow-up documentation creates perception of abandonment. Even a single missed follow-up entry undermines continuity-of-care defense [8].

- ***Step 7: Referral and Interdisciplinary Coordination***

When referring to specialists for complications (e.g., nerve injury or sinus repair), provide detailed written referral with diagnosis and treatment summary. Keep a copy in patient file.

Red flag: Verbal referral without documented proof shifts entire liability to referring dentist if outcome deteriorates [9].

- ***Step 8: Handling Complaints and Communication Records***

Respond to complaints in writing, maintaining factual tone and empathy. Preserve all communication, messages, and calls in file. Avoid alteration or deletion of messages.

Red flag: Defensive or emotional replies aggravate disputes. Altering records or deleting digital communication is treated as obstruction of justice [10].

- ***Step 9: Record Retention and Privacy***

Retain all extraction-related records (radiographs, notes, consent, referrals) for at least five years, longer in cases of complications or medico-legal inquiry. Secure files under restricted access.

Red flag: Premature disposal of records during active dispute is evidence destruction and can lead to suspension or criminal charges [11].

- ***Step 10: Audit and Continuous Training***

Conduct annual audits of surgical documentation and mock drills on informed consent. Keep attendance logs for legal defensibility training.

Red flag: Clinics without documentation audits or risk management training are considered institutionally negligent under clinical establishment regulations [12].

Defensibility and Documentation Anchors

For every extraction, the minimum legal file must include:

- Written, signed, and dated consent form mentioning all specific risks
- Preoperative radiographs and assessment notes

- Procedure notes with date and signature
- Postoperative instruction sheet acknowledged by patient
- Follow-up and complaint records
- Referral letters or specialist reports
- Record retention and privacy log

Properly filled, these documents transform a complication into a defendable event rather than a conviction.

Case Study

A 33-year-old patient filed a lawsuit alleging permanent numbness after wisdom tooth extraction. The dentist produced no signed consent form and no record mentioning nerve proximity or risk discussion. Radiographs were missing, and the first written note appeared only after the complaint. The court concluded that absence of consent and records reflected professional negligence, awarding compensation and disciplinary action.

Case Learnings

1. Informed consent must be detailed, procedure-specific, and dated before anesthesia.
2. Documentation must begin before incision and continue until review.
3. Concealment or delayed disclosure is legally worse than an actual mishap.
4. Signed acknowledgment of postoperative instructions is proof of patient education.
5. Continuous documentation training prevents lapses that cannot be repaired afterward.

Quick Checklist

- Consent form signed, dated, and specific
- Preoperative notes and radiographs attached
- Procedure details written and signed
- Complications disclosed and documented

- Written postoperative advice provided
- Follow-up entries complete and dated
- Referral letters issued when required
- All communication records preserved
- Records retained for minimum 5 years
- Audit and legal compliance training logged

References

1. *Dental Council of India. Clinical Establishment and Medico-Legal Standards. 2022.*
2. *Indian Medical Council. Legal Obligations and Professional Ethics in Clinical Practice. 2021.*
3. *General Dental Council (UK). Standards for the Dental Team: Consent and Disclosure. 2013.*
4. *World Health Organization. Health Record Documentation Standards. 2021.*
5. *Ministry of Health and Family Welfare, India. National Guidelines on Medical Record Maintenance. 2018.*
6. *Dental Protection Limited. Managing Adverse Incidents and Disclosure in Dental Practice. 2020.*
7. *Medical Defence Union (UK). Risk Management Handbook for Dental Practitioners. 2021.*
8. *American Dental Association. Documentation and Follow-Up Protocols. 2020.*
9. *Health Information Technology Act, India. Electronic Records and Legal Admissibility. 2019.*
10. *Government of India. Digital Evidence and Medical Documentation Regulations. 2020.*
11. *Ministry of Law and Justice, India. Indian Evidence Act - Electronic Record Amendments. 2021.*
12. *World Dental Federation (FDI). Global Guidelines for Dental Risk Management. 2022.*

SECTION 3

Endodontics - Pulpal and Periapical Decision Pathways

Inside every tooth lies a test of judgment. Endodontics isn't only about saving structure - it's about knowing when to stop, when to reopen, and when to accept that biology will not negotiate. The pulp chamber is small, but it's where technical precision and medico-legal accountability meet most sharply.

This section walks the reader from the first twinge of reversible pulpitis to the final radiograph that proves resolution. Each chapter builds a disciplined flow - diagnosis grounded in vitality testing and imaging, access designed to preserve enamel and reputation alike, instrumentation carried out with asepsis and traceability, obturation validated by radiographic proof, and coronal restoration that seals both tooth and case.

Here, the file is both instrument and evidence. Every millimeter entered, every irrigant used, every radiograph taken forms the audit trail that separates competence from carelessness. The section insists on contemporaneous documentation: working length notes, batch numbers, anesthetic volumes, and the sequence of every decision.

Complications - file separation, ledging, missed canals, flare-ups, and failed healing - are treated not as embarrassments but as responsibilities. The chapters teach disclosure, referral etiquette, and written acknowledgment, transforming crisis management into credibility.

By its close, this section gives the clinician a calm, methodical way to approach the most complex procedures - to act confidently within the tooth and defend decisively outside it. It proves that true endodontic success is not just radiographic; it's procedural, transparent, and recorded.

CHAPTER 15

Diagnosis of Pulpal Diseases - Clinical and Legal Relevance

Endodontic success begins long before the access cavity - in the precision of diagnosis. Misdiagnosis is not just a clinical error; it is a medicolegal trigger. Every failed root canal, unnecessary extraction, or lingering pain case traces back to diagnostic shortcuts. This chapter rebuilds diagnosis into a disciplined process anchored in documentation and informed reasoning.

Purpose and Indications

Accurate pulpal diagnosis differentiates reversible conditions from irreversible pulpitis, identifies necrosis, and guides correct treatment - whether conservative therapy, endodontic intervention, or extraction. It ensures that intervention is necessary, timed, and justified [1].

Preparation and Pre-Examination Steps

Obtain comprehensive medical and dental history. Record nature, duration, and triggers of pain - sharp, dull, spontaneous, lingering, or referred. Note any history of swelling, trauma, or previous dental treatment.

Red flag: Treating pain without recording its character, duration, or aggravating factors is diagnostic negligence. Courts regard "pain on and off" notes as inadequate documentation [2].

- ***Step 1: Visual and Clinical Inspection***

Inspect for discoloration, caries, restorations, fractures, and sinus openings. Test tooth mobility and percussion response.

Red flag: Skipping percussion and palpation leads to misdiagnosis between pulpal and periodontal pain. A neglected percussion finding has been cited in malpractice judgments as omission of standard diagnostic care [3].

- ***Step 2: Thermal Testing (Cold and Heat)***

Apply cold test using ethyl chloride or Endo-Ice and record patient response time and intensity. Compare with adjacent teeth. Use hot gutta-percha when indicated.

Red flag: Failure to test control teeth or record response duration makes interpretation speculative. A note that says "cold positive" without timing or reference teeth is meaningless in defense [4].

- ***Step 3: Electric Pulp Testing***

Use electronic pulp tester at increasing intensity until response occurs. Always compare with contralateral tooth.

Red flag: Over-reliance on pulp tester alone is flawed; false positives occur in inflamed pulp and false negatives in calcified teeth. No mention of calibration or comparison weakens credibility of diagnostic record [5].

- ***Step 4: Radiographic Examination***

Take periapical and bitewing radiographs. Evaluate lamina dura, periodontal ligament space, periapical radiolucency, and root morphology. Document radiographic findings with annotation or report.

Red flag: Performing endodontic therapy without baseline radiograph is indefensible. Even a technically perfect root canal cannot be defended if pretreatment imaging is missing [6].

- ***Step 5: Advanced Imaging and CBCT***

Use CBCT when radiographs are inconclusive or for complex canal morphology, resorption, or periapical pathology. Record reason for use and findings summary.

Red flag: Overuse of CBCT without justification exposes patient to unnecessary radiation and legal scrutiny. Each CBCT must have an indication note and signed acknowledgment [7].

- ***Step 6: Diagnostic Cavity and Test Drilling***

When results conflict, access pulp chamber under anesthesia and observe bleeding, color, and odor. This is reserved for diagnostic confirmation.

Red flag: Performing diagnostic drilling without anesthesia or consent for "exploratory opening" is unacceptable. The act constitutes invasive procedure without consent [8].

- ***Step 7: Correlation and Differential Diagnosis***

Combine clinical findings, tests, and radiographs to classify as:

- Normal pulp
- Reversible pulpitis
- Irreversible pulpitis
- Necrotic pulp
- Previously treated pulp

Red flag: Relying on single test to decide treatment type is indefensible. A valid diagnosis must have at least two convergent findings documented with interpretation [9].

- ***Step 8: Documentation and Record Keeping***

Record each test with date, method, result, and interpretation. Maintain radiographs in digital form with annotations.

Red flag: A treatment note stating only "RCT advised" without recorded findings and justification violates informed decision-making norms [10].

- ***Step 9: Communication and Informed Decision***

Explain diagnosis, prognosis, and alternatives - conservative therapy, endodontic treatment, or extraction. Obtain written consent with procedure name and expected outcomes.

Red flag: Absence of written consent for root canal or reliance on verbal "go ahead" invites disputes in cases of postoperative pain or failure [11].

- ***Step 10: Review and Second Opinion***

In uncertain cases, refer for specialist evaluation and record referral reason and outcome.

Red flag: Unrecorded second opinions or unacknowledged referrals create confusion in continuity of care and weaken defense in shared responsibility cases [12].

Defensibility and Documentation Anchors

Every diagnostic step must be traceable - from patient complaint to test results and final decision. Consent should reference diagnosis and chosen treatment. Radiographs and test records serve as primary proof of due diligence and professional reasoning.

Case Study

A 32-year-old patient presented with lingering pain in upper right first molar. The clinician diagnosed "irreversible pulpitis" and initiated RCT. Postoperatively, pain persisted. A specialist review revealed the maxillary sinus as the pain source. No documentation of pulp testing, radiograph, or sinus evaluation existed. The case was ruled as diagnostic negligence with compensation for unnecessary treatment.

Case Learnings

1. Pain pattern without test results is not diagnosis; it is assumption.
2. Radiographs and pulp tests are mandatory before any endodontic decision.
3. Documentation of findings and reasoning is legal evidence of judgment.
4. Consent for RCT must explicitly mention diagnostic basis.
5. Diagnostic diligence saves both patient and practitioner from avoidable harm.

Quick Checklist

- Pain history and duration recorded
- Visual inspection and percussion noted
- Thermal and electric pulp tests documented
- Radiographs taken and reported
- CBCT justified and recorded when used
- Diagnosis categorized and signed
- Consent obtained for planned treatment
- Referral and second opinions documented
- All data stored digitally and backed up
- Records retained minimum five years

References

1. *Hargreaves KM, Berman LH. Cohen's Pathways of the Pulp. 12th ed. Elsevier; 2022.*
2. *Abbott PV. Diagnosis and management of referred orofacial pain. Aust Dent J. 2016;61(Suppl 1):S14 - S22.*
3. *Seltzer S, Bender IB. Pulpal pain diagnosis and management. J Endod. 1984;10(9):390 - 397.*
4. *Petersson K et al. Evaluation of the ability of thermal and electric pulp tests to register pulp vitality. Int Endod J. 1999;32(1):1 - 6.*
5. *Weisleder R et al. Reliability of electric pulp testing in different pulpal and periapical conditions. Int Endod J. 2009;42(2):159 - 165.*
6. *Patel S et al. Radiographic assessment and documentation in endodontics. Int Endod J. 2019;52(7):1001 - 1013.*
7. *European Society of Endodontology. Use of CBCT in Endodontics: Position Statement. 2021.*
8. *American Association of Endodontists. Diagnostic Terminology and Guidelines. 2020.*
9. *Ricucci D, Siqueira JF. Biofilms and apical periodontitis. Endod Topics. 2010;22(1):33 - 49.*
10. *Dental Council of India. Documentation and Radiographic Standards in Endodontic Practice. 2022.*
11. *General Dental Council (UK). Standards for the Dental Team: Record Keeping and Consent. 2013.*
12. *Indian Medical Council. Shared Responsibility and Referral Documentation Advisory. 2021.*

CHAPTER 16

Access Cavity Preparation - Principles, Pitfalls, and Legal Safeguards

An access cavity is the gateway to endodontic success - or failure. It defines everything that follows: visibility, canal negotiation, irrigation, obturation, and long-term prognosis. Yet, most iatrogenic accidents in endodontics arise not from complex anatomy but from careless access - missed canals, perforations, or crown fractures. This chapter dissects the art and responsibility of access preparation as both a technical and legal act.

Purpose and Indications

The access cavity provides direct, unobstructed entry into the pulp chamber and canal system, allowing thorough cleaning and shaping while preserving tooth structure. It is indicated whenever endodontic therapy is planned or pulpal space must be examined diagnostically [1].

Preparation and Preoperative Planning

Obtain preoperative radiographs in at least two angulations. Assess tooth morphology, restorations, and previous treatments. Verify vitality, working diagnosis, and treatment plan in records before access.

Red flag: Starting access without radiograph or confirmed diagnosis turns a planned procedure into blind exploration. Any resulting perforation becomes indefensible due to lack of preoperative imaging [2].

- ***Step 1: Isolation and Field Control***

Apply rubber dam isolation to prevent contamination and instrument aspiration. Clean the crown surface and disinfect with chlorhexidine.

Red flag: Performing access without rubber dam, even in "short" cases, violates standard of care. In court, absence of rubber dam documentation is automatic negligence, regardless of outcome [3].

- ***Step 2: Outline Form Determination***

Visualize internal anatomy using radiographs and knowledge of typical pulp chamber morphology. Mark access outline on the occlusal or lingual surface before cutting.

Red flag: Guesswork leads to missed canals or structural overcutting. Over-enlarged access weakens crown and increases fracture risk; undersized access causes missed canal and persistent infection [4].

- ***Step 3: Initial Penetration***

Use high-speed round bur to penetrate enamel and superficial dentin until "drop-in" to pulp chamber is felt. Switch to slower speed to prevent perforation.

Red flag: Failure to change bur speed or direction leads to floor perforation or furcal entry. Every perforation is a permanent record of poor technique - and must be disclosed immediately [5].

- ***Step 4: Roof Removal and Chamber Clearance***

Use safe-ended bur to remove chamber roof and locate orifices under magnification. Clean all debris and rinse with sodium hypochlorite.

Red flag: Leaving residual pulp horns or ignoring hidden calcifications results in incomplete debridement and postoperative pain. Overzealous roof removal weakens crown and demands full coverage restoration later [6].

- ***Step 5: Canal Orifice Location***

Identify canal orifices using DG16 explorer, micro-openers, and dyes. Follow developmental lines and color changes on chamber floor.

Red flag: Skipping magnification or illumination risks missing accessory canals, especially MB2 in maxillary molars. Each missed canal is a potential source of reinfection and malpractice claim [7].

- ***Step 6: Preventing Perforations***

Maintain bur parallel to long axis of tooth and refer to radiographic guides frequently. Use apex locator and tactile sense when in doubt.

Red flag: Lateral or furcal perforation from angulation error is irreparable.

Concealing it or proceeding without informing patient is professional misconduct [8].

- ***Step 7: Pulp Chamber Irrigation and Debridement***

Irrigate chamber with sodium hypochlorite to remove debris and tissue remnants. Aspirate thoroughly and dry with paper points.

Red flag: Inadvertent extrusion of irrigant beyond apex due to overpressure causes chemical burn and swelling. Lack of irrigation record in notes exposes clinician to claims of chemical injury [9].

- ***Step 8: Access Refinement and Straight-Line Entry***

Refine walls for unobstructed canal access while preserving marginal ridges. Verify line of entry for each canal with small files.

Red flag: Over-enlargement for visibility weakens structure and predisposes to fracture. A tooth lost to fracture post-endodontic treatment often traces back to aggressive access [10].

- ***Step 9: Documentation and Radiographic Verification***

Take post-access radiograph to confirm chamber opening and initial file entry. Record instrument used, irrigation agent, and any complication.

Red flag: Proceeding to shaping without confirming canal trajectory or documenting radiograph breaks the chain of evidence for procedural care [11].

- ***Step 10: Patient Communication and Disclosure***

Explain access findings, canal variations, and any procedural events such as calcification, extra canal, or perforation. Obtain patient acknowledgment in writing.

Red flag: Concealing procedural incidents - however minor - voids legal defensibility. Disclosure with explanation and plan for correction sustains trust and protection [12].

Defensibility and Documentation Anchors

A defensible endodontic record for access cavity preparation includes:

- Preoperative and post-access radiographs
- Rubber dam use recorded with date and photo when possible

- Access design and instrument notes
- Irrigation protocol and chemical concentration
- Disclosure record of any complication

Each entry must be signed, dated, and filed in patient record. These simple elements transform technical precision into legal safety.

Case Study

A 40-year-old patient underwent root canal on a mandibular molar. The dentist performed access without radiograph or rubber dam. During entry, a furcal perforation occurred and was sealed without disclosure. Two months later, swelling and bone loss developed. Legal review confirmed absence of radiographs and written consent. The case was judged negligent for lack of standard isolation and concealment of intraoperative error.

Case Learnings

1. Radiographs and rubber dam are the twin pillars of defensibility in endodontics.
2. Every access shape and angulation should be deliberate and recorded.
3. Perforations are accidents; concealment is misconduct.
4. Documentation of irrigation and instrument use defines procedural competence.
5. Patient communication immediately after any event transforms potential litigation into transparency.

Quick Checklist

- Preoperative radiographs reviewed
- Rubber dam applied and logged
- Outline form marked and followed
- Penetration controlled under vision
- Roof removed with safe-ended bur
- Canal orifices located with magnification
- Irrigation documented with concentration

- Post-access radiograph confirmed
- All complications disclosed and recorded
- Patient informed and acknowledgment signed

References

1. *Hargreaves KM, Berman LH. Cohen's Pathways of the Pulp. 12th ed. Elsevier; 2022.*
2. *Patel S, Rhodes JS. Non-surgical retreatment: clinical procedures. Br Dent J. 2007;203(3):133 - 139.*
3. *General Dental Council (UK). Standards for the Dental Team: Clinical Safety and Isolation. 2013.*
4. *Krasner P, Rankow HJ. Anatomy of the pulp-chamber floor. J Endod. 2004;30(1):5 - 16.*
5. *Siqueira JF Jr, Rôças IN. Complications in endodontics: prevention and management. Int Endod J. 2008;41(7):593 - 604.*
6. *Ruddle CJ. Endodontic access preparation: anatomic considerations. Dent Today. 2001;20(6):66 - 73.*
7. *Wolcott J et al. MB2 canal detection rates: clinical significance. J Endod. 2005;31(4):264 - 268.*
8. *Tsesis I et al. Iatrogenic perforations: incidence, prognosis, and treatment. J Endod. 2010;36(3):475 - 479.*
9. *Hülsmann M, Hahn W. Complications during root canal irrigation. Endod Dent Traumatol. 2000;16(5):223 - 231.*
10. *Sedgley CM, Messer HH. Are endodontically treated teeth more brittle? J Endod. 1992;18(7):332 - 335.*
11. *Patel S et al. Radiographic documentation in endodontics. Int Endod J. 2019;52(7):1001 - 1013.*
12. *Dental Protection Limited. Disclosure and Management of Procedural Incidents. 2021.*

CHAPTER 17

Working Length Determination - Accuracy, Errors, and Legal Implications

Every millimeter in endodontics carries meaning. Stopping short leaves infection; going long invites injury. Determining working length is therefore not just a technical step but a legal statement - proof that the clinician respected anatomy, guidelines, and judgment. This chapter explains how to measure, verify, and document working length so that both the canal and the case file stay within limits.

Purpose and Indications

Working length (WL) is the distance from a coronal reference point to the point where canal preparation and obturation should end - ideally at the apical constriction, not beyond. Accurate WL ensures thorough cleaning while preventing periapical irritation or extrusion of materials [1].

Preparation and Preoperative Requirements

Take clear preoperative radiographs to assess root length, curvature, and periapical status. Calibrate apex locator and check file integrity. Document WL determination method in the procedure notes before shaping.

Red flag: Using "standard length" values or proceeding without radiographic verification transforms precision dentistry into guesswork - indefensible if postoperative pain or paresthesia occurs [2].

- ***Step 1: Establishing Glide Path and Canal Patency***

Use size 8 or 10 K-file to negotiate canal gently until slight resistance is felt. Confirm patency with tactile feedback and irrigation.

Red flag: Skipping glide path leads to inaccurate WL and instrument separation. A separated file without documented WL verification becomes an unexplainable error [3].

- ***Step 2: Radiographic Estimation of Initial Length***

Insert small K-file and take diagnostic radiograph with file in situ to approximate canal length. Record estimated distance from radiographic apex.

Red flag: Poor angulation or distorted image makes WL estimation unreliable. Absence of this radiograph before shaping implies procedural negligence [4].

- ***Step 3: Apex Locator Use***

Use electronic apex locator (EAL) under dry or minimally moist conditions. Record readings with file size and canal number.

Red flag: Relying solely on apex locator without correlating with radiograph is risky. Court evaluations consider EAL alone as insufficient proof of accuracy [5].

- ***Step 4: Cross-Verification and Final WL Fixation***

Correlate apex locator readings with radiographic estimation. Set WL 0.5 - 1 mm short of radiographic apex. Adjust as per canal curvature and apical constriction feedback.

Red flag: Over-instrumentation beyond apex results in periapical injury or extrusion. Lack of recorded WL adjustment note implies absence of re-evaluation during procedure [6].

- ***Step 5: Establishing Coronal Reference Point***

Mark WL from reproducible coronal landmark (cusp tip or incisal edge). Document which reference was used in notes.

Red flag: Unmarked or inconsistent reference points cause variable WL during instrumentation. Discrepancies across visits suggest procedural inconsistency and poor supervision [7].

- ***Step 6: Documentation of WL Determination***

Record methods used (EAL, radiograph), canal number, file size, and final WL in millimeters. Take working length confirmation radiograph.

Red flag: Missing WL record or radiograph voids defense in case of extrusion or postoperative pain. In court, absence of WL proof equates to no WL determination [8].

- ***Step 7: Continuous Verification During Preparation***

Reconfirm WL after coronal flaring or recapitulation since canal length may change. Record any adjustments.

Red flag: Not verifying WL after flaring causes inadvertent over-instrumentation. A perforation discovered later without adjustment record appears as operator carelessness [9].

- ***Step 8: Error Prevention and Correction***

If WL appears inconsistent, stop and repeat readings. Check for debris at file tip or device error. Use multiple methods before proceeding.

Red flag: Continuing procedure despite uncertain readings or malfunctioning EAL shows disregard for anatomical safety - a breach of standard of care [10].

- ***Step 9: Communication and Patient Transparency***

Explain that accurate length determination prevents pain and protects periapical tissues. In event of overextension, document patient notification and follow-up.

Red flag: Concealment of instrument or material extrusion is unethical and punishable under professional misconduct provisions [11].

- ***Step 10: Final Verification Before Obturation***

Take master cone radiograph confirming obturation length within apical constriction. Compare with documented WL.

Red flag: Obturation beyond apex due to mismatch between WL and cone length is entirely preventable. Lack of verification record eliminates defense of due diligence [12].

Defensibility and Documentation Anchors

Every WL determination must leave a trace - radiographs (initial and master cone), EAL readings, and procedural notes. These documents form the measurable proof of anatomical respect. Each canal length should be logged separately in the file or digital chart.

Case Study

A 35-year-old female underwent RCT on mandibular molar. The dentist relied only on apex locator readings without radiographs. Obturation material extruded beyond apex, causing chronic pain and paresthesia.

The court concluded that absence of WL radiographs and documentation showed procedural negligence. Compensation was granted for permanent nerve damage.

Case Learnings

1. Every WL must be proven by both electronic and radiographic evidence.
2. Over-instrumentation injuries stem from haste, not anatomy.
3. Each canal length should be written, signed, and confirmed with radiograph.
4. Documentation of reference point and method defines reproducibility.
5. The defense of "machine error" is invalid without corroborating records.

Quick Checklist

- Preoperative radiograph and EAL calibrated
- Glide path and patency confirmed
- Initial WL estimated radiographically
- Apex locator readings recorded per canal
- Cross-verification and adjustment logged
- Reference point documented
- WL confirmation radiograph taken
- Post-flaring WL rechecked
- Master cone fit verified within WL
- All notes signed, dated, and stored

References

1. *Hargreaves KM, Berman LH. Cohen's Pathways of the Pulp. 12th ed. Elsevier; 2022.*
2. *Patel S et al. Radiographic documentation in endodontics. Int Endod J. 2019;52(7):1001 - 1013.*
3. *Hülsmann M, Schinkel I. Influence of preparation technique on working length control. Int Endod J. 1994;27(5):254 - 260.*
4. *Forsberg J. Radiographic reproduction of root canal length measurement. Int Endod J.*

1987;20(3):135 - 142.

5. *Nekoofar MH et al. Accuracy of apex locators in different canal conditions. Int Endod J. 2006;39(6):483 - 489.*
6. *Ricucci D, Langeland K. Apical limit of root canal instrumentation. Int Endod J. 1998;31(6):384 - 393.*
7. *Ingle JI, Bakland LK, Baumgartner JC. Ingle's Endodontics. 7th ed. BC Decker; 2019.*
8. *Tsesis I et al. Outcome of overfilled and underfilled root canals. J Endod. 2013;39(6):632 - 639.*
9. *Canalda C et al. Changes in working length during instrumentation. Int Endod J. 1996;29(3):146 - 152.*
10. *Gordon MPJ, Chandler NP. Electronic apex locators-A review. Int Endod J. 2004;37(7):425 - 437.*
11. *Dental Protection Limited. Management of Procedural Accidents in Endodontics. 2021.*
12. *Dental Council of India. Clinical Documentation and Radiographic Protocols. 2022.*

CHAPTER 18

Cleaning and Shaping - Biomechanical Principles, Instrumentation Errors, and Medico-Legal Relevance

Cleaning and shaping transform a dark, infected space into a disinfected, biologically acceptable form. The canal is unseen, but the mistakes made inside it are painfully visible in postoperative pain, broken files, and litigation. This chapter translates biomechanics into a sequence of controlled actions that protect both periapical tissue and professional reputation.

Purpose and Indications

Cleaning and shaping remove necrotic pulp, bacteria, and debris while creating a continuously tapering canal that can be effectively irrigated and obturated. The goal is to disinfect without distortion, preserve anatomy without aggression, and document each step as reproducible evidence of diligence [1].

Preparation and Equipment Check

Confirm working length, isolate with rubber dam, and prepare irrigation solutions - sodium hypochlorite (2.5 - 5.25%), EDTA (17%), and saline. Inspect all files for defects under magnification.

Red flag: Using fatigued or reused rotary files without inspection is indefensible after a separation incident. Record batch numbers and discard after recommended use cycles [2].

- ***Step 1: Canal Patency and Glide Path Establishment***

Use small hand files (#8 - 15) to maintain canal patency and establish glide path with gentle watch-winding motion. Irrigate frequently.

Red flag: Forcing files into constricted canals without glide path causes ledge or perforation. A missed patency record in notes appears as procedural negligence [3].

- ***Step 2: Coronal Flaring and Pre-Enlargement***

Widen coronal third using Gates-Glidden drills or orifice openers to improve irrigant penetration and instrument control.

Red flag: Over-flaring weakens cervical dentin and predisposes to vertical fracture. Every flaring sequence should be logged in notes with instrument sizes [4].

- ***Step 3: Working Length Reconfirmation***

Recheck working length after coronal enlargement using apex locator or radiograph. Adjust if necessary.

Red flag: Failure to reconfirm WL after flaring leads to over-instrumentation and apical perforation - a classic preventable injury [5].

- ***Step 4: Step-Back or Crown-Down Technique Selection***

Choose technique according to canal anatomy and instrument system. Hand files suit narrow, curved canals; rotary NiTi files for wide, straight canals.

Red flag: Using rotary systems without understanding torque settings or anatomy leads to file separation. Each system used should be noted with manufacturer and size range [6].

- ***Step 5: Continuous Irrigation During Shaping***

Irrigate with sodium hypochlorite after each file. Activate irrigant using side-vented needles or sonic agitation for better debridement.

Red flag: Forcing irrigant under pressure can cause NaOCl extrusion and facial swelling. Courts view chemical injury as procedural negligence if irrigation method isn't recorded [7].

- ***Step 6: Recapitulation and Debris Control***

After each file, re-enter canal with small file to maintain patency. Flush debris and confirm smooth taper.

Red flag: Ignoring recapitulation leads to apical blockage and false WL readings. Subsequent over-instrumentation appears as lack of procedural sequence documentation [8].

- ***Step 7: Final Apical Preparation***

Prepare apical constriction to 0.25 - 0.40 mm diameter, maintaining smooth taper. Stop at established WL.

Red flag: Over-enlarging apex weakens seal and causes extrusion. In absence of WL record, apical transport becomes indefensible [9].

- ***Step 8: Final Irrigation Protocol***

Use sequence: NaOCl → EDTA → saline. Dry canal with sterile paper points.

Red flag: Failure to neutralize irrigants or leaving EDTA residue compromises obturation. Missing irrigation log is legally equivalent to incomplete cleaning [10].

- ***Step 9: Documentation and Procedural Notes***

Record file sizes, torque settings, sequence, irrigant concentration, and total volume used. Photograph or scan chart if digital.

Red flag: Absent procedural documentation renders endodontic sequence untraceable; in disputes, "no record" is read as "no step performed" [11].

- ***Step 10: Interim Medication and Temporary Seal***

Place calcium hydroxide or medicated dressing if obturation delayed. Seal access with sterile cotton and temporary restorative material.

Red flag: Leaving canal open to drain invites contamination. If patient returns with swelling or reinfection, absence of interim seal note negates defense [12].

Defensibility and Documentation Anchors

A defendable record must show:

- Rubber dam use and isolation note
- Working length confirmation before and after flaring
- File sequence, system, and sizes used
- Irrigation protocol with volumes and agents
- Notes on interim medication and temporary seal

All entries dated, signed, and supported with pre- and post-instrumentation radiographs.

Case Study

A 45-year-old patient developed persistent pain and swelling following RCT on a maxillary molar. Investigation revealed apical perforation and file extrusion. The dentist had no record of working length reconfirmation or file sequence. The consent form did not mention procedural risks. The court concluded lack of documentation proved absence of due care.

Case Learnings

1. Instrument sequence and WL reconfirmation define technical competence.
2. Chemical injury or extrusion without procedural notes is indefensible.
3. Documentation of every step protects even imperfect outcomes.
4. Isolation, irrigation, and patience build credibility.
5. Each radiograph and log entry is silent evidence of prudence.

Quick Checklist

- Rubber dam applied and noted
- Glide path established and recorded
- Coronal flaring sequence logged
- WL reconfirmed after flaring
- Rotary system and sizes documented
- Irrigation volume and concentration recorded
- Recapitulation ensured
- Apical preparation size within WL
- Interim medication and seal placed
- All data filed and radiographs stored

References

1. *Hargreaves KM, Berman LH. Cohen's Pathways of the Pulp. 12th ed. Elsevier; 2022.*
2. *Sattapan B, Nervo GJ, Palamara JE, Messer HH. Defects in rotary nickel-titanium files after clinical use. J Endod. 2000;26(3):161 - 165.*
3. *Hülsmann M, Schinkel I. Influence of preparation technique on working length control. Int Endod J. 1994;27(5):254 - 260.*
4. *Ingle JI, Bakland LK, Baumgartner JC. Ingle's Endodontics. 7th ed. BC Decker; 2019.*
5. *Ricucci D, Langeland K. Apical limit of root canal instrumentation. Int Endod J. 1998;31(6):384 - 393.*
6. *Peters OA. Current challenges and concepts in the preparation of root canal systems. J Endod. 2004;30(8):559 - 567.*
7. *Hülsmann M, Hahn W. Complications during root canal irrigation. Endod Dent Traumatol. 2000;16(5):223 - 231.*
8. *Siqueira JF Jr, Rôças IN. Debris extrusion: causes and prevention. Int Endod J. 2008;41(7):593 - 604.*
9. *Schilder H. Cleaning and shaping of the root canal. Dent Clin North Am. 1974;18(2):269 - 296.*
10. *Zehnder M. Root canal irrigants. J Endod. 2006;32(5):389 - 398.*
11. *Dental Council of India. Endodontic Procedural Documentation Standards. 2022.*
12. *Dental Protection Limited. Medico-Legal Aspects of Endodontic Complications. 2021.*

CHAPTER 19

Obturation - Techniques, Failures, and Legal Accountability

Obturation is the point where endodontics meets finality. The shape created must now be sealed - airtight, bacteria-tight, and legally watertight. This is where many clinicians relax; where most lawsuits begin. A root canal isn't judged by what's inside the canal, but by what escapes beyond it. This chapter aligns technical precision with legal defensibility - every cone, every sealer, every radiograph accounted for.

Purpose and Indications

Obturation seals the prepared canal system in three dimensions to prevent reinfection. It is indicated after thorough cleaning, shaping, and complete drying, once the tooth is symptom-free and ready for permanent restoration [1].

Preparation and Pre-Obturation Verification

Ensure canals are dry, free of debris, and within verified working length. Check master cone fit radiographically before final sealing. Confirm apical tug-back and coronal adaptation.

Red flag: Skipping master cone radiograph or obturating in wet canals ensures long-term failure. In absence of a pre-obturation image, claims of "correct length" cannot be defended [2].

- ***Step 1: Sealer Selection and Mixing***

Use an accepted biocompatible sealer - zinc oxide eugenol, epoxy resin, calcium silicate, or bioceramic. Mix per manufacturer's ratio and record batch number.

Red flag: Using unapproved sealers or expired materials can cause chemical irritation or systemic allergy. Absence of material log nullifies traceability [3].

- ***Step 2: Master Cone Fitting***

Select gutta-percha cone matching master apical file size. Verify tug-back at working length with radiograph. Adjust if necessary.

Red flag: Loose or overextended master cone allows sealer extrusion and postoperative pain. Lack of verification image negates the claim of accuracy [4].

- ***Step 3: Sealer Application***

Coat canal walls and cone lightly using lentulo spiral or file. Avoid overfilling.

Red flag: Excessive sealer pressure forces material through apex, causing inflammation. Radiographic overfill with missing irrigation and WL documentation is direct evidence of poor control [5].

- ***Step 4: Obturation Technique (Cold or Warm)***

Adopt consistent technique - lateral condensation, vertical compaction, thermoplasticized flow, or single-cone with bioceramic sealer. Record method used and temperature if applicable.

Red flag: Using advanced heating techniques without training or documentation exposes clinician to malpractice risk when burns or extrusion occur [6].

- ***Step 5: Compaction and Coronal Seal***

Compact gutta-percha vertically or laterally ensuring dense fill and coronal seal integrity. Clean chamber floor and seal orifices with glass ionomer or resin-modified cement.

Red flag: Leaving coronal gap or debris causes microleakage and reinfection. No note on final restoration equates to incomplete treatment [7].

- ***Step 6: Post-Obturation Radiograph***

Take immediate postoperative radiograph to confirm obturation level and homogeneity. Compare with pre-obturation image.

Red flag: Absence of post-obturation radiograph makes procedural evaluation impossible. Courts view this as abandonment of follow-up documentation [8].

- ***Step 7: Managing Overfills and Underfills***

Overfills within 2 mm beyond apex may be tolerated if asymptomatic, but large extrusions require monitoring. Underfills beyond 2 mm of working length indicate incomplete cleaning.

Red flag: Failure to disclose overfill or underfill to the patient constitutes concealment. Every deviation must be explained, documented, and reviewed clinically [9].

- ***Step 8: Temporary or Permanent Coronal Restoration***

Seal access cavity immediately to prevent reinfection. Use IRM, GIC, or bonded resin as temporary measure; plan full crown within two weeks for posterior teeth.

Red flag: Leaving tooth unsealed or delaying restoration invites contamination. Documentation of patient instruction and referral to prosthodontist must be in notes [10].

- ***Step 9: Post-Operative Review***

Review patient after 7 - 14 days. Record pain, tenderness, and radiographic healing over time.

Red flag: Ignoring or failing to schedule review breaks continuity of care. A "one-visit" RCT without review note cannot claim completion of treatment [11].

- ***Step 10: Legal Documentation and Case Closure***

Document:

- Master cone and post-obturation radiographs
- Sealer brand, batch, and expiry
- Technique and compaction method
- Final restoration advice and follow-up plan

Sign and date each entry. Maintain these records for at least five years.

Red flag: Destroying or misplacing endodontic images during dispute constitutes evidence destruction and invites disciplinary action [12].

Defensibility and Documentation Anchors

A legally secure obturation case file includes: pre- and post-obturation radiographs, consent for procedure, detailed sealer and technique log, postoperative instruction sheet, and follow-up record. These establish continuity, caution, and competence - the three pillars of defense.

Case Study

A 38-year-old male underwent RCT on a mandibular second premolar. No pre- or post-obturation radiographs were taken. The patient returned with severe pain and paresthesia; imaging later revealed gross overfill of gutta-percha into the mental foramen. The dentist had no documentation of working length verification or sealer type. The case was ruled negligent for over-instrumentation, inadequate records, and lack of disclosure.

Case Learnings

1. Radiographs before and after obturation are mandatory proof of correctness.
2. Sealer and gutta-percha logs establish material traceability.
3. Overfill is not malpractice; hiding it is.
4. Coronal seal determines long-term success - document it.
5. Legal closure equals procedural closure plus follow-up evidence.

Quick Checklist

- Canal dried and debris-free
- Sealer type, batch, expiry recorded
- Master cone fit verified radiographically
- Sealer applied evenly without pressure
- Technique documented (cold/warm)
- Post-obturation radiograph taken
- Coronal seal achieved and noted
- Follow-up scheduled and recorded

- All notes signed and dated
- Records stored minimum five years

References

1. *Hargreaves KM, Berman LH. Cohen's Pathways of the Pulp. 12th ed. Elsevier; 2022.*
2. *Ingle JI, Bakland LK, Baumgartner JC. Ingle's Endodontics. 7th ed. BC Decker; 2019.*
3. *Grossman LI. Endodontic Practice. 12th ed. Lea & Febiger; 1988.*
4. *Schilder H. Filling root canals in three dimensions. Dent Clin North Am. 1967;723 - 744.*
5. *Siqueira JF Jr, Rôças IN. Root canal filling materials and techniques. Int Endod J. 2008;41(10):846 - 868.*
6. *Whitworth J. Methods of filling root canals. Br Dent J. 2005;198(9):529 - 536.*
7. *Saunders WP, Saunders EM. Coronal leakage as a cause of failure in endodontics. Endod Dent Traumatol. 1994;10(3):105 - 108.*
8. *Patel S et al. Radiographic standards for endodontic documentation. Int Endod J. 2019;52(7):1001 - 1013.*
9. *Tsesis I et al. Outcome of overfilled and underfilled root canals. J Endod. 2013;39(6):632 - 639.*
10. *Dental Council of India. Post-Endodontic Restoration Guidelines. 2022.*
11. *American Association of Endodontists. Post-treatment evaluation and documentation standards. 2020.*
12. *Dental Protection Limited. Handling Complaints and Records in Endodontic Practice. 2021.*

CHAPTER 20

Post-Endodontic Restoration - Structural Integrity, Documentation, and Legal Continuity

A root canal without a proper restoration is like a lock without a key - it protects nothing. Once obturation is complete, the real question begins: can this tooth survive the pressures of daily function, or will it fracture and fail? The biological cure is meaningless without mechanical continuity. This chapter defines how to rebuild strength, ensure seal, and document the restoration so that no claim of "incomplete treatment" ever holds.

Purpose and Indications

Post-endodontic restoration seals the canal coronally and restores functional strength. It is indicated immediately after obturation to prevent microleakage, contamination, and structural failure. The restoration also completes the legal cycle of treatment continuity [1].

Preparation and Immediate Coronal Seal

After obturation, clean the chamber of gutta-percha remnants and sealer using alcohol or cotton pellets. Place a 2 - 3 mm thick base of glass ionomer or bonded resin over canal orifices before final buildup.

Red flag: Leaving access unsealed, even for a few days, allows reinfection. When reinfection occurs and records show no coronal seal note, the entire root canal is deemed incomplete [2].

- ***Step 1: Assessment of Remaining Tooth Structure***

Evaluate cuspal integrity, marginal ridges, and ferrule effect. Record percentage of coronal structure lost. Decide between direct restoration and full coverage crown.

Red flag: Restoring a structurally compromised tooth with only composite filling leads to fracture and liability. Absence of pre-restoration photograph or structural note negates evidence of due diligence [3].

- ***Step 2: Choice of Restorative Material***

Select restorative material based on occlusal load and location - resin composite for anterior, amalgam or composite with onlay for posterior. Use bonded systems whenever possible.

Red flag: Using outdated or non-bonded restorative material violates standard protocols. In fracture cases, unrecorded material brand or type removes traceability [4].

- ***Step 3: Core Buildup Protocol***

For teeth with significant loss, place post and core using fiber or metal posts only after confirming at least 4 mm apical gutta-percha seal. Record post length and cement type.

Red flag: Removing entire gutta-percha column for post placement causes apical leakage. Failure to document post type and cement used makes subsequent root fracture indefensible [5].

- ***Step 4: Occlusal Adjustment***

Check occlusion under articulating paper and adjust premature contacts. Document that occlusion was balanced and patient comfort confirmed.

Red flag: Ignoring occlusal stress on endodontically treated teeth is a common reason for vertical fracture. Absence of occlusal record shows procedural oversight [6].

- ***Step 5: Full Coverage Crown Recommendation***

Advise full coverage crown for all posterior endodontically treated teeth within 2 - 3 weeks. Record this advice and obtain patient acknowledgment in writing.

Red flag: Failure to recommend crown protection is legally interpreted as incomplete treatment. If fracture occurs later, liability remains even after perfect obturation [7].

- ***Step 6: Temporary Restoration for Deferred Crowns***

If crown placement is delayed, seal access cavity with dual-layer temporary restoration (IRM plus composite overlay).

Red flag: Using single-layer temporary without documented advice to return for crown constitutes negligence through omission. Every "temporary" must have timeline noted [8].

- ***Step 7: Documentation of Final Restoration***

Note restorative material, brand, batch number, curing time, and shade. Attach post-restoration photograph or intraoral image if available.

Red flag: Lack of documentation allows patient to allege "filling fell out" due to improper technique. Every restored tooth must have a clear record of material and method [9].

- ***Step 8: Postoperative Radiograph***

Take final radiograph showing obturation and coronal restoration integrity. Compare with pre-obturation image and file under same patient ID.

Red flag: Missing final radiograph invites doubt whether restoration ever sealed the canal completely. Legal defensibility depends on visible closure proof [10].

- ***Step 9: Patient Education and Maintenance Instructions***

Instruct patient on avoiding hard biting for 24 hours, crown placement schedule, and need for follow-up imaging. Provide printed aftercare sheet signed by both parties.

Red flag: Verbal-only instructions fail in disputes about delayed crown or failed filling. Written acknowledgment protects clinician even if patient ignores advice [11].

- ***Step 10: Follow-Up and Review***

Schedule review after one month to assess marginal seal and function. Record findings and radiographs if symptoms persist.

Red flag: Lack of follow-up entry converts an avoidable crown fracture into an "abandoned case." Review logs confirm continuity of care and professional vigilance [12].

Defensibility and Documentation Anchors

Defensible post-endodontic documentation includes:

- Immediate coronal seal record
- Structural assessment and photo
- Restorative material and batch details
- Post or core placement note with cement type
- Written crown recommendation and patient acknowledgment
- Final radiograph
- Postoperative instruction sheet and review log

These ensure traceability and show that the clinician completed not just the canal but the commitment.

Case Study

A 42-year-old woman underwent RCT on maxillary first molar. The dentist filled the access cavity with composite but did not advise a crown in writing. Six months later, the tooth fractured at gingival level. She alleged incomplete treatment. With no record of crown recommendation or postoperative advice, the court ruled that the dentist had failed to provide standard post-endodontic care.

Case Learnings

1. Endodontic therapy is legally incomplete until coronal coverage is documented.
2. Written advice for crown placement is the most protective legal document after obturation.
3. Material and technique logs transform craftsmanship into evidence.
4. Every radiograph and photograph prevents speculative claims.
5. A follow-up entry is as vital as a perfect seal - both show continuity of care.

Quick Checklist

- Chamber cleaned and coronal seal placed
- Structural assessment and photograph recorded
- Restorative material, brand, and batch logged
- Post/core placement within apical seal
- Occlusal adjustment verified and noted
- Full coverage crown advised and signed
- Final radiograph confirming restoration taken
- Aftercare instructions given in writing
- Follow-up scheduled and logged
- Records securely filed for 5+ years

References

1. *Hargreaves KM, Berman LH. Cohen's Pathways of the Pulp. 12th ed. Elsevier; 2022.*
2. *Saunders WP, Saunders EM. Coronal leakage as a cause of failure in endodontics. Endod Dent Traumatol. 1994;10(3):105 - 108.*
3. *Ferrari M et al. Influence of coronal restoration on success of endodontically treated teeth. J Dent Res. 2000;79(9):1563 - 1568.*
4. *Opdam NJ et al. Longevity of posterior composite restorations: a systematic review. J Dent Res. 2014;93(10):943 - 949.*
5. *Morgano SM, Brackett SE. Foundation restorations in fixed prosthodontics. J Prosthet Dent. 1999;82(6):643 - 657.*
6. *Fuss Z, Lustig J, Tamse A. Prevalence of vertical root fractures in extracted endodontically treated teeth. Int Endod J. 1999;32(4):283 - 286.*
7. *Aquilino SA, Caplan DJ. Relationship between crown placement and root canal - treated teeth survival. J Prosthet Dent. 2002;87(3):256 - 263.*
8. *Dental Council of India. Post-Endodontic Restoration and Crown Advisory. 2022.*
9. *Dental Protection Limited. Legal Accountability in Endodontic Restoration Failures. 2021.*
10. *Patel S et al. Radiographic standards for endodontic documentation. Int Endod J. 2019;52(7):1001 - 1013.*
11. *General Dental Council (UK). Patient Information and Consent Standards. 2013.*
12. *Ministry of Health and Family Welfare, India. Clinical Documentation and Review Protocols. 2020.*

CHAPTER 21

Instrument Separation and Procedural Mishaps - Disclosure, Documentation, and Defense

In endodontics, the file is your scalpel - delicate, precise, and unforgiving. Instrument separation, ledging, or canal transportation can happen even in the most skilled hands. What defines professionalism is not avoidance but response. This chapter shows how to manage the complication clinically, communicate transparently, and document defensively so that a procedural mishap never becomes a medico-legal disaster.

Purpose and Context

Instrument fracture is the most common cause of post-treatment disputes in endodontics. Courts rarely penalize a separated file - they penalize concealment, poor disclosure, or missing documentation. Your aim is to prove awareness, competence, and honesty.

- ***Step 1: Recognition and Immediate Assessment***

Identify separation during instrumentation through tactile loss of working length or radiographic evidence.

Red flag: Continuing instrumentation blindly after tactile change causes canal deviation or perforation, making retrieval impossible.

- ***Step 2: Record Exact Location and Size***

Take intraoperative radiographs or digital imaging. Document tooth number, canal, and fragment length.

Red flag: Vague chart entries like "file broke" without location data weaken defense and invite assumptions of negligence.

- ***Step 3: Evaluate Retrieval Feasibility***

Decide if retrieval, bypassing, or sealing beyond fragment is safer. Record rationale and inform patient before proceeding.

Red flag: Attempting aggressive retrieval without documentation of informed risk can be construed as recklessness.

- ***Step 4: Patient Disclosure and Consent Update***

Explain cause, consequence, and management plan clearly. Obtain written acknowledgment for any additional procedure or referral.

Red flag: Verbal disclosure without written update is treated as concealment even if intent was honest.

- ***Step 5: Management and Referral***

If retrieval attempt fails, seal canal appropriately and refer to endodontic specialist with full record transfer. Keep copy of referral note and acknowledgment.

Red flag: Absence of referral documentation converts professional collaboration into apparent neglect.

- ***Step 6: Post-Event Reporting***

Note time, instruments used, magnification, and irrigants. Attach radiographs and file batch numbers. Sign and date all notes.

Red flag: Missing signatures or undated entries break the chain of record authenticity.

- ***Step 7: Communication and Follow-Up***

Schedule review for symptom check and radiographic monitoring. Document patient response and satisfaction post-disclosure.

Red flag: Ignoring follow-up after mishap implies avoidance; absence of re-evaluation weakens defense.

Legal and Ethical Anchors

A separated file is not proof of negligence; silence is. Courts look for honesty, competence, and evidence of patient involvement. Maintain a "Mishap Register" for all procedural deviations-signed, time-stamped, and transparent.

Case Study

A 33-year-old patient complained of pain after RCT elsewhere. The radiograph revealed a fractured NiTi file in the apical third. The treating dentist had documented the event, obtained written consent for referral, and sealed the canal. The tribunal ruled no negligence, citing timely disclosure and complete records.

Case Learnings

1. Immediate recognition and open disclosure build trust.
2. Written updates prevent verbal misinterpretation.
3. Mishap documentation is part of the clinical record, not a confession.
4. Radiographic proof of position is vital for defense.
5. Referral communication must always be on record.

Quick Checklist

- Separation detected and documented
- Radiograph showing fragment position
- Feasibility and options recorded
- Patient informed and written acknowledgment obtained
- Referral made if indicated
- Mishap report filed and signed
- Follow-up radiograph attached
- All entries time-stamped and authenticated

References

1. *American Association of Endodontists. Managing Mishaps and Procedural Accidents. 2022.*
2. *Dental Council of India. Documentation Standards for Endodontic Complications. 2022.*
3. *National Medical Commission (India). Disclosure and Consent Update Guidelines. 2021.*
4. *Dental Protection Limited. Instrument Fracture and Risk Communication. 2021.*
5. *Ministry of Health and Family Welfare, India. Clinical Records and Incident Reporting Rules. 2020.*

CHAPTER 22

Endodontic Failure and Retreatment - Ethics, Communication, and Legal Safeguards

Failure in endodontics is not always a fault - it is often biology's reminder that healing cannot be forced. Yet when symptoms recur or radiolucency persists, the patient rarely sees biology; they see blame. This chapter shows how to manage failure as both a clinical event and a communication test, ensuring transparency, documentation, and dignity throughout.

Purpose and Context

Endodontic retreatment sits at the junction of science and reputation. It demands diagnostic humility, technical competence, and absolute honesty. Legally, failure becomes defensible only if the clinician can prove three things - accurate diagnosis, timely disclosure, and reasonable effort.

- ***Step 1: Recognition and Diagnosis***

Identify failure through persistent pain, swelling, sinus tract, or radiographic non-healing. Compare new findings with pre- and post-obturation images.

Red flag: Initiating retreatment without baseline radiograph or old record review exposes you to claims of unnecessary intervention.

- ***Step 2: Review of Prior Documentation***

Obtain the original endodontic record - preoperative chart, working length notes, obturation radiographs, and patient consent.

Red flag: Criticizing the previous dentist in writing or verbally breaches professional ethics and often becomes a litigation trigger.

- ***Step 3: Patient Communication and Disclosure***

Explain that failure does not automatically mean error. Discuss biological and procedural causes, success rates, and possible outcomes of retreatment. Obtain written acknowledgment of discussion and new consent for retreatment.

Red flag: Using phrases like "the earlier doctor did it wrong" can be interpreted as defamation; instead, use objective terms like "previous treatment appears incomplete radiographically."

- ***Step 4: Retreatment Planning and Justification***

Record the reason for retreatment - missed canal, overfill, perforation, or coronal leakage. Outline stepwise plan, materials, and referral options if microsurgery is anticipated.

Red flag: Proceeding without explaining reduced prognosis or increased cost invites consumer court complaints.

- ***Step 5: Retreatment Procedure and Documentation***

Use magnification, ultrasonic retrieval, and irrigation protocols. Document each stage with radiographs and clinical notes. Record file separation, obturation quality, and temporary seal integrity.

Red flag: Omitting intraoperative radiographs makes it impossible to prove thoroughness later.

- ***Step 6: Postoperative Review and Follow-Up***

Schedule radiographic checkups at 3, 6, and 12 months. Record healing, patient satisfaction, and symptom regression.

Red flag: Discharging the case without formal recall note breaks the chain of continuity and weakens your defense if healing stalls later.

- ***Step 7: When Retreatment Fails Again***

If persistent lesions remain, discuss surgical options (apicoectomy, hemisection) or extraction. Provide written referral and copy of radiographs.

Red flag: Ignoring repeated complaints or avoiding follow-up messages is often interpreted as abandonment of care.

Legal and Ethical Anchors

Every failure should leave a clear audit trail - initial diagnosis, new consent, stepwise treatment, and periodic follow-up. If questioned later, these prove you acted within standard of care and maintained patient communication. Honesty in prognosis transforms potential conflict into collaboration.

Case Study

A 45-year-old woman presented with persistent swelling two years after RCT. The radiograph showed a missed palatal canal. The clinician reviewed prior records, explained the biological cause, and obtained fresh consent for retreatment. Follow-up radiographs at six months showed healing. Despite the previous complaint, the consumer forum dismissed negligence, citing full disclosure and documented communication.

Case Learnings

1. Failure ≠ Negligence if documentation is complete.
2. Always review and retain prior records before re-intervention.
3. Communicate objectively, not emotionally.
4. Retreatment consent must clearly state "reduced prognosis."
5. Healing documentation is as important as treatment documentation.

Quick Checklist

- Previous records reviewed and copied
- Baseline radiograph taken
- Failure cause identified and recorded
- Written disclosure and fresh consent obtained
- Retreatment steps fully documented with radiographs
- Post-op recall schedule given and signed
- Follow-up results charted and authenticated

References

1. *American Association of Endodontists. Endodontic Retreatment Guidelines. 2022.*
2. *Dental Council of India. Ethical and Legal Code for Secondary Endodontic Care. 2022.*
3. *European Society of Endodontology. Quality Guidelines for Endodontic Retreatment. 2021.*
4. *Dental Protection Limited. Communication and Disclosure after Endodontic Failure. 2021.*
5. *Consumer Protection Act, 2019 - Interpretation in Dental Negligence Cases.*

SECTION 4

Periodontics - Soft Tissue Integrity, Disease Management, and Legal Safeguards

Gingiva and bone form the quiet stage on which every other specialty performs. Ignore them, and every crown, root canal, or implant will fail in silence first — then loudly in court later. Periodontics teaches the discipline of maintenance: the unglamorous, essential work that keeps all else standing.

This section begins where most clinicians rush — with the first signs of inflammation. It teaches the anatomy of diligence: probing depths measured, bleeding charted, radiographs compared, and advice repeated until it becomes recordable behavior change. Each chapter transforms routine cleaning into accountable therapy — scaling documented site-wise, flap surgery justified by numbers, grafting made traceable by material batch and consent wording.

Soft-tissue management is also human management. You'll see how to discuss recession, sensitivity, or post-surgical appearance without defensiveness, and how to record those conversations so they become protection, not exposure. The same principles extend to peri-implant tissues — where biofilm and expectation collide, and where every recall visit must read like a contract renewed.

Finally, the section distills decades of litigation into patterns: missed diagnosis, vague notes, absent follow-up. By showing where others fell, it teaches how not to. Periodontal care is more than mechanical debridement; it is a slow, steady act of documentation, empathy, and foresight.

By the end, you will understand that periodontics is not a subset of dentistry — it is its conscience. The clinician who measures gums measures judgment itself.

CHAPTER 23

Gingival Inflammation and Periodontal Pocket - Diagnosis, Treatment, and Legal Responsibility

Gingival inflammation is the beginning of most periodontal tragedies. What starts as bleeding on brushing ends as tooth loss and, too often, allegations of "missed diagnosis." The true failure is rarely in treatment - it lies in absence of records, recall, and advice. This chapter restores the fundamentals of periodontal vigilance.

Purpose and Indications

Diagnosis and management of gingival inflammation prevent progression to periodontitis. Early detection through bleeding scores, probing depths, and plaque indices allows reversible treatment and documentation of preventive diligence [1].

Preparation and Initial Assessment

Take full medical and dental history. Record smoking status, diabetes, medications, and previous periodontal therapy. Perform visual inspection for color, contour, and texture changes. Document findings on periodontal chart.

Red flag: Proceeding to scaling without baseline charting or bleeding index invalidates future claims of "disease progression despite care." Absence of such record is construed as neglect of diagnosis [2].

- ***Step 1: Probing and Charting***

Measure probing pocket depth (PPD) and clinical attachment loss (CAL) at six points per tooth using standardized probe with controlled force. Record bleeding on probing (BOP) and plaque index (PI).

Red flag: Relying on visual inspection without probing is substandard practice. Missing or unsigned periodontal chart negates proof of baseline condition in medico-legal review [3].

- ***Step 2: Radiographic Evaluation***

Obtain periapical or bitewing radiographs to assess crestal bone loss pattern. In advanced cases, use full-mouth series or digital panoramic imaging.

Red flag: Performing deep cleaning or flap surgery without radiographic confirmation of bone loss violates standard diagnostic protocol. Courts consider "blind treatment" evidence of recklessness [4].

- ***Step 3: Risk Factor Identification and Documentation***

Note systemic diseases, smoking, hormonal changes, and drug-induced gingival enlargement. Counsel patient on modifiable factors and record advice.

Red flag: Failing to document advice regarding smoking or diabetes control voids preventive care defense when disease advances despite treatment [5].

- ***Step 4: Initial Therapy - Scaling and Root Planing (SRP)***

Perform thorough ultrasonic scaling and subgingival debridement. Irrigate pockets with chlorhexidine. Record sites treated, instruments used, and time spent.

Red flag: Incomplete quadrant documentation or failure to note anesthesia use in sensitive cases counts as substandard recordkeeping. "Full-mouth scaling" without details lacks legal weight [6].

- ***Step 5: Re-Evaluation and Recall Scheduling***

Reassess PPD and BOP after 4 - 6 weeks. Compare with initial readings. Adjust maintenance interval based on response.

Red flag: Failure to document re-evaluation dates or results constitutes "treatment without follow-up." Most legal cases stem from missing recall records, not missed cleanings [7].

- ***Step 6: Patient Motivation and Home Care Instruction***

Educate patient on brushing technique, floss use, interdental cleaning, and mouthwash. Provide printed care sheet signed by patient.

Red flag: Verbal advice without written reinforcement cannot be proven in disputes of "lack of instruction." Courts treat missing education records as omission of preventive duty [8].

- ***Step 7: Adjunctive Therapy***

Prescribe systemic antibiotics or local antimicrobials when indicated. Record drug, dose, duration, and reason for use.

Red flag: Prescribing antibiotics without documented indication exposes clinician to allegations of overuse or adverse reaction negligence [9].

- ***Step 8: Maintenance and Long-Term Follow-Up***

Schedule maintenance every 3 - 6 months depending on risk profile. Record findings, plaque control, and any new pockets.

Red flag: No recall entry for over a year after SRP shows professional abandonment. Every visit should bear date, findings, and signature [10].

- ***Step 9: Communication and Consent***

Explain to patient that periodontal disease is chronic and requires maintenance. Obtain written consent for SRP and re-evaluation plan.

Red flag: Lack of signed consent for deep cleaning or curettage eliminates protection if patient develops postoperative sensitivity or recession [11].

- ***Step 10: Legal Record Assembly***

Include in patient file:

- Baseline chart with pocket depth and BOP
- Radiographs labeled and dated
- Consent for therapy
- Re-evaluation and recall entries
- Home-care instructions signed by patient

Red flag: Fragmented or unsigned charts are legally equivalent to absence of documentation [12].

Defensibility and Documentation Anchors

Each periodontal case should have a complete paper trail from first bleeding report to final review. Document disease stage (I - IV), grade (A - C), and systemic associations. Keep before-and-after photos of gingiva and radiographs. Maintenance schedule with patient acknowledgment completes the legal chain.

Case Study

A 48-year-old male presented with mobile lower incisors. He had undergone "scaling" a year earlier but no records existed. The dentist claimed patient ignored maintenance. The court observed that no baseline probing chart or written advice existed; thus, progression could not be proven as patient negligence. Compensation was granted for "failure to diagnose and monitor periodontal disease."

Case Learnings

1. Diagnosis begins with charting, not cleaning.
2. Every measurement must have numbers, not memories.
3. Documentation of risk factors and advice defines professionalism.
4. Recall and re-evaluation records protect clinicians more than any treatment note.
5. In periodontal care, silence in files equals absence of care.

Quick Checklist

- Medical and dental history documented
- PPD, CAL, BOP, PI recorded at baseline
- Radiographs taken and labeled
- Risk factors identified and advice noted
- Scaling and root planing documented quadrant-wise
- Re-evaluation after 4 - 6 weeks recorded
- Written home-care instruction signed
- Maintenance schedule fixed and logged
- Consent forms filed
- Records retained minimum five years

References

1. *Lindhe J, Lang NP, Karring T. Clinical Periodontology and Implant Dentistry. 7th ed. Wiley-Blackwell; 2022.*
2. *Newman MG, Takei H, Klokkevold PR, Carranza FA. Carranza's Clinical Periodontology. 13th ed. Elsevier; 2021.*
3. *Chapple ILC et al. Periodontal diagnosis in the context of the 2018 classification. J Clin Periodontol. 2018;45(Suppl 20):S9 - S16.*
4. *Mealey BL. Periodontal-systemic interrelationships. Periodontol 2000. 2013;62(1):59 - 94.*
5. *Kinane DF, Stathopoulou PG, Papapanou PN. Periodontal diseases. Nat Rev Dis Primers. 2017;3:17038.*
6. *Cobb CM. Clinical significance of non-surgical periodontal therapy. J Clin Periodontol. 2002;29(Suppl 2):6 - 16.*
7. *Pihlstrom BL, Michalowicz BS, Johnson NW. Periodontal diseases. Lancet. 2005;366(9499):1809 - 1820.*
8. *Dental Council of India. Guidelines for Periodontal Documentation and Consent. 2022.*
9. *Herrera D et al. Adjunctive therapies in non-surgical periodontal treatment. J Clin Periodontol. 2019;46(Suppl 21):74 - 91.*
10. *Lang NP, Tonetti MS. Periodontal risk assessment (PRA) model. J Clin Periodontol. 2003;30(7):589 - 599.*
11. *General Dental Council (UK). Standards for Record Keeping and Consent. 2013.*
12. *Dental Protection Limited. Periodontal Negligence and Legal Defensibility in Dental Practice. 2021.*

CHAPTER 24

Scaling and Root Planing - Technique, Tissue Response, and Legal Defensibility

Scaling and root planing (SRP) is often called "routine" treatment, but it's never minor in the eyes of law or biology. It is the first surgical act most patients undergo - blood, anesthesia, and sometimes pain. The moment tissue is breached, the clinician steps into the realm of consent, infection control, and professional accountability. This chapter builds the full sequence of SRP as a clinical and medico-legal procedure: methodical, measured, and fully documented.

Purpose and Indications

SRP removes plaque, calculus, and contaminated cementum to eliminate inflammation and create a biologically compatible root surface. It is indicated in gingivitis, early and moderate periodontitis, or as pre-surgical therapy to reduce bacterial load [1].

Preparation and Patient Readiness

Review medical history for bleeding disorders, diabetes, or cardiac conditions requiring prophylaxis. Obtain written consent outlining procedure, discomfort, and possible sensitivity. Record baseline probing depths and bleeding scores.

Red flag: Performing SRP without consent or ignoring systemic risk (e.g., anticoagulants) may lead to bleeding complications and litigation. Courts treat absence of signed consent as omission of standard care [2].

- ***Step 1: Infection Control and Field Setup***

Wear full barrier protection - gloves, mask, eyewear, and face shield. Disinfect unit surfaces and prepare sterile instruments.

Red flag: Cross-infection events during scaling due to poor sterilization are strictly punishable. Absence of sterilization log implies breach of universal precautions [3].

- ***Step 2: Anesthesia and Pain Control***

Administer local or topical anesthesia for deep pockets or sensitive patients. Record dose, site, and anesthetic used.

Red flag: Administering anesthetic without documentation or exceeding recommended dosage violates procedural safety and legal record standards [4].

- ***Step 3: Supragingival Scaling***

Use ultrasonic or hand scalers to remove visible calculus and plaque above the gingival margin. Employ controlled strokes and adequate irrigation.

Red flag: Using excessive pressure or dull instruments causes enamel abrasion and cervical notching. Any soft tissue injury during scaling must be noted in record [5].

- ***Step 4: Subgingival Scaling***

Insert curette gently under the gingival margin. Use short, overlapping strokes to remove calculus from root surface. Maintain finger rest and adapt blade angle (70 - 80 degrees).

Red flag: Blind or forceful insertion results in tissue laceration and postoperative bleeding. Failure to record subgingival procedure invites dispute about completeness of cleaning [6].

- ***Step 5: Root Planing***

Smooth root surface to remove endotoxin-contaminated cementum. Check with explorer for glassy smoothness. Rinse with saline or chlorhexidine.

Red flag: Overzealous planing causes root sensitivity and dentin exposure. Lack of documented discussion about potential sensitivity becomes a "failure to warn" claim [7].

- ***Step 6: Irrigation and Local Drug Delivery (If Indicated)***

Use chlorhexidine or povidone-iodine for irrigation. For persistent pockets, apply local antibiotic gels or microspheres. Record product name, concentration, and site.

Red flag: Administering local antimicrobials without recording site or product batch violates traceability; allergic reactions then become undefendable [8].

- ***Step 7: Hemostasis and Debridement Check***

After scaling, control bleeding with pressure or local hemostatic solution. Recheck pocket for remaining deposits using explorer.

Red flag: Discharging patient with active bleeding or tissue tags indicates incomplete debridement. Any uncontrolled bleeding must be recorded with vitals and management steps [9].

- ***Step 8: Postoperative Instructions***

Provide written instructions: avoid hard foods, use antiseptic mouthwash, gentle brushing, and analgesics as needed. Inform about possible transient bleeding or sensitivity.

Red flag: Verbal-only instructions are legally weak; failure to warn about postoperative discomfort often results in patient complaints of "botched scaling" [10].

- ***Step 9: Recall and Reevaluation***

Schedule re-evaluation after 4 - 6 weeks. Record improvement in probing depth, bleeding, and plaque control.

Red flag: Failure to record recall appointment is one of the most common reasons for lost medico-legal defense in periodontal care [11].

- ***Step 10: Documentation and Maintenance Plan***

Include in patient file: preoperative chart, anesthesia record, sites treated, instruments used, and postoperative instructions. Add before-and-after photos if possible.

Red flag: Vague entries like "scaling done" are unacceptable; courts expect site-specific, signed records of procedure, duration, and follow-up plan [12].

Defensibility and Documentation Anchors

Defensible SRP records contain:

- Signed consent and risk acknowledgment
- Preoperative pocket chart and bleeding index
- Local anesthesia log (if used)

- Documentation of scaling instruments and areas treated
- Written postoperative advice and re-evaluation schedule
- Follow-up entry at 4 - 6 weeks

These elements prove that the clinician performed within standard care and maintained communication.

Case Study

A 50-year-old diabetic underwent full-mouth scaling and root planing without medical clearance or anesthesia record. Postoperative bleeding occurred, leading to emergency hospital visit. The patient sued for negligence. The court found no consent form, no procedure notes, and no postoperative instructions. The dentist was held liable for failing to recognize and document systemic risk.

Case Learnings

1. Even “routine” scaling requires consent, documentation, and aftercare records.
2. Bleeding events are defensible only when risk and management are documented.
3. Written postoperative instructions prevent exaggerated claims of pain or bleeding.
4. Maintenance and recall prove continuity of care - absence suggests neglect.
5. Every SRP must read like a small surgery on paper - detailed, timed, and signed.

Quick Checklist

- Medical history and consent verified
- Sterilization log and setup ready
- Anesthesia recorded (if given)
- Quadrants treated documented
- Subgingival scaling confirmed

- Irrigation and drug use recorded
- Hemostasis achieved before discharge
- Written instructions provided
- Recall visit scheduled and noted
- Follow-up entry signed and dated

References

1. *Lindhe J, Lang NP, Karring T. Clinical Periodontology and Implant Dentistry. 7th ed. Wiley-Blackwell; 2022.*
2. *Newman MG, Takei H, Klokkevold PR, Carranza FA. Carranza's Clinical Periodontology. 13th ed. Elsevier; 2021.*
3. *Ministry of Health and Family Welfare, India. National Guidelines for Infection Control in Dental Practice. 2020.*
4. *Malamed SF. Handbook of Local Anesthesia. 7th ed. Elsevier; 2019.*
5. *Cobb CM. Clinical significance of non-surgical periodontal therapy. J Clin Periodontol. 2002;29(Suppl 2):6 - 16.*
6. *Pihlstrom BL, Michalowicz BS, Johnson NW. Periodontal diseases. Lancet. 2005;366(9499):1809 - 1820.*
7. *Axelsson P, Lindhe J. Effect of controlled oral hygiene on caries and periodontal disease. J Clin Periodontol. 1981;8(3):239 - 248.*
8. *Herrera D et al. Adjunctive therapies in non-surgical periodontal treatment. J Clin Periodontol. 2019;46(Suppl 21):74 - 91.*
9. *Kinane DF et al. Periodontal emergencies and management. Br Dent J. 2012;213(4):163 - 170.*
10. *General Dental Council (UK). Communication and Patient Information Standards. 2013.*
11. *Lang NP, Tonetti MS. Periodontal risk assessment (PRA) model. J Clin Periodontol. 2003;30(7):589 - 599.*
12. *Dental Protection Limited. Periodontal Documentation and Legal Standards. 2021.*

CHAPTER 25

Periodontal Flap Surgery - Indications, Stepwise Technique, and Legal Documentation

When nonsurgical care cannot reach the depth of disease, a flap is not an option - it is an obligation. Flap surgery exposes the truth beneath the gingiva: calculus, bone loss, and judgment. A well-executed flap not only cleans but restores architecture; a poorly planned one exposes roots, nerves, and the clinician to litigation. This chapter breaks down every step, from consent to closure, into reproducible, legally secure actions.

Purpose and Indications

Periodontal flap surgery provides direct access for debridement, root planing, and bone reshaping. It is indicated in pocket depths greater than 5 mm unresponsive to scaling and root planing, furcation involvement, or osseous defects requiring visualization [1].

Preparation and Preoperative Protocol

Obtain thorough medical clearance for bleeding disorders, diabetes, or cardiac risks. Explain procedure, risks, alternatives, and postoperative expectations. Obtain signed surgical consent and preoperative photographs.

Red flag: Failure to record informed consent or pre-surgical clearance transforms any intraoperative complication into malpractice. Even perfect surgery is indefensible without a documented pre-op record [2].

- ***Step 1: Anesthesia and Field Isolation***

Administer local anesthesia using infiltration or nerve block as appropriate. Confirm anesthesia before incision.

Red flag: Commencing incision before complete anesthesia or neglecting to record anesthetic type and dose violates standard of care and patient rights [3].

- ***Step 2: Incision Design***

Mark internal bevel incision 0.5 - 1 mm from gingival margin using No. 15 blade, extending interdentally. Add vertical releasing incisions if needed.

Red flag: Incorrect incision design leading to tissue tears or gingival recession is avoidable. If flap tear occurs, immediate notation and photographic record must be made [4].

- ***Step 3: Flap Reflection***

Reflect full-thickness mucoperiosteal flap using periosteal elevator. Maintain gentle retraction to prevent tearing.

Red flag: Forceful retraction causing flap necrosis or nerve exposure is a documented surgical injury. Absence of flap design notes invalidates defense if postoperative paresthesia develops [5].

- ***Step 4: Debridement and Root Planing Under Direct Vision***

Remove granulation tissue, calculus, and residual cementum. Irrigate with saline or chlorhexidine. Verify root smoothness with explorer.

Red flag: Incomplete debridement or failure to irrigate properly is a leading cause of postoperative infection. "Flap raised and cleaned" without details is legally weak documentation [6].

- ***Step 5: Osseous Correction (If Indicated)***

Perform osteoplasty or ostectomy to correct bone architecture using rotary or hand instruments. Preserve natural contours.

Red flag: Overzealous bone removal causing root exposure or tooth mobility is indefensible without radiographic and written justification for the correction [7].

- ***Step 6: Flap Repositioning and Suturing***

Reposition flap at original or apical level depending on indication. Secure with interrupted or sling sutures using non-resorbable suture material. Record suture type and number.

Red flag: Neglecting to document suture type or placement leads to disputes when delayed healing or stitch abscess occurs [8].

- ***Step 7: Hemostasis and Dressing***

Achieve hemostasis with pressure or local hemostatic agent. Apply periodontal dressing over surgical site.

Red flag: Discharging patient with active oozing or without dressing record is equivalent to incomplete surgery. Bleeding complications post-discharge are defensible only if hemostasis and dressing were recorded [9].

- ***Step 8: Postoperative Care and Medication***

Prescribe antibiotics, analgesics, and chlorhexidine rinse. Provide written postoperative instructions - diet, oral hygiene, and follow-up schedule.

Red flag: Failure to provide written instructions or medication record converts normal healing complications into claims of negligence [10].

- ***Step 9: Review and Suture Removal***

Review patient after 7 - 10 days for suture removal. Examine healing and record findings with photograph.

Red flag: Absence of review record implies neglect. Every postoperative infection case without review note is legally undefendable [11].

- ***Step 10: Long-Term Maintenance and Documentation***

Re-chart pockets after 6 - 8 weeks, compare with preoperative values, and update maintenance schedule. Store all radiographs, photos, and consent in digital archive.

Red flag: Failing to record postoperative improvement nullifies claim of successful treatment and exposes clinician to allegations of "ineffective surgery" [12].

Defensibility and Documentation Anchors

A defensible flap surgery record must include:

- Written and signed surgical consent
- Medical clearance and anesthesia record
- Incision and flap design documentation
- Intraoperative photos (where feasible)
- Suture and dressing notes
- Postoperative instructions sheet signed by patient

- Follow-up and re-evaluation entries

This record proves professional thoroughness and transparency in surgical conduct.

Case Study

A 46-year-old diabetic underwent flap surgery without medical clearance. Postoperative bleeding led to hospitalization. The dentist had no consent form or medication record. Despite technically proper surgery, the court ruled negligence due to lack of systemic risk assessment and informed consent documentation.

Case Learnings

1. A perfect flap without paperwork is still malpractice.
2. Surgical consent and medical clearance are non-negotiable.
3. Each incision and suture should leave both a clinical and documentary trace.
4. Written postoperative instruction sheets protect against exaggerated claims.
5. In surgery, recordkeeping equals half the operation.

Quick Checklist

- Medical clearance and consent obtained
- Preoperative radiographs and photos taken
- Anesthesia documented
- Flap design and incision recorded
- Debridement and irrigation completed
- Osseous correction justified and noted
- Suture type and count documented
- Hemostasis achieved and dressing placed
- Postoperative instructions written and signed
- Follow-up and re-evaluation entries stored

References

1. *Lindhe J, Lang NP, Karring T. Clinical Periodontology and Implant Dentistry. 7th ed. Wiley-Blackwell; 2022.*
2. *Newman MG, Takei H, Klokkevold PR, Carranza FA. Carranza's Clinical Periodontology. 13th ed. Elsevier; 2021.*
3. *Malamed SF. Handbook of Local Anesthesia. 7th ed. Elsevier; 2019.*
4. *Waerhaug J. Healing of the dento-epithelial junction following subgingival plaque control. J Periodontol. 1978;49(3):119 - 134.*
5. *Ramfjord SP, Nissle RR. The modified Widman flap procedure. J Periodontol. 1974;45(8):601 - 607.*
6. *Kaldahl WB et al. Long-term evaluation of periodontal therapy. J Clin Periodontol. 1996;23(3 Pt 2):290 - 295.*
7. *Glickman I. Clinical Periodontology. 4th ed. Saunders; 1972.*
8. *Lang NP, Tonetti MS. Periodontal risk assessment (PRA) model. J Clin Periodontol. 2003;30(7):589 - 599.*
9. *Kinane DF et al. Periodontal emergencies and management. Br Dent J. 2012;213(4):163 - 170.*
10. *Dental Council of India. Surgical Consent and Documentation Protocols in Dentistry. 2022.*
11. *General Dental Council (UK). Standards for Surgical Recordkeeping. 2013.*
12. *Dental Protection Limited. Legal Management of Periodontal Surgical Complications. 2021.*

CHAPTER 26

Mucogingival and Reconstructive Procedures - Soft Tissue Grafts, Esthetic Balance, and Legal Consent Standards

Gingival recession, inadequate keratinized tissue, and mucogingival defects are as much psychological concerns as biological ones. Patients seek reconstruction not just for function but for appearance - and expectation is where litigation hides. Mucogingival surgery, when performed with care and documented with clarity, restores both tissue and trust. When performed casually, it risks exposure of root, bone, and practitioner alike. This chapter aligns technique with transparency.

Purpose and Indications

Mucogingival and reconstructive procedures aim to increase attached gingiva, cover exposed roots, correct shallow vestibules, and enhance esthetics. They are indicated in Miller Class I - III recession, inadequate keratinized tissue, or high frenum attachment compromising hygiene [1].

Preparation and Preoperative Evaluation

Evaluate defect dimensions, width of attached gingiva, and plaque control status. Record medical history, gingival biotype, and patient's esthetic expectations. Obtain preoperative photographs and signed consent clearly explaining limitations and possible graft color mismatch or incomplete coverage.

Red flag: Promise of "complete root coverage" or failure to document patient expectations invites litigation when esthetic results vary. Every esthetic surgery needs written consent specifying "improvement, not perfection" [2].

- ***Step 1: Recipient Site Preparation***

Administer local anesthesia and mark the recipient area. Make horizontal and vertical incisions at the recession margins. Elevate partial-thickness flap to expose periosteum without bone exposure.

Red flag: Over-thinning flap or full-thickness reflection leads to necrosis. Any intraoperative tear must be recorded, photographed if possible, and managed immediately [3].

- ***Step 2: Donor Site Selection (Palatal or Adjacent Area)***

Select donor area between canine and first molar on palate, 2 mm away from gingival margin. Determine graft dimensions matching recipient defect.

Red flag: Harvesting without assessing palatal vessel course can cause hemorrhage. No documented donor-site anesthesia or design note nullifies defense for bleeding complications [4].

- ***Step 3: Graft Harvesting***

Raise split-thickness flap using scalpel or tissue punch. Harvest free gingival graft (FGG) or subepithelial connective tissue graft (SCTG) based on indication. Achieve hemostasis with pressure pack.

Red flag: Excessive graft thickness or uncontrolled bleeding, if undocumented, implies poor surgical judgment. All donor grafts must be labeled in operative note as FGG or SCTG [5].

- ***Step 4: Graft Stabilization and Adaptation***

Place graft on recipient bed ensuring intimate contact. Secure with interrupted or sling sutures using fine monofilament. Apply gentle pressure for adaptation.

Red flag: Loose or mobile grafts cause necrosis and failure. Absence of suture details in records raises doubts about procedural competence [6].

- ***Step 5: Flap Repositioning and Dressing***

Reposition flap coronally or apically depending on defect type. Apply periodontal dressing or light pressure pack.

Red flag: Discharging patient without recording dressing placement or coverage technique is a recurrent legal oversight in graft failures [7].

- ***Step 6: Postoperative Medication and Care***

Prescribe antibiotics, analgesics, and chlorhexidine rinse. Instruct on diet (soft, non-spicy foods), avoid brushing near graft for 10 - 14 days. Provide written instructions.

Red flag: Failing to issue printed postoperative instructions converts ordinary healing discomfort into claims of "improper advice" [8].

- ***Step 7: Donor Site Management***

Check for bleeding after 30 minutes, apply pressure dressing if required. Schedule review after 48 hours.

Red flag: Secondary hemorrhage or infection at donor site without postoperative follow-up record is indefensible. Both sites require separate entries in surgical note [9].

- ***Step 8: Review and Suture Removal***

Assess graft attachment, color match, and healing after 10 - 14 days. Remove sutures carefully, record healing status, and photograph result.

Red flag: Omission of postoperative photo and measurement prevents demonstration of improvement if the patient alleges poor cosmetic outcome [10].

- ***Step 9: Long-Term Evaluation***

Reassess gingival margin stability after 3 - 6 months. Record final measurements, plaque control, and tissue thickness.

Red flag: Absence of long-term follow-up nullifies proof of graft success. A good surgery without follow-up record reads as incomplete treatment [11].

- ***Step 10: Documentation and Legal Anchors***

Attach to patient file:

- Pre- and postoperative photographs
- Signed esthetic consent with specific disclaimers
- Operative note with graft type, donor site, and suture details
- Medication record and follow-up entries
- Review photographs with date and measurement

Red flag: Lack of photographic evidence or unsigned consent is the single biggest weakness in esthetic surgery defense [12].

Defensibility and Documentation Anchors

Every mucogingival case must show the chain of informed expectation, precise execution, and verifiable improvement. Photographs, consent forms, and donor site records are not extras - they are shields. Patient expectations must be defined, not assumed.

Case Study

A 34-year-old woman underwent root coverage for upper canine recession. Graft survived partially, leaving 1 mm residual exposure. Patient alleged "cosmetic failure." Investigation revealed no written consent and no postoperative photograph. Though the result was clinically satisfactory, the absence of visual documentation and consent clause led to settlement for "dissatisfaction and miscommunication."

Case Learnings

1. Every esthetic procedure must begin with written boundaries of expectation.
2. Photos are proof of improvement; words are not.
3. Donor and recipient sites must both have independent records.
4. Informed consent with esthetic disclaimer is non-negotiable.
5. Follow-up photos complete the legal loop of success.

Quick Checklist

- Preoperative measurements and photos recorded
- Informed esthetic consent signed
- Recipient and donor sites documented
- Anesthesia and flap design recorded
- Graft labeled and sutures detailed
- Hemostasis and dressing confirmed
- Written postoperative instructions given
- Follow-up visits logged with photos

- Final results measured and stored
- Records retained minimum five years

References

1. *Lindhe J, Lang NP, Karring T. Clinical Periodontology and Implant Dentistry. 7th ed. Wiley-Blackwell; 2022.*
2. *American Academy of Periodontology. Consensus report on mucogingival therapy. J Periodontol. 1996;67(8):859 - 862.*
3. *Zucchelli G, De Sanctis M. Treatment of multiple recession-type defects. J Periodontol. 2000;71(9):1506 - 1514.*
4. *Reiser GM, Bruno JF, Mahan PE, Larkin LH. The subepithelial connective tissue graft: surgical anatomy and technique. J Periodontol. 1996;67(1):28 - 36.*
5. *Harris RJ. Root coverage with connective tissue grafts: review of literature. J Periodontol. 2002;73(9):1057 - 1069.*
6. *Cairo F et al. Root coverage procedures: systematic review of long-term outcomes. J Clin Periodontol. 2016;43(Suppl 16):S286 - S302.*
7. *Miller PD Jr. Classification of marginal tissue recession. Int J Periodontics Restorative Dent. 1985;5(2):8 - 13.*
8. *Dental Council of India. Documentation of Esthetic and Mucogingival Surgery. 2022.*
9. *General Dental Council (UK). Standards for Consent and Recordkeeping in Elective Dental Procedures. 2013.*
10. *Dental Protection Limited. Handling Complaints in Esthetic Dental Practice. 2021.*
11. *Newman MG, Takei H, Klokkevold PR, Carranza FA. Carranza's Clinical Periodontology. 13th ed. Elsevier; 2021.*
12. *Ministry of Health and Family Welfare, India. Clinical Photography and Documentation Guidelines. 2020.*

CHAPTER 27

Frenectomy and Vestibuloplasty - Functional Correction, Procedural Steps, and Legal Essentials

A tight frenum or shallow vestibule is a small defect with large consequences. They distort speech, pull gingiva, open gaps, and make prosthetic work impossible. Yet these are among the most underestimated surgical procedures - simple in execution, but often the cause of avoidable disputes. The difference lies not in the scalpel, but in documentation: who decided, who consented, and what was explained. This chapter turns these minor surgeries into structured, accountable procedures.

Purpose and Indications

Frenectomy removes an aberrant frenum that interferes with speech, esthetics, or gingival attachment. Vestibuloplasty deepens the vestibule to improve prosthesis retention or oral hygiene. Indications include high frenum causing midline diastema, tension on marginal gingiva, shallow sulcus hindering brushing, and pre-prosthetic preparation [1].

Preparation and Preoperative Evaluation

Assess frenum attachment level, tissue thickness, and vestibular depth. Take preoperative photographs and record functional disturbance - speech, brushing difficulty, or prosthesis instability. Obtain informed consent with a clear note that minor swelling, relapse, or scar formation may occur.

Red flag: Failure to document preoperative photographs or expected outcomes leads to patient dissatisfaction claims. Even simple surgeries require esthetic and functional expectation documentation [2].

- ***Step 1: Anesthesia and Field Preparation***

Administer local anesthesia with infiltration at the base of frenum or vestibular mucosa. Stretch tissue gently to visualize the attachment.

Red flag: Omitting anesthesia record or dosage details invalidates the surgical log and weakens medico-legal defense in any postoperative complaint [3].

- ***Step 2: Frenum Identification and Tension Test***

Pull upper or lower lip outward and upward to visualize frenum tension. Mark the base of attachment using indelible pencil or tissue marker.

Red flag: Performing incision without prior tension assessment can result in incomplete release and recurrence. Absence of recorded indication appears as unjustified surgery [4].

- ***Step 3: Incision and Excision (Conventional Frenectomy)***

Make a V-shaped or elliptical incision around the frenum with scalpel or laser. Excise fibrous band and underlying muscle attachment. Achieve hemostasis.

Red flag: Deep dissection causing labial artery injury or excessive bleeding, if unrecorded, will appear as procedural carelessness. Every intraoperative bleeding event must be entered in surgical note [5].

- ***Step 4: Z-Plasty or Frenotomy (If Indicated)***

In cases requiring tissue lengthening, perform Z-plasty or simple frenotomy with lateral repositioning. Ensure relaxed closure without tension.

Red flag: Incorrect technique selection leading to scarring or restricted mobility must be justified by preoperative findings in the file. Otherwise, it reads as poor judgment [6].

- ***Step 5: Vestibuloplasty (If Required)***

For shallow vestibules, raise mucosal flap, dissect muscle attachment apically, and secure flap with periosteal sutures. Cover raw surface with graft or pack.

Red flag: Failure to maintain moist dressing or note graft coverage results in infection or relapse. Every vestibuloplasty must have coverage method documented [7].

- ***Step 6: Suturing and Dressing***

Approximate wound edges with fine interrupted sutures. Apply pressure pack or periodontal dressing to prevent hematoma.

Red flag: Not recording suture type or number leaves postoperative dehiscence indefensible. Courts interpret absent suture documentation as incomplete surgery [8].

- ***Step 7: Postoperative Instructions***

Advise cold compresses for first 24 hours, soft diet, and chlorhexidine rinse twice daily. Avoid lip pulling for a week. Provide written instruction sheet signed by patient.

Red flag: Absence of written postoperative advice is a standard feature in malpractice complaints alleging "excessive swelling" or "lip deformity" [9].

- ***Step 8: Medication and Follow-Up***

Prescribe analgesics and mild antibiotics if indicated. Schedule review at 7 - 10 days for suture removal and healing assessment.

Red flag: No documentation of review appointment equals lack of continuity. Even uncomplicated healing needs an entry and signature [10].

- ***Step 9: Healing Documentation and Evaluation***

At review, record photograph, tissue color, and mobility improvement. Measure vestibular depth if vestibuloplasty performed.

Red flag: Omission of postoperative photograph or note of improvement prevents demonstration of success when patient disputes result [11].

- ***Step 10: Legal Documentation and Closure***

Each case file must contain:

- Written informed consent
- Pre- and postoperative photographs
- Operative notes (technique, anesthesia, sutures, medications)
- Postoperative instruction sheet signed
- Review entry with final photograph and remarks

Red flag: In absence of signed consent and photo sequence, even a successful surgery can be questioned as "unnecessary" [12].

Defensibility and Documentation Anchors

Every soft tissue corrective procedure is a visible act - easily appreciated, easily criticized. Visual proof is the clinician's defense. Record indications, technique, and outcomes with precision; maintain signed acknowledgments for every discussion and instruction.

Case Study

A 22-year-old female underwent frenectomy to close midline diastema before orthodontic treatment. After two weeks, slight scarring and asymmetry developed. The patient alleged "cosmetic disfigurement." The clinician had no preoperative photographs, consent, or postoperative documentation. Although the procedure was technically sound, absence of visual and written records led to an unfavorable ruling and compensation.

Case Learnings

1. Always record the indication and objective before performing minor oral surgery.
2. Photographs before and after are indispensable.
3. Document anesthesia, technique, and suture details precisely.
4. Written postoperative instructions are evidence of care.
5. No documentation equals no defense - regardless of surgical success.

Quick Checklist

- Preoperative photographs taken
- Indications and consent recorded
- Anesthesia dose and site noted
- Frenum or vestibule marked and tested
- Technique type and instruments documented
- Suture details and dressing logged
- Written postoperative instructions signed
- Follow-up and review photos recorded

- Final healing measured and filed
- Records archived for minimum five years

References

1. *Lindhe J, Lang NP, Karring T. Clinical Periodontology and Implant Dentistry. 7th ed. Wiley-Blackwell; 2022.*
2. *Devishree SK et al. Frenectomy: a review with the reports of surgical techniques. J Clin Diagn Res. 2012;6(9):1581 - 1585.*
3. *Malamed SF. Handbook of Local Anesthesia. 7th ed. Elsevier; 2019.*
4. *Dolich CJ et al. Surgical management of the maxillary labial frenum. J Am Dent Assoc. 1994;125(4):414 - 419.*
5. *Patel RM, Varma S. Laser vs conventional frenectomy: comparative evaluation. J Periodontol. 2019;90(10):1147 - 1154.*
6. *Edwards JG. The diastema, the frenum, the frenectomy: a clinical study. Am J Orthod. 1977;71(5):489 - 508.*
7. *Obwegeser H. Vestibuloplasty techniques revisited. J Oral Maxillofac Surg. 1996;54(11):1466 - 1472.*
8. *Ministry of Health and Family Welfare, India. Documentation Standards for Minor Oral Surgeries. 2020.*
9. *Dental Council of India. Consent and Postoperative Care Guidelines for Oral Surgery. 2022.*
10. *General Dental Council (UK). Patient Records and Follow-up Standards. 2013.*
11. *Dental Protection Limited. Medico-Legal Issues in Soft Tissue and Minor Oral Surgery. 2021.*
12. *Newman MG, Takei H, Klokkevold PR, Carranza FA. Carranza's Clinical Periodontology. 13th ed. Elsevier; 2021.*

CHAPTER 28

Guided Tissue Regeneration and Bone Grafting - Biological Principles, Technique Mastery, and Legal Boundaries

Regenerating lost bone and attachment is the highest test of both skill and accountability in periodontics. Every graft placed is a promise - to restore not only form but trust. The technique demands precision, sterility, and documentation equal to any major surgery. Bone and membrane failures are not judged by healing alone, but by whether the clinician followed protocol, maintained asepsis, and obtained fully informed consent.

Purpose and Indications

Guided tissue regeneration (GTR) and bone grafting aim to restore lost periodontal support by promoting new bone, cementum, and ligament formation. Indicated in vertical bone defects, class II furcations, and peri-implant bone loss. Success depends on patient selection, aseptic technique, and postoperative compliance [1].

Preparation and Preoperative Evaluation

Record systemic history - diabetes, smoking, bisphosphonate use - and perform full-mouth radiographs or CBCT. Measure defect depth and classify defect morphology. Explain realistic outcomes, donor sources, membrane materials, and possible resorption or infection risks. Obtain signed consent explicitly noting "regenerative attempt, not guarantee."

Red flag: Failing to mention limited predictability in consent converts biologic variation into legal liability. Written expectation control is mandatory [2].

- ***Step 1: Surgical Field Preparation***

Ensure strict asepsis. Use sterile drapes, gloves, and surgical instruments. Administer anesthesia, confirm hemostasis, and retract gently to expose defect.

Red flag: Performing regenerative surgery under routine chairside asepsis invites contamination. Infection post-grafting is indefensible without sterile protocol record [3].

- ***Step 2: Flap Reflection and Defect Exposure***

Raise full-thickness flap beyond defect margin for adequate access. Remove granulation tissue completely and rinse with saline.

Red flag: Incomplete debridement or retained epithelium blocks regeneration. Absence of recorded flap type and reflection method weakens defense in postoperative infection [4].

- ***Step 3: Root Surface and Defect Preparation***

Smooth root surface using curettes or rotary instruments. Demineralize with tetracycline or EDTA for biologic conditioning if indicated.

Red flag: Applying chemical agents without documented indication or concentration is malpractice if tissue necrosis occurs. Always note material, strength, and duration in surgical log [5].

- ***Step 4: Graft Material Selection and Preparation***

Select graft based on defect and patient profile - autograft, allograft, xenograft, or synthetic substitute. Record brand, batch number, and expiry. Moisten graft with sterile saline before placement.

Red flag: Using unverified or expired material, or failing to document product details, violates biomedical traceability laws. Every graft must be traceable to source [6].

- ***Step 5: Graft Placement***

Pack graft gently into defect without compression. Avoid overfilling and ensure contact with root and bone walls.

Red flag: Overfilling or dislodged grafts cause flap tension and dehiscence. If graft exposure occurs, record incident and management plan immediately [7].

- ***Step 6: Barrier Membrane Adaptation***

Trim and secure membrane over graft, extending 2 - 3 mm beyond defect margins. Fix with tacks or sutures to prevent displacement.

Red flag: Skipping membrane fixation or failing to document membrane type and batch voids proof of proper GTR execution. Any membrane exposure must be logged [8].

- ***Step 7: Flap Closure and Suturing***

Reposition flap for passive closure without tension. Use interrupted or horizontal mattress sutures. Check stability and apply pressure pack.

Red flag: Tension closure failure leading to graft exposure can occur even in skilled hands, but lack of intraoperative notes or photos will imply technical negligence [9].

- ***Step 8: Postoperative Medication and Care***

Prescribe antibiotics, analgesics, and chlorhexidine rinse. Advise soft diet, gentle cleaning, and avoidance of brushing in surgical area for 10 - 14 days. Provide written instructions and review schedule.

Red flag: Verbal-only instructions for graft care lead to contamination and exposure disputes. Written and signed postoperative sheet is essential [10].

- ***Step 9: Follow-Up and Evaluation***

Review at 7, 14, and 30 days, then at 3 and 6 months. Record healing, soft tissue stability, and radiographic bone fill. Photograph each visit.

Red flag: Missing review documentation at any stage forfeits proof of progressive healing. Litigation often focuses on "missing middle records," not failure itself [11].

- ***Step 10: Long-Term Maintenance***

After 6 months, re-chart pocket depth and radiographically assess bone regeneration. Plan supportive therapy every 3 - 6 months.

Red flag: Absence of maintenance record suggests procedural abandonment. Each review should be dated, signed, and compared with baseline images [12].

Defensibility and Documentation Anchors

Defensible regenerative surgery documentation includes:

- Preoperative radiographs or CBCT
- Informed consent with limited success clause
- Operative note detailing defect, materials, and technique
- Batch numbers and expiry of graft/membrane
- Photographic evidence (pre-, intra-, and post-operative)
- Postoperative instructions and signed review entries
- Radiographic follow-up proof of healing

These establish both clinical credibility and medico-legal protection.

Case Study

A 45-year-old smoker underwent GTR with xenograft and collagen membrane. Postoperative infection developed with graft exposure. The clinician had not recorded smoking status or membrane batch number. The patient sued, alleging "foreign material reaction." The court concluded inadequate consent and documentation failure - negligence by omission, not by outcome.

Case Learnings

1. Success in regeneration is uncertain; documentation must never be.
2. Always record medical risk factors, materials, and consent limitations.
3. Infection or exposure becomes defensible only when asepsis and review logs are present.
4. Every photograph, radiograph, and label is a line of protection.
5. Transparency in uncertainty is the most effective legal safeguard.

Quick Checklist

- Systemic risks and defect assessment documented
- Preoperative radiographs/CBCT stored
- Consent signed with limited outcome clause
- Aseptic setup confirmed
- Graft and membrane type, batch, and expiry recorded
- Flap closure tension-free and documented
- Written postoperative instructions signed
- Scheduled reviews logged with photographs
- Radiographic follow-up at 6 months
- Maintenance plan initiated and recorded

References

1. *Lindhe J, Lang NP, Karring T. Clinical Periodontology and Implant Dentistry. 7th ed. Wiley-Blackwell; 2022.*
2. *Mellonig JT. Regeneration of alveolar bone with GTR. J Periodontol. 1995;66(6):507 - 514.*
3. *Simion M et al. Prevention of membrane exposure in GTR. Int J Periodontics Restorative Dent. 1994;14(6):497 - 505.*
4. *Karring T, Nyman S, Lindhe J. Healing following guided tissue regeneration. J Clin Periodontol. 1980;7(2):96 - 105.*
5. *Yukna RA. Root surface demineralization in periodontal therapy. J Periodontol. 1994;65(10):1017 - 1025.*
6. *Mellonig JT. Bone graft materials in periodontal therapy. J Periodontol. 1991;62(8):570 - 578.*
7. *Buser D et al. Membrane exposure and regenerative outcome. Clin Oral Implants Res. 1990;1(3):133 - 142.*
8. *American Academy of Periodontology. GTR and bone grafting position paper. J Periodontol. 2005;76(9):1601 - 1622.*
9. *Cortellini P, Tonetti MS. Clinical outcomes of regenerative therapy. J Clin Periodontol. 2004;31(9):817 - 826.*
10. *Dental Council of India. Surgical Regeneration and Documentation Protocols. 2022.*
11. *General Dental Council (UK). Surgical Follow-up Standards. 2013.*
12. *Dental Protection Limited. Regenerative and Implant Complications: Legal Management Guide. 2021.*

CHAPTER 29

Peri-Implantitis and Mucosal Complications - Diagnosis, Intervention, and Legal Implications

Implants promise permanence, but biology keeps its veto. Peri-implantitis sits at the junction of technology, technique, and tissue - and every failure is personal to the patient. When an implant fails, the patient doesn't blame titanium; they blame the clinician. This chapter defines how to diagnose, intervene, and document peri-implant disease so that when failure occurs, it is understood as biological, not professional.

Purpose and Indications

Peri-implant mucositis and peri-implantitis are inflammatory conditions affecting the soft and hard tissues around osseointegrated implants. Early diagnosis through probing, radiographs, and documentation prevents progression to bone loss or implant mobility. Legal safety depends on periodic recordkeeping, not just clinical correction [1].

Preparation and Risk Assessment

Evaluate systemic factors (diabetes, smoking), oral hygiene, implant age, and prosthetic design. Record probing depth, bleeding, and radiographic bone levels at baseline and every review. Obtain signed informed consent noting maintenance dependency and potential for long-term complications.

Red flag: Implant placement or maintenance without risk documentation converts biological variability into negligence. Every implant record must begin with baseline probing and bone height documentation [2].

- ***Step 1: Diagnosis and Documentation***

Use plastic probe around implants to measure depth, bleeding, and suppuration. Compare with baseline values. Take standardized periapical radiograph using parallel technique.

Red flag: Diagnosing "peri-implantitis" without baseline chart or radiograph is speculation. Courts dismiss unsubstantiated claims of disease or defense alike [3].

- ***Step 2: Non-Surgical Intervention***

Perform mechanical debridement with titanium or plastic curettes. Irrigate with chlorhexidine or saline. Use air-abrasive or ultrasonic devices designed for implants.

Red flag: Using steel instruments or abrasive powders causes surface damage and worsens inflammation. Absence of instrument log makes damage causation indefensible [4].

- ***Step 3: Adjunctive Antimicrobial Therapy***

Apply local antibiotics (minocycline or chlorhexidine chips) or prescribe systemic therapy when suppuration is evident. Record drug, dose, and duration.

Red flag: Empirical antibiotic use without culture or indication record invites scrutiny for irrational prescribing. Every antimicrobial intervention must cite evidence in notes [5].

- ***Step 4: Surgical Intervention - Flap Access and Debridement***

When bone loss exceeds 3 mm or pockets >5 mm persist, raise full-thickness flap. Remove granulation tissue and polish implant surface using titanium brushes or lasers.

Red flag: Failure to note flap design, surface decontamination method, and irrigants leaves no trace of due care. If bone loss progresses later, undocumented procedure equals no defense [6].

- ***Step 5: Regenerative or Resective Approach***

For crater defects, place bone graft and membrane; for horizontal loss, perform resective contouring. Document materials used and technique.

Red flag: Using bone grafts or membranes without traceability records violates medical device regulations. Batch and brand details must be written in surgical log [7].

- ***Step 6: Flap Closure and Postoperative Care***

Achieve tension-free closure. Prescribe antibiotics and chlorhexidine rinse. Provide written instructions for hygiene and soft diet.

Red flag: Neglecting written aftercare leads to contamination and relapse. Every implant surgery must end with signed postoperative instruction sheet [8].

- ***Step 7: Prosthetic Evaluation***

Assess occlusal load, screw tightness, and prosthetic contour. Document correction or referral if overload detected.

Red flag: Ignoring prosthetic interference or poor access for hygiene is negligence in maintenance, not implantology. Documenting correction shows continuity of care [9].

- ***Step 8: Maintenance and Recall Schedule***

Schedule follow-up every 3 - 6 months. Record probing depth, radiographic bone levels, and hygiene status at each visit.

Red flag: Implant patients lost to follow-up due to clinician inaction reflect abandonment. Every recall reminder or note demonstrates ongoing responsibility [10].

- ***Step 9: Communication of Risk and Prognosis***

Discuss disease stage, prognosis, and long-term expectations with patient. Note communication in file and obtain acknowledgment.

Red flag: Failure to warn that peri-implantitis may recur is treated as concealment. A signed discussion note prevents disputes about "unexpected relapse" [11].

- ***Step 10: Legal Record Assembly and Retention***

Each implant file must contain:

- Baseline probing and radiographs
- Maintenance and review charts
- Surgical and material details with batch numbers
- Signed informed consent and postoperative instruction sheet
- Communication notes regarding prognosis

Red flag: Missing any part of this chain renders the case indefensible, even if implant survival rates are acceptable [12].

Defensibility and Documentation Anchors

A legally secure implant case has evidence of care before, during, and after placement. The law does not require perfection - only traceability. Baseline records, follow-ups, and transparent communication convert an adverse outcome into an understood complication.

Case Study

A 55-year-old patient developed peri-implant bone loss two years after crown delivery. The dentist had no baseline probing or radiographs, and no maintenance records. The defense of "biological variability" failed; absence of documentation was treated as absence of maintenance. Compensation was ordered for implant failure and prosthesis loss.

Case Learnings

1. Implant success is measured not only in bone but in paperwork.
2. Baseline charts and radiographs are non-negotiable.
3. Each material and intervention must be traceable.
4. Maintenance reminders are legal protection, not courtesy.
5. Transparency about disease risk is the clinician's strongest defense.

Quick Checklist

- Baseline probing and radiographs taken
- Risk factors documented and consent signed
- Instrument type and method recorded
- Antimicrobial use justified and noted
- Flap design and technique described
- Graft and membrane batch recorded
- Postoperative instructions signed
- Maintenance reviews logged
- Prosthetic adjustment documented
- Records retained minimum five years

References

1. *Lindhe J, Lang NP, Karring T. Clinical Periodontology and Implant Dentistry. 7th ed. Wiley-Blackwell; 2022.*
2. *Berglundh T et al. Peri-implant diseases and conditions: Consensus report of the 2017 World Workshop. J Periodontol. 2018;89(Suppl 1):S313 - S318.*
3. *Schwarz F, Derks J. Peri-implantitis: clinical diagnosis and management. Periodontol 2000. 2022;89(1):66 - 84.*
4. *Louropoulou A, Slot DE, Van der Weijden F. Mechanical cleaning of implants: review. Clin Oral Implants Res. 2014;25(2):114 - 124.*
5. *Mombelli A, Décaillet F. Antimicrobial therapy for peri-implant diseases. Int J Oral Maxillofac Implants. 2011;26(1):169 - 176.*
6. *Renvert S, Polyzois I. Treatment modalities for peri-implant mucositis and peri-implantitis. Periodontol 2000. 2018;76(1):163 - 175.*
7. *Schwarz F et al. Regenerative approaches in peri-implantitis defects. Clin Oral Investig. 2017;21(2):601 - 610.*
8. *Dental Council of India. Implant Surgery Documentation Standards. 2022.*
9. *General Dental Council (UK). Maintenance and Recordkeeping for Implant Patients. 2013.*
10. *Tonetti MS, Schmid J. Pathogenesis of peri-implantitis. Clin Oral Implants Res. 1994;5(4):230 - 238.*
11. *Dental Protection Limited. Managing Implant Complications and Legal Risk. 2021.*
12. *Ministry of Health and Family Welfare, India. Clinical Record Standards for Implant Dentistry. 2020.*

CHAPTER 30

Periodontal Emergencies - Abscesses, Acute Necrotizing Conditions, and Legal Duty of Immediate Care

Emergencies test reflexes, not routines. A swollen gingiva or sudden pain may seem minor until systemic infection, trismus, or airway compromise follow. Periodontal emergencies require immediate clinical judgment, antiseptic precision, and meticulous records. In such moments, the patient remembers pain; the law remembers paperwork. This chapter details how to manage acute periodontal conditions with clarity, speed, and legal defensibility.

Purpose and Indications

Periodontal emergencies include gingival abscess, periodontal abscess, pericoronitis, acute necrotizing ulcerative gingivitis (ANUG), and post-surgical infections. Each demands rapid diagnosis, drainage, and antibiotic coverage. The clinician's duty is both therapeutic and legal: to stabilize, document, and communicate clearly [1].

Preparation and Initial Response

Take concise medical history - allergies, diabetes, anticoagulants - and note vitals (temperature, pulse, BP). Assess facial swelling, trismus, lymphadenopathy, and systemic signs. Document findings before any incision or prescription.

Red flag: Starting antibiotics without examination or written record violates medical ethics. In court, undocumented prescriptions are treated as blind treatment [2].

- ***Step 1: Diagnostic Differentiation***

Differentiate abscess types - gingival (localized marginal), periodontal (deep pocket), and pericoronal (around erupting tooth). Use probing, radiographs, and vitality testing.

Red flag: Confusing endodontic and periodontal abscess leads to unnecessary RCT or extraction. Absent documentation of probing or vitality tests shows diagnostic negligence [3].

- ***Step 2: Local Anesthesia and Asepsis***

Administer local anesthesia and disinfect site with povidone-iodine. Use suction and protective eyewear.

Red flag: Failing to record anesthetic type and dose converts any adverse reaction into indefensible error [4].

- ***Step 3: Drainage and Debridement***

Make vertical incision at most fluctuant point. Gently express pus and irrigate with saline or chlorhexidine. For periodontal abscess, debride pocket and remove calculus.

Red flag: Performing incision without asepsis or consent is surgical assault. A simple signed emergency consent is essential for every invasive act [5].

- ***Step 4: Antibiotic and Analgesic Prescription***

Prescribe amoxicillin (500 mg TID) or clindamycin for allergic patients; analgesic per pain tolerance. Record drug name, dose, duration, and rationale.

Red flag: Overprescribing or undocumented antibiotic use is legally punishable under rational drug use laws. Prescription records protect against both infection claims and drug reactions [6].

- ***Step 5: Occlusal Adjustment and Relief***

Reduce traumatic occlusion if mobility or tenderness exists. Advise soft diet and warm saline rinses.

Red flag: Ignoring occlusal trauma when evident implies incomplete emergency care. Every step must be entered in patient file [7].

- ***Step 6: Systemic Evaluation and Referral***

Refer for medical evaluation if fever >101°F, cellulitis, or lymph node involvement present.

Red flag: Retaining patient in clinic despite spreading infection constitutes negligence by delay. Referral letters and timing notes are vital evidence of appropriate judgment [8].

- ***Step 7: Management of ANUG and Ulcerative Lesions***

Clean necrotic pseudomembrane gently with cotton pellet and chlorhexidine. Prescribe metronidazole if systemic signs present. Counsel on nutrition and oral hygiene.

Red flag: Overzealous debridement of ulcerated tissue causes severe pain and bleeding. Every ulcerative condition must have a clear diagnosis and record of minimal intervention [9].

- ***Step 8: Postoperative Care and Follow-Up***

Advise cold compresses for swelling, analgesics as prescribed, and soft diet. Re-evaluate after 48 - 72 hours. Record reduction in pain and swelling.

Red flag: Failure to document review makes clinician liable for recurrence or spread, as continuity of care is part of legal duty [10].

- ***Step 9: Patient Communication and Disclosure***

Explain diagnosis, cause, and home-care instructions. Provide written leaflet on oral hygiene and recall.

Red flag: No written communication allows patient to allege "no advice given." A signed instruction sheet closes this gap [11].

- ***Step 10: Definitive Treatment and Documentation***

After infection subsides, plan scaling, root planing, or surgical correction. Update periodontal chart and store emergency record with progress notes.

Red flag: Completing drainage but omitting definitive plan reads as abandonment. Every emergency entry must show next step and follow-up schedule [12].

Defensibility and Documentation Anchors

Every periodontal emergency must leave a verifiable trail - from first complaint to resolution. Mandatory elements include:

- Vitals and brief medical history
- Diagnosis and differentiation notes

- Signed emergency consent
- Medication log with rationale
- Referral or review entry
- Follow-up record with outcome

This sequence converts reactive care into traceable professionalism.

Case Study

A 40-year-old diabetic presented with facial swelling due to periodontal abscess. The dentist prescribed antibiotics by phone without examination or record. The infection spread, requiring hospitalization. The court ruled negligence due to lack of documentation and absence of referral. Even though medication was appropriate, absence of examination note invalidated the defense.

Case Learnings

1. Emergency care begins with a record, not a scalpel.
2. Documentation of vitals and consent is critical even in urgency.
3. Telephone or verbal prescriptions are indefensible.
4. Early referral with written note proves judgment and prudence.
5. Continuity of care - from incision to healing - defines legal protection.

Quick Checklist

- Vitals and medical history recorded
- Diagnosis confirmed and type of abscess noted
- Anesthesia documented
- Drainage and irrigation performed aseptically
- Antibiotic and analgesic prescription logged
- Occlusal relief and home-care advised
- Referral or hospitalization if systemic signs
- Written postoperative instructions given

- Follow-up at 48 - 72 hours recorded
- Definitive care planned and documented

References

1. *Lindhe J, Lang NP, Karring T. Clinical Periodontology and Implant Dentistry. 7th ed. Wiley-Blackwell; 2022.*
2. *Herrera D, Roldán S, Sanz M. The periodontal abscess: a review. J Clin Periodontol. 2000;27(6):377 - 386.*
3. *Pihlstrom BL, Michalowicz BS, Johnson NW. Periodontal diseases. Lancet. 2005;366(9499):1809 - 1820.*
4. *Malamed SF. Handbook of Local Anesthesia. 7th ed. Elsevier; 2019.*
5. *Kinane DF, Lindhe J. Acute periodontal conditions. In: Lindhe J et al. Clinical Periodontology. 7th ed. Wiley-Blackwell; 2022.*
6. *Dental Council of India. Prescription Writing and Antibiotic Stewardship in Dentistry. 2022.*
7. *Slots J. Periodontal infections: systemic antibiotics and treatment strategies. J Periodontol. 2004;75(11):1552 - 1566.*
8. *General Dental Council (UK). Emergency Referral and Recordkeeping Standards. 2013.*
9. *Rowland RW. Necrotizing ulcerative gingivitis. Ann Periodontol. 1999;4(1):65 - 73.*
10. *Dental Protection Limited. Emergency Documentation and Continuity of Care. 2021.*
11. *Ministry of Health and Family Welfare, India. Clinical Documentation for Dental Emergencies. 2020.*
12. *Newman MG, Takei H, Klokkevold PR, Carranza FA. Carranza's Clinical Periodontology. 13th ed. Elsevier; 2021.*

CHAPTER 31

Negligence and Litigation in Periodontics - Patterns, Prevention, and Learning

*Periodontics sits quietly at the crossroads of prevention and accountability. Gum disease rarely kills, but in law it often condemns. The courts see every lost tooth, bone defect, or untreated pocket as something that *should have been detected earlier.* Negligence in periodontics is seldom about surgical failure - it's about missing the signs, failing to warn, or not keeping a record. This chapter exposes the recurring medico-legal traps and turns them into lessons for daily defense.*

Purpose and Context

The objective here is to recognize patterns of litigation in periodontal care and to prevent them through systematic documentation, timely referral, and ethical communication. Each complaint begins where diligence ends.

- ***Step 1: Recognize Common Allegations***

The most frequent charges include:

- Failure to diagnose or record periodontal disease during routine checkups.
- Inadequate scaling or incomplete debridement.
- Tooth mobility or loss after "cleaning" without prior risk disclosure.
- Undocumented surgical consent or graft details.
- Inadequate postoperative follow-up or recall reminders.

Red flag: Patients claim "my tooth became loose after cleaning" - without baseline charting, you cannot prove it was already compromised.

- ***Step 2: Establish Baseline Proof***

Every patient above 18 should have a recorded periodontal status - probing depths, bleeding index, and radiographs when indicated. Baseline photographs and charts prove pre-existing disease.

Red flag: Starting therapy without dated measurements removes your defense; the court assumes you never assessed.

- ***Step 3: Record Consent Specific to Periodontal Procedures***

Each scaling, flap surgery, or graft must have its own consent specifying potential sensitivity, bleeding, or mobility changes.

Red flag: Generic "dental treatment" consent is invalid for invasive soft-tissue procedures.

- ***Step 4: Maintain Full Traceability of Materials***

When bone grafts or membranes are used, record batch number, expiry, and manufacturer certificate. Keep copies of invoices in a traceability folder.

Red flag: Missing batch details converts any infection claim into presumed negligence.

- ***Step 5: Manage Communication Failures***

Many lawsuits stem from silence. Patients interpret absence of explanation as concealment. Always inform them of expected bleeding, transient sensitivity, or temporary recession, both verbally and in writing.

Red flag: A postoperative complaint handled over the phone without entry in notes equals unrecorded event - legally invisible.

- ***Step 6: Timely Referral and Shared Responsibility***

If disease persists or worsens, document referral to a periodontist and obtain written acknowledgment from both the specialist and the patient.

Red flag: Late or undocumented referral is treated as delay, not discretion.

- ***Step 7: Legal Procedural View***

When cases reach inquiry, defense depends on contemporaneous notes, dated radiographs, and signed consents. Retrospective entries or unspecific "improvement noted" remarks lack credibility. Maintain chronological continuity - baseline, therapy, re-evaluation, recall. The file should read like a timeline, not a collection of random sheets.

Case Study

A 52-year-old diabetic visited a clinic for bleeding gums over three years. The dentist repeatedly performed scaling without recording pocket depths or blood sugar control. Later, when multiple teeth were lost, the patient alleged negligence. The tribunal found against the dentist, citing lack of baseline charting, absent risk disclosure, and no written referral to a specialist. Compensation was awarded despite acceptable technical care.

Case Learnings

1. Courts equate missing records with missing care.
2. Proper documentation of systemic factors like diabetes proves awareness, not omission.
3. Referral letters and compliance notes carry the same legal weight as treatment records.
4. Objective re-evaluation numbers trump vague descriptors.
5. Defensive dentistry is not defensive practice - it's deliberate practice.

- ***Step 8: Preventive Framework - The "Four D" Model***
- **Detect:** Chart every bleeding point, even if mild.
- **Document:** Photograph, measure, and log findings by date.
- **Disclose:** Explain disease, risks, and treatment options with written acknowledgment.
- **Defend:** Review and audit records monthly; maintain separate consent and traceability files.

Key Message

In periodontics, negligence is not what happens to the tissues - it's what doesn't happen on paper. Every pocket you probe, every graft you place, every recall you suggest should leave a visible mark in your records. Prevention and documentation are not two tasks; they are the same act performed through two hands - one on the curette, one on the pen.

References

1. *Dental Council of India. Ethical and Legal Responsibilities in Periodontal Care. 2022.*
2. *Ministry of Health and Family Welfare, India. Clinical Documentation Standards for Dental Practitioners. 2020.*
3. *American Academy of Periodontology. Guidelines for Comprehensive Periodontal Therapy. 2021.*
4. *National Medical Commission (India). Medico-Legal Framework for Dental Negligence. 2021.*
5. *Consumer Protection Act, 2019 - Relevant Sections on Medical Negligence and Record Retention.*

SECTION 5

Oral and Maxillofacial Surgery - Extractions, Flaps, and Medico-Legal Protocols

Surgery is dentistry's most visible truth. It leaves marks - on tissue, on records, and on reputation. Every incision and suture is both an act of healing and a legal document in flesh. This section brings discipline to that double responsibility: the hand that cuts must also record.

It begins with the universal grammar of safe surgery - preoperative assessment, aseptic setup, and consent that speaks the patient's language as clearly as it satisfies the law's. From there, it moves through flap design, impaction removal, cyst and tumor management, fracture stabilization, and maxillofacial infections. Each step carries two simultaneous demands: anatomical precision and procedural traceability.

The chapters highlight how easily surgical brilliance can be undone by poor documentation - a missing batch number on a graft, an unsigned operative note, or an unrecorded warning about paresthesia. They teach the rhythm of writing as you work: note it, photograph it, and sign it before moving on.

Emergency control - bleeding, airway compromise, nerve injury - is shown as both medical reflex and legal proof of preparedness. You will see how to record communication with anesthetists, referrals to hospitals, and even phone calls to families after complex surgery.

By the end, this section turns oral surgery from a sequence of procedures into a system of accountability. You'll leave with more than confidence under the light - you'll leave with clarity under scrutiny.

CHAPTER 32

Principles of Exodontia and Legal Accountability

Extraction remains the most common oral surgical procedure and the most litigated. Patients often recall pain, swelling, or a "piece left behind," but rarely the medical complexities that justify those outcomes. This chapter restores order to extraction - making it not a mechanical act but a reasoned, legally sound intervention.

Purpose and Indications

Exodontia removes teeth that are non-restorable, infected, or impeding other treatments. It must achieve complete removal with minimal trauma and full documentation of indication, method, and consent [1].

Preparation and Preoperative Evaluation

Obtain comprehensive medical history - hypertension, bleeding disorders, diabetes, medications (especially anticoagulants and bisphosphonates). Record radiographic evaluation, tooth anatomy, root curvature, and relation to vital structures.

Red flag: Extracting without preoperative radiograph or medical history is indefensible. Postoperative complications such as nerve injury or excessive bleeding without baseline record are classified as negligent omission [2].

- ***Step 1: Informed Consent and Documentation***

Explain indication, risks (bleeding, pain, infection, dry socket, nerve injury), and alternatives. Obtain written consent and note patient's questions and your responses.

Redflag: Verbal consent alone invalidates defense. Courts require written acknowledgment of risk explanation [3].

- ***Step 2: Infection Control and Field Preparation***

Use sterile gloves, instruments, and suction. Disinfect perioral area with antiseptic.

Red flag: Failure to record sterilization and barrier use can convert a postoperative infection into a case of "unsanitary surgical practice" [4].

- ***Step 3: Anesthesia Administration***

Administer local anesthesia - type, volume, site, and batch number documented. Confirm onset before proceeding.

Red flag: Missing anesthesia record negates due diligence; any adverse reaction becomes indefensible [5].

- ***Step 4: Tooth Luxation and Elevation***

Loosen soft tissue attachment with periosteal elevator. Use appropriate force and angulation to expand socket.

Red flag: Excessive force causing root or alveolar fracture is a known risk but becomes malpractice if radiographic complexity was not noted beforehand [6].

- ***Step 5: Extraction and Delivery***

Use forceps suited for tooth morphology. Support alveolar bone and maintain controlled motion. Remove tooth entirely, inspecting for retained roots.

Red flag: Retained fragments without mention of difficulty or fractured root note imply operator carelessness. Every breakage must be documented immediately [7].

- ***Step 6: Socket Debridement and Inspection***

Curette socket gently, irrigate with saline, and inspect for debris or bony spicules.

Red flag: Failing to examine socket or record inspection note invites infection and legal reproach for incomplete surgery [8].

- ***Step 7: Hemostasis and Closure***

Achieve hemostasis using pressure, sutures, or hemostatic agents. Provide postoperative instructions for bleeding control.

Red flag: Leaving socket oozing or failing to document hemostasis violates surgical completeness. A bleeding emergency the next day is indefensible without closure record [9].

- ***Step 8: Postoperative Instructions and Medication***

Prescribe analgesics and antibiotics only if indicated. Advise cold compresses, soft diet, and no smoking for 24 hours. Provide written instruction sheet.

Red flag: Verbal-only instructions are legally meaningless. Signed discharge notes are protection against miscommunication claims [10].

- ***Step 9: Follow-Up and Complication Monitoring***

Review after 48 - 72 hours to assess pain, bleeding, and healing. Note findings and photograph site if needed.

Red flag: No follow-up entry equals procedural abandonment. Most medico-legal complaints arise when clinicians fail to record postoperative interaction [11].

- ***Step 10: Complication Management and Disclosure***

If root fracture, sinus exposure, or nerve injury occurs, disclose immediately, manage conservatively, and document fully. Referral to specialist if needed.

Red flag: Concealment of intraoperative accident converts a procedural mishap into ethical misconduct. Disclosure and referral are non-negotiable [12].

Defensibility and Documentation Anchors

A defendable extraction record contains:

- Indication and preoperative radiograph
- Written consent
- Anesthesia type and dose
- Procedure notes with tooth number and technique
- Complication or fragment note
- Hemostasis and postoperative instruction record
- Follow-up entry and closure status

Such records convert even complex extractions into defensible, accountable care.

Case Study

A 56-year-old woman underwent lower third molar extraction without radiographic evaluation. Lingual nerve paresthesia followed. No anesthesia record or consent existed. The court ruled that lack of radiograph and written consent constituted breach of standard care, regardless of technical skill.

Case Learnings

1. Every extraction must have a radiograph and written consent before it begins.
2. Surgical accidents are defensible; concealment is not.
3. Documentation turns clinical honesty into protection.
4. Written postoperative instructions prevent miscommunication.
5. The patient's perception of negligence is erased only by documented transparency.

Quick Checklist

- Medical and radiographic evaluation recorded
- Written consent signed
- Aseptic preparation confirmed
- Anesthesia type, dose, batch noted
- Tooth number and difficulty recorded
- Socket inspected and irrigated
- Hemostasis achieved and noted
- Written postoperative instructions given
- Follow-up review recorded
- Complication, if any, disclosed and documented

References

1. *Peterson LJ et al. Contemporary Oral and Maxillofacial Surgery. 7th ed. Elsevier; 2022.*
2. *Pogrel MA. Damage to the inferior alveolar and lingual nerves after third molar removal. J Oral Maxillofac Surg. 2012;70(2):438 - 444.*
3. *General Dental Council (UK). Consent and Patient Communication Standards. 2013.*
4. *Ministry of Health and Family Welfare, India. National Guidelines for Infection Control in Dental Practice. 2020.*
5. *Malamed SF. Handbook of Local Anesthesia. 7th ed. Elsevier; 2019.*
6. *Howe GL. The Extraction of Teeth. 3rd ed. Wright; 1991.*
7. *Renton T. Management of third molar surgery complications. Oral Surg Oral Med Oral Pathol Oral Radiol. 2017;123(3):327 - 333.*
8. *Dental Protection Limited. Recordkeeping in Oral Surgery: Legal Guidance. 2021.*
9. *Blondeau F, Daniel NG. Inferior alveolar nerve injuries: prevention and management. Oral Maxillofac Surg Clin North Am. 2007;19(1):175 - 186.*
10. *Dental Council of India. Standard of Care in Exodontia and Minor Oral Surgery. 2022.*
11. *Bouloux GF. Complications of third molar surgery. Oral Maxillofac Surg Clin North Am. 2007;19(1):117 - 128.*
12. *National Medical Commission (India). Guidelines for Disclosure and Referral in Surgical Complications. 2021.*

CHAPTER 33

Surgical Extractions and Flap Management - Technique, Risk Avoidance, and Legal Documentation

Every tooth that resists simple elevation asks the same question: how far will you go safely? Surgical extractions convert a mechanical problem into an anatomical one - and every incision, flap, or bone cut must be deliberate, defensible, and documented. The technical act is brief; the medicolegal footprint lasts years. This chapter defines surgical extraction as a measured operation - not just removal, but responsibility.

Purpose and Indications

Surgical extraction is indicated for teeth with curved or divergent roots, hypercementosis, ankylosis, retained roots, or impacted position. It requires flap reflection, bone removal, and sometimes sectioning. The purpose is controlled access - not force, but visibility [1].

Preparation and Preoperative Requirements

Take detailed medical history and obtain radiograph or CBCT showing root anatomy and proximity to sinus, nerve canal, or adjacent teeth. Explain risks (bleeding, nerve injury, sinus communication) and obtain written surgical consent.

Red flag: Absence of radiographic evidence or signed consent before flap incision is indefensible. These are the first documents requested in any surgical claim [2].

- ***Step 1: Asepsis and Anesthesia***

Disinfect surgical field, drape patient, and use sterile instruments.

Administer local anesthesia - record agent, dose, and site.

Red flag: Operating without recorded anesthesia details or aseptic preparation breaches both surgical and medico-legal standards [3].

- ***Step 2: Flap Design and Incision***

Design envelope, triangular, or semilunar flap ensuring broad base and minimal tension. Incise cleanly using No. 15 blade.

Red flag: Ragged or poorly planned flap causing delayed healing or scarring is not a complication - it is a preventable error. Absence of flap design note removes defense against claims of "cosmetic deformity" [4].

- ***Step 3: Flap Reflection and Exposure***

Reflect full-thickness mucoperiosteal flap using periosteal elevator, maintaining contact with bone. Retract gently with appropriate instrument.

Red flag: Tearing or excessive retraction leading to tissue necrosis must be recorded immediately. Silence in operative note equals concealment [5].

- ***Step 4: Bone Removal (Osteotomy)***

Remove overlying bone with bur under saline irrigation. Expose crown or root up to cementoenamel junction.

Red flag: Overzealous bone removal weakening adjacent teeth or perforating sinus is indefensible without record of controlled, irrigated technique. Always note bur type and irrigation used [6].

- ***Step 5: Tooth Sectioning***

Section tooth into manageable fragments using straight bur. Remove segments individually with elevators.

Red flag: Attempting extraction without sectioning and fracturing alveolus is procedural negligence. Record every sectioning step with justification ("curved root" or "ankylosed segment") [7].

- ***Step 6: Debridement and Socket Smoothing***

Curette socket, remove debris, smooth sharp bone edges, and irrigate thoroughly.

Red flag: Leaving root tips or bony spicules unrecorded leads to postoperative infection and litigation. Always note "socket inspected and irrigated" [8].

- ***Step 7: Hemostasis and Closure***

Achieve hemostasis using pressure, bone wax, or sutures. Reposition flap and close with interrupted or figure-of-eight sutures. Record suture material, size, and number.

Red flag: Uncontrolled bleeding or missing closure note implies incomplete surgery. Every hemostatic measure must be logged [9].

- ***Step 8: Postoperative Instructions and Medication***

Prescribe analgesics and antibiotics as indicated. Advise cold compresses, soft diet, and avoid rinsing for 24 hours. Provide written instruction sheet signed by patient.

Red flag: Verbal instructions carry no legal weight. Absence of a signed discharge record invites miscommunication claims [10].

- ***Step 9: Follow-Up and Review***

Re-evaluate in 3 - 5 days for pain, swelling, and healing. Remove sutures after 7 - 10 days. Record findings and photograph if any complication arises.

Red flag: Failure to document follow-up equals procedural abandonment. A simple "review attended" note prevents liability for delayed infection [11].

- ***Step 10: Management of Intraoperative Complications***

If root fracture, sinus perforation, or nerve exposure occurs, document immediately. Inform patient, manage conservatively, and record all measures taken and referrals.

Red flag: Concealment or silence in notes is fatal in legal defense. Even small perforations are forgivable; nondisclosure is not [12].

Defensibility and Documentation Anchors

A defensible surgical extraction record must contain:

- Radiograph or CBCT and indication
- Written consent and anesthesia log
- Flap design and suture record
- Intraoperative notes with any complications
- Postoperative instruction sheet signed

- Follow-up and healing record

These form a complete chain of procedural evidence that proves skill, consent, and continuity.

Case Study

A 37-year-old patient developed oroantral communication after maxillary molar extraction. The dentist had no radiograph or consent form. The operative note stated only "surgical extraction done." The patient required sinus repair. The court ruled that the absence of imaging and consent violated standard care, awarding damages for "avoidable sinus injury."

Case Learnings

1. Every surgical extraction must be preceded by radiograph and written consent.
2. Flap design and suture details must be part of the record.
3. Complications are defensible when documented in real time.
4. Follow-up visits are proof of continuity and care.
5. In surgery, absence of records is worse than presence of error.

Quick Checklist

- Radiograph/CBCT reviewed and filed
- Written surgical consent obtained
- Asepsis confirmed and anesthesia recorded
- Flap design and incision noted
- Bone removal method and bur type recorded
- Sectioning justified and documented
- Socket inspected and irrigated
- Hemostasis achieved and sutures logged
- Written postoperative instructions provided
- Follow-up and complication management recorded

References

1. *Peterson LJ et al. Contemporary Oral and Maxillofacial Surgery. 7th ed. Elsevier; 2022.*
2. *Renton T. Management of third molar surgery complications. Oral Surg Oral Med Oral Pathol Oral Radiol. 2017;123(3):327 - 333.*
3. *Ministry of Health and Family Welfare, India. National Guidelines for Infection Control in Dental Practice. 2020.*
4. *Howe GL. Minor Oral Surgery. 3rd ed. Wright; 1985.*
5. *Bouloux GF. Complications of third molar surgery. Oral Maxillofac Surg Clin North Am. 2007;19(1):117 - 128.*
6. *Blondeau F, Daniel NG. Inferior alveolar nerve injuries: prevention and management. Oral Maxillofac Surg Clin North Am. 2007;19(1):175 - 186.*
7. *Pogrel MA. Damage to the inferior alveolar and lingual nerves after third molar removal. J Oral Maxillofac Surg. 2012;70(2):438 - 444.*
8. *Dental Council of India. Recordkeeping in Oral and Maxillofacial Surgery. 2022.*
9. *General Dental Council (UK). Standards for Surgical Documentation and Consent. 2013.*
10. *Dental Protection Limited. Surgical Complications and Legal Responsibility. 2021.*
11. *Peterson LJ. Principles of Surgical Exodontia. In: Contemporary Oral Surgery, 7th ed. Elsevier; 2022.*
12. *National Medical Commission (India). Disclosure and Referral Guidelines for Surgical Complications. 2021.*

CHAPTER 33

Third Molar Surgery - Assessment, Operative Safety, and Legal Defensibility

Third molar surgery is where surgical skill, anatomy, and law intersect. Most claims in oral surgery arise not from difficulty, but from surprise - a nerve injury unanticipated, a sinus opened without warning, a patient left uninformed. The challenge isn't the impaction; it's the expectation. This chapter sets the clinical and legal rhythm for safe, reproducible, and defendable third molar removal.

Purpose and Indications

Removal of impacted third molars prevents or resolves pain, pericoronitis, cysts, or resorption of adjacent teeth. Indications include recurrent infection, caries, pathology, orthodontic interference, or prosthetic planning. Legal defensibility requires radiographic assessment and documented justification for surgery [1].

Preparation and Preoperative Evaluation

Record detailed medical history, focusing on systemic disease, medications, and bleeding risk. Obtain panoramic radiograph or CBCT to assess impaction type (mesioangular, vertical, horizontal, distoangular) and relation to inferior alveolar canal or maxillary sinus.

Red flag: Proceeding without imaging or written indication converts any complication into negligence. Radiographic documentation is the single most critical medicolegal safeguard [2].

- ***Step 1: Patient Information and Consent***

Explain procedure, risks (pain, swelling, infection, nerve injury, trismus, dry socket, sinus exposure), and alternatives. Provide a printed consent form with illustrations and obtain signature.

Red flag: Verbal explanations without written acknowledgment carry no evidentiary value. Even when skillful, unconsented surgery equals assault in legal interpretation [3].

- ***Step 2: Anesthesia and Asepsis***

Administer local anesthesia (inferior alveolar, lingual, and buccal infiltration). Note anesthetic type, dose, and batch. Maintain sterile field and drape.

Red flag: Failure to document anesthesia brand or volume nullifies safety record. In event of paresthesia, lack of this record erases proof of due care [4].

- ***Step 3: Flap Design and Incision***

Design triangular or envelope flap with broad base, preserving vital structures. Incise along external oblique ridge using No. 15 blade.

Red flag: Flap tears, tissue burns, or careless incision angles leading to scarring or poor healing become indefensible without flap design notes and photographs [5].

- ***Step 4: Bone Removal (Osteotomy)***

Expose crown by removing minimal buccal bone under continuous saline irrigation using round or fissure bur.

Red flag: No record of irrigation use leads to claims of "burning pain" or osteonecrosis. Bur type and irrigation must appear in operative notes [6].

- ***Step 5: Tooth Sectioning and Delivery***

Section crown from roots if angulated. Remove in fragments with elevators. Inspect socket for remaining fragments.

Red flag: Root tip retention without documentation of difficulty suggests incomplete procedure. Every retained fragment must be recorded with rationale ("apical fragment left to prevent nerve damage") [7].

- ***Step 6: Hemostasis and Wound Closure***

Irrigate, achieve hemostasis, reposition flap, and suture with 3-0 or 4-0 silk. Note suture type, number, and closure method.

Red flag: Persistent bleeding without hemostasis record invites liability. Every closure detail should be traceable [8].

- ***Step 7: Postoperative Instructions and Medication***

Prescribe analgesics, anti-inflammatory, and antibiotics as indicated. Advise ice packs, soft diet, and no spitting or smoking for 24 hours. Provide printed instruction sheet signed by patient.

Red flag: Verbal-only postoperative advice is legally void. Written discharge forms are your only admissible defense in patient complaints [9].

- ***Step 8: Follow-Up and Review***

Review after 48 - 72 hours and at one week for swelling, pain, or infection. Remove sutures after 7 - 10 days. Document all findings with photographs if swelling persists.

Red flag: Failure to document reviews or record delayed healing converts biological variation into alleged negligence [10].

- ***Step 9: Management of Complications***

If dry socket, infection, or trismus occurs, record date of onset, management steps, and patient communication. For paresthesia, conduct neurosensory evaluation and referral within 24 hours.

Red flag: Concealing complications or lack of referral documentation is unethical and indefensible. Transparency equals protection [11].

- ***Step 10: Long-Term Record Maintenance***

Store all radiographs, consent forms, prescriptions, and follow-up records for minimum five years.

Red flag: Disposing of or losing surgical documentation before the statutory retention period invalidates legal defense, regardless of procedural success [12].

Defensibility and Documentation Anchors

A defensible third molar case includes:

- Preoperative imaging (OPG or CBCT)
- Clear surgical indication and written consent
- Recorded anesthesia details
- Flap design and bone removal notes
- Suture record and closure method

- Postoperative instructions signed
- Complication management and follow-up documentation

The written chain of events converts surgery into defensible judgment.

Case Study

A 29-year-old male developed inferior alveolar nerve paresthesia after lower third molar surgery. The dentist had taken no preoperative CBCT and lacked a signed consent form. Though the technique was sound, the court concluded breach of standard care for absence of risk disclosure. Compensation was granted based on "failure to warn," not technical failure.

Case Learnings

1. No imaging, no defense - radiographic proof precedes incision.
2. Written consent with explicit nerve injury clause is essential.
3. Paresthesia and sinus exposure must be disclosed and managed immediately.
4. Every anesthetic, flap, and closure detail matters.
5. Complication transparency prevents escalation to litigation.

Quick Checklist

- Preoperative radiograph or CBCT obtained
- Written consent signed and filed
- Anesthesia type and dose recorded
- Flap design and irrigation method noted
- Bone removal technique documented
- Root sectioning justification recorded
- Hemostasis achieved and sutures logged
- Printed postoperative instructions provided
- Follow-up and review records maintained
- Complication management documented

References

1. *Peterson LJ et al. Contemporary Oral and Maxillofacial Surgery. 7th ed. Elsevier; 2022.*
2. *Renton T. Inferior alveolar nerve injury in relation to mandibular third molar surgery. Oral Surg Oral Med Oral Pathol Oral Radiol Endod. 2004;98(3):263 - 273.*
3. *General Dental Council (UK). Consent and Disclosure Standards. 2013.*
4. *Malamed SF. Handbook of Local Anesthesia. 7th ed. Elsevier; 2019.*
5. *Howe GL. Minor Oral Surgery. 3rd ed. Wright; 1985.*
6. *Blondeau F, Daniel NG. Prevention and management of third molar surgery complications. Oral Maxillofac Surg Clin North Am. 2007;19(1):117 - 128.*
7. *Pogrel MA. Nerve injuries in mandibular third molar surgery. J Oral Maxillofac Surg. 2012;70(2):438 - 444.*
8. *Dental Council of India. Surgical Extraction and Flap Documentation Standards. 2022.*
9. *Dental Protection Limited. Managing Complications and Patient Communication. 2021.*
10. *Ministry of Health and Family Welfare, India. Postoperative Care and Recordkeeping Protocols. 2020.*
11. *National Medical Commission (India). Disclosure and Referral in Postoperative Complications. 2021.*
12. *General Dental Council (UK). Record Retention and Legal Protection. 2013.*

CHAPTER 34

Oroantral Communication and Sinus Management - Prevention, Repair, and Legal Obligations

Every maxillary molar extraction is a quiet negotiation with the sinus. The surgeon works in millimeters; the law judges in hindsight. Oroantral communication (OAC) is not rare - but unrecognized or undocumented, it becomes a permanent scar on reputation. This chapter unpacks how to foresee, prevent, and manage sinus openings while keeping the procedure legally airtight.

Purpose and Indications

OAC is a pathological connection between the oral cavity and maxillary sinus, usually following extraction of maxillary molars or premolars. Prompt recognition and closure prevent sinusitis and oroantral fistula (OAF) formation. The clinician's duty extends beyond closure - to document recognition, action, and communication [1].

Preparation and Preoperative Evaluation

Preoperative radiographs or CBCT are mandatory to determine root - sinus proximity and sinus floor thickness. Explain this risk in the consent, especially for second molar or first molar extractions.

Red flag: Failure to warn of sinus involvement or to record radiographic assessment makes even an unavoidable perforation legally indefensible [2].

- ***Step 1: Pre-Surgical Planning***

Mark high-risk teeth on radiograph and prepare sinus management instruments (resorbable membrane, suture, flap materials).

Red flag: Operating without ready closure materials leads to improvisation under stress, which courts interpret as unpreparedness [3].

- ***Step 2: Asepsis and Anesthesia***

Maintain sterile field and drape the operative area. Administer local anesthesia - document type, concentration, and site.

Red flag: Neglecting aseptic field documentation converts any postoperative sinusitis into a presumption of poor infection control [4].

- ***Step 3: Extraction Technique and Prevention***

During maxillary posterior extraction, use controlled force, avoiding excessive apical pressure. Luxate gently and rotate within bone contour.

Red flag: Applying uncontrolled force resulting in perforation, without radiographic complexity note, implies procedural negligence [5].

- ***Step 4: Recognition of Oroantral Communication***

After extraction, inspect socket for sinus exposure, bubbling on exhalation, or nasal fluid leakage. Confirm by Valsalva test (gently).

Red flag: Discharging patient without assessing sinus integrity is professional omission. "Did not notice communication" is not a defense - documentation of inspection is [6].

- ***Step 5: Immediate Management (Small OAC <2 mm)***

If exposure is minimal and no infection, place absorbable gelatin sponge in socket and suture for primary closure. Advise sinus precautions - no nose blowing, sneezing with closed mouth.

Red flag: Failure to provide written sinus precautions turns predictable sinusitis into malpractice [7].

- ***Step 6: Primary Surgical Closure (Moderate to Large OAC)***

For OAC >2 mm, perform buccal advancement flap, palatal rotational flap, or buccal fat pad graft depending on size and location. Ensure tension-free closure and confirm hemostasis.

Red flag: Attempting closure under tension or using unsuitable flap without record of choice rationale is indefensible when dehiscence occurs. Technique justification must appear in notes [8].

- ***Step 7: Postoperative Medication and Instructions***

Prescribe antibiotics (amoxicillin-clavulanate or clindamycin for allergy), nasal decongestant spray, and analgesics. Provide printed instructions emphasizing sinus precautions and review schedule.

Red flag: No record of nasal advice (no nose blowing, no straw use) equals failure of postoperative duty. Written handouts serve as evidence of care [9].

- ***Step 8: Follow-Up and Radiographic Review***

Review after 3 - 5 days for symptoms of sinus infection - nasal discharge, foul smell, or facial pain. Repeat radiograph if sinusitis suspected.

Red flag: Failure to record follow-up examination and radiograph forfeits defense if chronic OAF develops later [10].

- ***Step 9: Management of Chronic Oroantral Fistula***

If epithelialized tract forms after 3 - 4 weeks, excise fistula margins and perform flap closure under antibiotic cover. Record surgical technique, medications, and photos.

Red flag: Attempting fistula closure without culture or sinus control first is negligence by omission. Always confirm sinus sterility before surgery [11].

- ***Step 10: Referral and Legal Documentation***

In complex or recurrent cases, refer to ENT specialist. Document date, referral note, and reason.

Red flag: No referral documentation suggests concealment. Shared care proves responsibility; silence suggests guilt [12].

Defensibility and Documentation Anchors

To legally secure every sinus-related case:

- • Record preoperative imaging with sinus relation marked
- Include sinus risk clause in consent
- Note inspection of sinus integrity post-extraction
- Record method of closure and materials used
- Provide printed sinus precautions
- Document every review or ENT referral

These six steps alone can neutralize most OAC-related litigation.

Case Study

A 52-year-old woman developed chronic sinus discharge after maxillary molar extraction. The dentist had neither radiographs nor consent mentioning sinus risk. OAC was not recognized or recorded. ENT later confirmed OAF requiring surgical repair. The dentist was held negligent for lack of preoperative disclosure and intraoperative recognition.

Case Learnings

1. Every upper molar extraction carries potential sinus risk - anticipate and document.
2. Recognition and closure matter more than perfection of technique.
3. Postoperative written sinus precautions are a legal must.
4. Radiographs and consent are not optional formalities; they are the foundation of defense.
5. Silence in notes equals admission of ignorance in court.

Quick Checklist

- Preoperative radiograph/CBCT taken
- Sinus risk explained and consent signed
- Asepsis and anesthesia recorded
- Socket inspected for sinus exposure
- OAC size and closure technique documented
- Hemostasis achieved and closure tension-free
- Postoperative sinus precautions printed and signed
- Follow-up examination recorded
- Referral to ENT noted if persistent
- Records stored minimum five years

References

1. *Peterson LJ et al. Contemporary Oral and Maxillofacial Surgery. 7th ed. Elsevier; 2022.*
2. *Punwutikorn J, Waikakul A, Pairuchvej V. Clinically significant oroantral communications. Int J Oral Maxillofac Surg. 1994;23(1):19 - 21.*
3. *Visscher SH, van Minnen B, Bos RR. Closure of oroantral communications: a review. Int J Oral Maxillofac Surg. 2010;39(4):361 - 369.*
4. *Ministry of Health and Family Welfare, India. National Guidelines for Surgical Asepsis in Dentistry. 2020.*
5. *Khandelwal P, Hajira N. Management of oroantral communication and fistula: review. J Oral Maxillofac Surg. 2016;74(5):940 - 948.*
6. *Hirata Y et al. Prevention and management of oroantral perforations. Oral Surg Oral Med Oral Pathol. 1980;49(6):479 - 483.*
7. *Ehrl PA. Oroantral communications: a clinical study of 175 cases. J Oral Surg. 1980;38(8):613 - 617.*
8. *Sailer HF, Pajarola GF. Oral Surgery for the General Dentist. Thieme; 1999.*
9. *Dental Council of India. Clinical Documentation and Postoperative Instructions Guidelines. 2022.*
10. *Dental Protection Limited. Sinus Injuries and Legal Implications. 2021.*
11. *General Dental Council (UK). Complication Disclosure Standards. 2013.*
12. *National Medical Commission (India). Referral and Interdisciplinary Care Standards. 2021.*

CHAPTER 35

Mandibular Fracture Management - Stabilization, Documentation, and Medico-Legal Precautions

Fracture of the mandible is both a surgical and legal emergency. It tests the surgeon's grasp of anatomy, airway, and accountability. The treatment outcome is judged not merely by bone union, but by how the airway was secured, the occlusion restored, and the records maintained. This chapter outlines the systematic, legally defensible approach to diagnosing and managing mandibular fractures in clinical or emergency settings.

Purpose and Indications

Mandibular fracture management aims to restore function, esthetics, and occlusion through reduction and immobilization. Indications include trauma with mobility, malocclusion, pain on movement, or radiographic evidence of discontinuity. The medico-legal obligation is to document injury extent, airway stability, and consent for surgical intervention [1].

Preparation and Initial Assessment

Assess airway, breathing, and circulation before examining the fracture. Document time of injury, mechanism (assault, accident, fall), and associated injuries. Photograph swelling, bruising, and lacerations before manipulation.

Red flag: Failure to record history and mechanism of injury violates medico-legal protocols. Every trauma case must have documented history of event and timing - absence implies concealment or poor triage [2].

- ***Step 1: Clinical and Radiographic Evaluation***

Inspect for deviation, occlusal derangement, step deformity, and paresthesia. Obtain panoramic and PA mandible radiographs; use CBCT when available.

Red flag: Starting reduction or wiring before imaging is indefensible. Radiographic record must precede intervention, even in emergencies [3].

- ***Step 2: Airway and Pain Management***

Ensure airway patency before manipulation. Administer local or general anesthesia as indicated; record drug, dose, and route.

Red flag: Administering anesthesia without airway assessment or recorded vitals converts routine care into unsafe practice. Always record baseline vitals and anesthesia details [4].

- ***Step 3: Temporary Stabilization***

Apply Barton's bandage, intermaxillary fixation (IMF) with Erich arch bars, or eyelet wiring as temporary stabilization.

Red flag: Improper or unrecorded stabilization that leads to airway compromise is indefensible. Document device type, side applied, and fixation duration [5].

- ***Step 4: Definitive Reduction (Closed or Open)***

Perform closed reduction with IMF in simple fractures. For displaced or multiple fractures, perform open reduction and internal fixation (ORIF) using plates and screws under sterile conditions. Record implant type, size, and number.

Red flag: Failure to record hardware specifications violates traceability norms under medical device regulations. Every screw and plate used must be documented with batch and manufacturer details [6].

- ***Step 5: Intraoperative Asepsis and Instrument Record***

Maintain sterile draping and instrument count. Use suction judiciously to prevent aspiration.

Red flag: Absence of aseptic record or sponge count in surgical notes converts postoperative infection into a procedural negligence claim [7].

- ***Step 6: Occlusal Verification and Functional Check***

Before closure, verify occlusion alignment and mandibular movement. Document "occlusion restored intraoperatively."

Red flag: Postoperative malocclusion without intraoperative record implies lack of verification - indefensible in outcome disputes [8].

- ***Step 7: Wound Closure and Hemostasis***

Irrigate with saline, achieve hemostasis, and close in layers using resorbable sutures. Record closure type and suture material.

Red flag: Persistent postoperative bleeding or dehiscence without documented closure method is interpreted as incomplete surgery [9].

- ***Step 8: Postoperative Medication and Care***

Prescribe antibiotics, analgesics, and antiseptic mouth rinse. Advise soft diet, limited jaw movement, and maintenance of oral hygiene with syringe irrigation. Provide written instructions signed by patient or attendant.

Red flag: Failure to issue written discharge advice leads to noncompliance and infection disputes - verbal advice carries no legal value [10].

- ***Step 9: Follow-Up and Radiographic Review***

Review at one week and one month to assess healing, occlusion, and implant stability. Record findings and compare radiographs.

Red flag: Absence of documented follow-up undermines defense even if bone healing occurs. Every visit must be dated and signed [11].

- ***Step 10: Medico-Legal Documentation and Reporting***

For trauma from assault, road accident, or industrial injury, issue medico-legal certificate (MLC) and inform authorities as per law. Record patient identification, injury description, and attending personnel names.

Red flag: Failure to file MLC when indicated is a legal offence under Indian Penal Code Sections 201 and 202 (suppression of evidence). Proper reporting protects both patient and clinician [12].

Defensibility and Documentation Anchors

To establish procedural and legal integrity, every mandibular fracture case file must include:

- Injury history and mechanism
- Radiographs or CBCT before reduction
- Airway and anesthesia record
- Temporary stabilization note

- ORIF details with implant log
- Occlusal verification statement
- Written postoperative instructions
- Follow-up radiographs
- MLC copy (if applicable)

This documentation chain demonstrates professionalism, compliance, and accountability.

Case Study

A 30-year-old male with road accident injury underwent mandibular fixation. No MLC was filed and no implant log maintained. Postoperative infection developed and the patient alleged improper fixation. Court proceedings found procedural negligence due to lack of reporting and missing implant records. Despite good alignment on radiograph, absence of documentation led to disciplinary action.

Case Learnings

1. Every trauma case is a potential legal case - file MLC early.
2. Implant traceability protects against manufacturing and procedural disputes.
3. Documentation of airway assessment is as critical as bone alignment.
4. Written discharge instructions are proof of communication, not formality.
5. Records are the bridge between surgical integrity and legal defense.

Quick Checklist

- Injury history and timing recorded
- Preoperative imaging and MLC filed
- Airway and anesthesia log maintained
- Temporary stabilization documented
- Definitive fixation with implant details noted
- Asepsis and instrument count recorded

- Occlusal alignment confirmed
- Written discharge advice issued
- Follow-up radiographs filed
- All records retained for legal and audit use

References

1. *Fonseca RJ et al. Oral and Maxillofacial Trauma. 5th ed. Elsevier; 2022.*
2. *Ministry of Health and Family Welfare, India. Medico-Legal Documentation Standards in Trauma Cases. 2021.*
3. *Peterson LJ et al. Contemporary Oral and Maxillofacial Surgery. 7th ed. Elsevier; 2022.*
4. *Malamed SF. Medical Emergencies in the Dental Office. 8th ed. Elsevier; 2020.*
5. *Banks P, Brown A. Fractures of the Facial Skeleton. 3rd ed. Wright; 2001.*
6. *General Dental Council (UK). Traceability of Surgical Materials and Implants. 2013.*
7. *Dental Council of India. Operative and Aseptic Recordkeeping Protocols. 2022.*
8. *Ellis E, Walker L. Treatment of mandibular angle fractures. J Oral Maxillofac Surg. 1994;52(9):1032 - 1041.*
9. *Dental Protection Limited. Postoperative Complications: Legal and Clinical Considerations. 2021.*
10. *Ministry of Health and Family Welfare, India. Postoperative Discharge and Documentation Guidelines. 2020.*
11. *General Dental Council (UK). Surgical Follow-Up and Audit Standards. 2013.*
12. *National Medical Commission (India). Mandatory Reporting and Medico-Legal Duty in Trauma Care. 2021.*

CHAPTER 36

Maxillary Fractures and Midface Injuries - Stabilization, Airway Management, and Legal Reporting Protocols

Midface trauma carries two distinct dangers: airway loss and accountability loss. The clinician's first duty is to preserve life, not symmetry. Yet, in court, documentation of those first ten minutes is scrutinized more closely than the fixation technique that followed. This chapter merges surgical clarity with medico-legal vigilance - ensuring every decision is traceable and defensible.

Purpose and Indications

Maxillary and midface fractures require prompt stabilization to restore occlusion, aesthetics, and airway integrity. Indications include facial asymmetry, epistaxis, infraorbital step deformity, malocclusion, nasal flattening, or ocular disturbances. Proper documentation of airway, neurological status, and radiographic findings is the foundation for both clinical and legal protection [1].

Preparation and Initial Evaluation

Assess airway, breathing, and circulation immediately. Document consciousness level using Glasgow Coma Scale (GCS). Note mechanism of injury - assault, road traffic accident, or fall - and time since trauma.

Red flag: Failure to document initial airway status or GCS score before sedation or intubation is legally interpreted as neglect of resuscitation protocol [2].

- ***Step 1: Clinical Examination and Documentation***

Inspect facial swelling, asymmetry, and ecchymosis. Palpate infraorbital rim, zygomatic arch, and maxillary alveolus for step deformity or mobility. Record occlusal derangement and paresthesia.

Red flag: Beginning fixation without documenting preoperative occlusion forfeits defense in any postoperative malalignment claim [3].

- ***Step 2: Radiographic and Imaging Assessment***

Obtain Waters, Caldwell, and lateral skull views or CT scan for definitive diagnosis. Annotate fracture line, displacement, and sinus involvement.

Red flag: Proceeding with reduction without imaging constitutes procedural negligence. No radiograph means no defense [4].

- ***Step 3: Airway and Hemodynamic Stabilization***

Secure airway through endotracheal intubation or tracheostomy if obstruction risk exists. Control bleeding from nasal or oral cavity. Document vitals pre- and post-airway management.

Red flag: Missing airway documentation before surgery is considered professional misconduct in trauma care. A clear note "airway secured, vitals stable" is mandatory [5].

- ***Step 4: Temporary Stabilization***

Apply intermaxillary fixation (IMF) using arch bars or eyelets to maintain occlusion before definitive surgery.

Red flag: No preoperative occlusal record or photograph renders postoperative correction indefensible. IMF record must include wire gauge and fixation points [6].

- ***Step 5: Surgical Exposure and Reduction***

Under general anesthesia and strict asepsis, expose fracture line via intraoral or transconjunctival approach. Reposition segments using bone clamps or forceps under direct vision.

Red flag: Unrecorded approach or intraoperative difficulty note weakens surgical credibility. Each incision route and fixation point must be written in operative record [7].

- ***Step 6: Fixation and Stabilization***

Use miniplates and screws for rigid fixation. Document plate type, manufacturer, batch, number of screws, and torque used.

Red flag: Missing implant traceability details violates biomedical device laws. Every fixation hardware used must have complete labeling recorded [8].

- ***Step 7: Occlusion Verification and Sinus Care***

Verify occlusion and ensure maxillary alignment with mandibular arch. Irrigate sinuses with saline to clear blood clots.

Red flag: Failure to confirm occlusion intraoperatively is a frequent source of malpractice suits claiming "altered bite post-surgery." Documentation of occlusal verification is non-negotiable [9].

- ***Step 8: Wound Closure and Hemostasis***

Close incisions in layers, ensuring no dead space. Achieve hemostasis and maintain suction for airway protection.

Red flag: Postoperative epistaxis without closure details or hemostasis record implies incomplete surgery [10].

- ***Step 9: Postoperative Care and Discharge***

Prescribe antibiotics, analgesics, nasal decongestants, and instruct avoidance of nose blowing. Provide written discharge instructions and soft diet advice.

Red flag: Absence of written discharge note invalidates defense in postoperative sinusitis or infection cases [11].

- ***Step 10: Medico-Legal Documentation and Reporting***

File medico-legal case (MLC) report with date, injury description, and referral details to trauma or ENT department. Attach radiographs, consent, anesthesia record, and implant log.

Red flag: Non-reporting of trauma cases is a punishable offence under Indian law (Sections 201 - 202 IPC). MLC filing is both ethical and mandatory [12].

Defensibility and Documentation Anchors

A defensible maxillary fracture case must contain:

- Airway and GCS documentation
- Imaging and fracture annotation
- Surgical plan and incision record

- Implant log with manufacturer and batch
- Occlusal verification entry
- Discharge and follow-up documentation
- MLC registration copy

These collectively establish procedural transparency, technical diligence, and legal compliance.

Case Study

A 27-year-old male with zygomaticomaxillary complex fracture underwent fixation without MLC filing. Postoperative complaint of "flattened cheek and sinus discharge" was made. No imaging, airway, or occlusion record existed. The court declared negligence by omission, citing missing MLC and incomplete operative notes as primary failures.

Case Learnings

1. Every maxillofacial trauma is a medico-legal case until proven otherwise.
2. Airway and occlusion documentation are parallel lifesaving acts - one clinical, one legal.
3. Implant traceability and radiographic proof are non-negotiable.
4. Written discharge instructions and follow-ups preserve professional credibility.
5. In facial trauma, it's not only what you fix - it's what you file.

Quick Checklist

- Airway secured and GCS recorded
- Imaging done and fracture annotated
- Consent and MLC report filed
- IMF or temporary stabilization applied
- Surgical approach and fixation logged
- Implant traceability recorded
- Occlusion verified intraoperatively

- Hemostasis and closure documented
- Written discharge advice provided
- Follow-up and review notes maintained

References

1. *Fonseca RJ et al. Oral and Maxillofacial Trauma. 5th ed. Elsevier; 2022.*
2. *Ministry of Health and Family Welfare, India. National Trauma Care Guidelines. 2021.*
3. *Banks P, Brown A. Fractures of the Facial Skeleton. 3rd ed. Wright; 2001.*
4. *Peterson LJ et al. Contemporary Oral and Maxillofacial Surgery. 7th ed. Elsevier; 2022.*
5. *Malamed SF. Medical Emergencies in the Dental Office. 8th ed. Elsevier; 2020.*
6. *Ellis E, Zide MF. Surgical Approaches to the Facial Skeleton. 3rd ed. Lippincott; 2012.*
7. *General Dental Council (UK). Documentation and Surgical Record Standards. 2013.*
8. *Dental Council of India. Surgical Material Traceability Guidelines. 2022.*
9. *Dental Protection Limited. Legal Risk in Maxillofacial Surgery. 2021.*
10. *Ministry of Health and Family Welfare, India. Documentation in Surgical Trauma Cases. 2020.*
11. *General Dental Council (UK). Postoperative Care and Communication Standards. 2013.*
12. *National Medical Commission (India). Reporting Duties in Medico-Legal Trauma. 2021.*

CHAPTER 37

Nerve Injuries in Oral and Maxillofacial Surgery - Prevention, Documentation, and Consent Protocols

Every nerve injury is an invisible fracture - unseen, silent, and often permanent. The patient feels it immediately; the surgeon only later, in the form of a complaint. Inferior alveolar, lingual, and mental nerve injuries are among the most common sources of medico-legal action in oral surgery. This chapter focuses on prevention, recognition, and rigorous documentation - because in nerve injury cases, written consent and clear communication often carry more weight than surgical skill.

Purpose and Indications

Nerve preservation governs every surgical act in the mandible and posterior maxilla. Awareness of nerve pathways, radiographic proximity, and surgical control defines both outcome and accountability. The goal is not only to avoid injury but to ensure the record reflects anticipation and informed consent for risk [1].

Preparation and Risk Assessment

Before any mandibular, implant, or third molar surgery, obtain radiographs or CBCT clearly showing the nerve canal's course and proximity. Record risk classification (low, moderate, high) and note this in consent.

Red flag: Performing high-risk procedures without radiographic proximity assessment is indefensible. "I didn't see it" is never an acceptable defense when imaging was omitted [2].

- ***Step 1: Informed Consent and Communication***

Explain to the patient, both verbally and in writing, the possibility of temporary or permanent numbness, altered taste, or pain in the lip, chin, or tongue. Obtain signed consent with the phrase "nerve injury discussed and understood."

Red flag: Absence of nerve injury clause in consent nullifies defense, even if injury occurred despite due care. Consent must include the specific nerve at risk [3].

- ***Step 2: Preoperative Imaging and Planning***

Analyze CBCT to assess canal position, cortical thickness, and surgical entry angle. For implants, measure 2 mm clearance above the canal.

Red flag: Implant encroachment claims are indefensible without documented 3D imaging and planning notes. CBCT findings must be attached to case record [4].

- ***Step 3: Surgical Field and Instrument Control***

Maintain asepsis, visibility, and controlled instrumentation. Use round burs with irrigation for bone removal and elevators with tactile restraint.

Red flag: Using uncontrolled rotary instruments without irrigation or depth marker constitutes procedural negligence if nerve damage follows [5].

- ***Step 4: Identification and Protection During Exposure***

If the nerve is visible, maintain a 1 - 2 mm safety zone, protect with saline-moistened gauze, and avoid compression.

Red flag: Contact or manipulation of exposed nerve without notation or protective measures is indefensible. Every intraoperative nerve exposure must be described in the operative note [6].

- ***Step 5: Immediate Recognition and Intraoperative Documentation***

If nerve injury is suspected (bleeding from canal, sharp pain despite anesthesia), stop immediately, record event, and photograph if possible.

Red flag: Proceeding without documenting intraoperative suspicion suggests concealment. Timely recognition and written entry prove honesty and diligence [7].

- ***Step 6: Postoperative Evaluation and Patient Communication***

Test for altered sensation using light touch, pinprick, and two-point discrimination within 24 hours. Inform the patient, explain possible recovery timeline, and document findings.

Red flag: Ignoring complaints of numbness or dismissing them without record implies neglect. Early documentation converts allegation into an acknowledged complication [8].

- ***Step 7: Referral to Specialist***

If paresthesia persists beyond 48 hours, refer to oral surgeon or neurologist. Record date, specialist name, and communication summary.

Red flag: Delayed referral or lack of written record is viewed as cover-up, not caution. Documented referral shows professional responsibility [9].

- ***Step 8: Follow-Up and Progress Records***

Review patient weekly for four weeks, then monthly until resolution or stabilization. Record sensory improvement scale and photographs where possible.

Red flag: Missing follow-up data in nerve injury cases is fatal in litigation - absence of progress notes equals abandonment [10].

- ***Step 9: Medico-Legal Documentation and Communication***

If injury persists beyond three months, provide written report summarizing history, procedure, and steps taken. Include copy of consent, imaging, and correspondence.

Red flag: Refusal to issue written summary to patient can be interpreted as concealment of injury. Transparency is legal armor [11].

- ***Step 10: Legal Disclosure and Record Preservation***

All nerve injury cases must retain documentation for at least 10 years. Records must include imaging, consent, operative notes, sensory charts, and correspondence.

Red flag: Destroying or misplacing nerve injury records violates medico-legal data retention norms and professional conduct standards [12].

Legal Defensibility and Documentation Anchors

A defendable nerve injury case demonstrates:

- Preoperative imaging and risk documentation
- Explicit consent mentioning nerve at risk
- Detailed operative note and intraoperative findings
- Early recognition and patient disclosure
- Written referrals and progress reports
- Record retention for 10 years

These confirm anticipation, communication, and continuous care - the pillars of legal defense in sensory nerve injuries.

Case Study

A 42-year-old patient underwent implant placement in the mandibular premolar region. Postoperative lip numbness developed. The dentist had no CBCT, no written consent, and no nerve risk disclosure. Neurological evaluation confirmed inferior alveolar nerve damage. Court ruled negligence for lack of preoperative imaging and absence of informed consent, awarding compensation for sensory disability.

Case Learnings

1. Radiographic anticipation is the surgeon's best protection.
2. Every consent for mandibular surgery must mention nerve injury specifically.
3. Early documentation of paresthesia converts accident into accountable care.
4. Referral timing is as crucial as diagnosis.
5. Honesty and paperwork repair what anatomy sometimes cannot.

Quick Checklist

- Radiograph/CBCT showing nerve proximity filed
- Risk classification and consent clause recorded

- Controlled surgical access and irrigation confirmed
- Intraoperative nerve contact documented if occurred
- Postoperative sensory tests recorded
- Referral within 48 hours if paresthesia persists
- Progress notes maintained until recovery
- Written report provided to patient
- Records preserved minimum 10 years
- All communications transparent and signed

References

1. *Renton T. Prevention of iatrogenic inferior alveolar nerve injuries. Br Dent J. 2010;209(10):525 - 532.*
2. *Pogrel MA. Permanent nerve injury after implant placement. J Oral Maxillofac Surg. 2012;70(2):511 - 517.*
3. *General Dental Council (UK). Consent and Disclosure Guidelines. 2013.*
4. *Greenstein G, Tarnow D. The mental foramen and nerve: implant considerations. J Periodontol. 2006;77(12):1933 - 1943.*
5. *Malamed SF. Handbook of Local Anesthesia. 7th ed. Elsevier; 2019.*
6. *Hillerup S. Iatrogenic injury to oral sensory nerves: a clinical study. J Oral Maxillofac Surg. 2007;65(7):1333 - 1339.*
7. *Dental Protection Limited. Nerve Injury: Legal and Clinical Guidance. 2021.*
8. *Dental Council of India. Recordkeeping in Sensory Nerve Injury Cases. 2022.*
9. *National Medical Commission (India). Referral Standards in Neurological Complications. 2021.*
10. *Ministry of Health and Family Welfare, India. Long-Term Follow-up and Documentation Norms. 2020.*
11. *General Dental Council (UK). Transparency and Patient Communication Protocols. 2013.*
12. *National Medical Commission (India). Clinical Data Retention and Legal Compliance Guidelines. 2021.*

CHAPTER 38

Hemorrhage and Bleeding Disorders in Oral Surgery - Management, Documentation, and Legal Responsibility

In oral surgery, bleeding is the line between control and chaos. What appears minor in the operatory can escalate into airway obstruction or hypovolemic collapse in minutes. Most bleeding complications are not from surgical ignorance but from missing history, rushed consent, or undocumented drug use. This chapter defines how to manage bleeding - both physiologically and legally - so that every drop has context, and every event has a record.

Purpose and Indications

The goal of hemorrhage control is to prevent uncontrolled blood loss during or after oral surgical procedures while maintaining patient safety and medico-legal transparency. This includes recognizing systemic causes (anticoagulant therapy, coagulopathies, liver disease) and procedural triggers (flap tears, vessel laceration, incomplete hemostasis) [1].

Preparation and Risk Assessment

Record medical history in detail - including hypertension, bleeding disorders, liver disease, and all current medications (especially warfarin, clopidogrel, aspirin, or DOACs). Obtain INR and platelet count for at-risk patients.

Red flag: Proceeding without documenting coagulation status or medication history in an anticoagulated patient is indefensible. "I didn't know" is never a defense when records show omission [2].

- ***Step 1: Preoperative Screening and Consent***

Document patient's bleeding history, any prior excessive bleeding episodes, and current hematological values. Include "risk of bleeding" in consent with explanation of emergency plan.

Red flag: No written consent acknowledging bleeding risk invalidates defense if postoperative hemorrhage occurs, even when standard care was followed [3].

- ***Step 2: Surgical Planning and Asepsis***

Schedule high-risk patients for morning procedures. Keep hemostatic agents (oxidized cellulose, gelatin sponge, tranexamic acid) ready. Use atraumatic techniques.

Red flag: Absence of recorded preparation or unavailable hemostatic materials suggests procedural unpreparedness - a major factor in negligence claims [4].

- ***Step 3: Intraoperative Hemostasis***

Use suction and gauze pressure to localize bleeding. Control with pressure, sutures, or hemostatic agents. Maintain irrigation with saline to identify active bleeders.

Red flag: Leaving socket oozing without confirming cessation or recording control measures implies incomplete surgery. Every hemostatic step must be noted [5].

- ***Step 4: Management of Intraoperative Vessel Injury***

If arterial spurting occurs, clamp and ligate under direct vision or apply pressure for 10 minutes. Use absorbable hemostats for inaccessible areas.

Red flag: Panicked management without note of vessel identification or ligature method leaves no defense if bleeding recurs. Written intraoperative note is essential [6].

- ***Step 5: Postoperative Hemostasis and Verification***

Inspect surgical field before closure for active bleeding. Achieve tension-free flap closure. Record "hemostasis achieved" and method used (pressure, sutures, gelatin sponge, etc.).

Red flag: "Bleeding noted" without "hemostasis confirmed" is legally equivalent to leaving the case unfinished [7].

- ***Step 6: Immediate Postoperative Instructions***

Provide written sheet instructing patient to:

- Apply firm pressure with gauze for 30 minutes
- Avoid spitting, rinsing, or smoking for 24 hours
- Report if bleeding persists beyond one hour

Red flag: Verbal instructions without printed handout invalidate defense when bleeding recurs at home. Signed acknowledgment of instructions is required [8].

- ***Step 7: Management of Postoperative Bleeding***

If bleeding occurs after discharge, document onset time, amount, and measures taken (re-suturing, packing, tranexamic rinse). Record vitals and photographs.

Red flag: Failing to record re-admission vitals or management steps is interpreted as unmonitored complication. The file must reflect urgency and care [9].

- ***Step 8: Medical Consultation and Referral***

If systemic cause suspected, refer for hematology opinion and record communication.

Red flag: Failure to refer promptly in uncontrolled bleeding equals professional neglect. Referral letter is legal evidence of prudence [10].

- ***Step 9: Documentation and Incident Reporting***

Every bleeding episode (even minor) must be documented in operative log and patient file, stating "cause identified" and "action taken."

Red flag: Absence of bleeding incident documentation during audit appears as suppression of facts - a disciplinary violation [11].

- ***Step 10: Follow-Up and Preventive Review***

Schedule review within 48 hours. Note tissue color, swelling, and clot integrity. Reinforce oral hygiene and medication compliance.

Red flag: Missing follow-up record after bleeding incident gives impression of procedural abandonment - indefensible if complications arise [12].

Legal Defensibility and Documentation Anchors

A defendable hemorrhage management record contains:

- Medical and medication history with INR values
- Written consent with bleeding risk clause
- Description of intraoperative hemostasis methods
- Postoperative instruction sheet signed
- Bleeding incident report (if any)
- Referral or hematology opinion documentation
- Follow-up notes with vitals and outcome

This chain demonstrates anticipation, control, and continuity - the three legal pillars in surgical bleeding management.

Case Study

A 68-year-old man on warfarin underwent tooth extraction. No INR check or written consent was obtained. Postoperative bleeding continued overnight; the patient required hospital transfusion. The dentist's file contained no medication history or documentation of control measures. The court ruled negligence by omission of preoperative screening, not by act of surgery.

Case Learnings

1. No anticoagulant patient should be treated without a documented INR value.
2. Every consent for extraction must mention bleeding risk specifically.
3. Intraoperative hemostasis must be recorded stepwise.
4. Verbal postoperative advice is worthless in legal defense.
5. Documentation and communication stop the bleeding of blame.

Quick Checklist

- Medical and drug history recorded
- INR or coagulation tests reviewed
- Consent includes bleeding risk clause
- Hemostatic agents and plan prepared
- Hemostasis achieved and recorded
- Postoperative written instructions signed
- Bleeding incidents documented in log
- Referral issued for systemic causes
- Follow-up within 48 hours recorded
- Records archived for legal verification

References

1. *Peterson LJ et al. Contemporary Oral and Maxillofacial Surgery. 7th ed. Elsevier; 2022.*
2. *Wahl MJ. Myths of dental surgery in anticoagulated patients. J Am Dent Assoc. 2000;131(1):77 - 81.*
3. *National Medical Commission (India). Informed Consent and Risk Disclosure Guidelines. 2021.*
4. *Dental Council of India. Surgical Preparedness and Asepsis Protocols. 2022.*
5. *Malamed SF. Handbook of Local Anesthesia. 7th ed. Elsevier; 2019.*
6. *Pogrel MA. Hemorrhage in oral and maxillofacial surgery. Oral Surg Oral Med Oral Pathol. 1990;69(4):473 - 478.*
7. *Ministry of Health and Family Welfare, India. Surgical Documentation Standards. 2020.*
8. *General Dental Council (UK). Postoperative Care and Instruction Standards. 2013.*
9. *Dental Protection Limited. Managing Surgical Complications and Incident Reports. 2021.*
10. *British Committee for Standards in Haematology. Management of Anticoagulated Dental Patients. Br J Haematol. 2016;175(4):602 - 610.*
11. *Ministry of Health and Family Welfare, India. Clinical Incident and Audit Reporting Norms. 2021.*
12. *Dental Council of India. Surgical Follow-Up and Record Maintenance. 2022.*

CHAPTER 39

Osteomyelitis of the Jaws - Surgical Management, Antibiotic Stewardship, and Legal Accountability

Osteomyelitis is the meeting point of infection, ischemia, and inattention. It is slow to appear, stubborn to heal, and quick to become a legal wound if mismanaged. Every case demands patience, precision, and proof - proof that the infection was identified early, treated aggressively, and documented without gaps. This chapter presents the practical steps and medico-legal imperatives for managing jaw osteomyelitis, from first suspicion to final discharge.

Purpose and Indications

Osteomyelitis of the jaws is an inflammatory process of bone and marrow caused by microbial invasion following trauma, extraction, or systemic infection. Early recognition and surgical debridement prevent chronicity. Indications for intervention include pain, swelling, suppuration, non-healing sockets, or radiographic sequestrum formation. The legal safeguard lies in timely diagnosis, rational antibiotic use, and meticulous documentation [1].

Preparation and Diagnostic Evaluation

Record complete medical history including diabetes, immunosuppression, bisphosphonate therapy, or radiation exposure. Obtain radiographs and CBCT to assess sequestra and cortical perforation. Collect pus for culture and sensitivity before starting antibiotics.

Red flag: Initiating empirical antibiotics without culture report or radiographic record is a common and indefensible error. Treatment without diagnosis is interpreted as guesswork [2].

- ***Step 1: Medical Stabilization and Consent***

Optimize systemic conditions such as diabetes and nutrition before surgery. Obtain written informed consent clearly mentioning "possible need for multiple debridements" and "long-term antibiotic therapy."

Red flag: Failure to include chronic or recurrent risk in consent converts a biological persistence into alleged incomplete treatment [3].

- ***Step 2: Preoperative Imaging and Blood Investigations***

Perform orthopantomogram (OPG) and CBCT for local assessment; order complete blood count, ESR, and CRP.

Red flag: Proceeding without inflammatory marker baseline prevents tracking of progress - an omission that appears as clinical laxity during audit [4].

- ***Step 3: Asepsis and Anesthesia***

Use sterile setup under local or general anesthesia. Record anesthetic drug, dose, and route.

Red flag: Postoperative infection following unrecorded asepsis status or missing anesthesia entry leads to assumption of breach of protocol [5].

- ***Step 4: Surgical Exposure and Drainage***

Reflect mucoperiosteal flap, establish drainage through cortical window, remove pus and necrotic tissue. Collect specimen for microbiology.

Red flag: Absence of intraoperative culture report or specimen note implies blind surgery - indefensible when infection recurs [6].

- ***Step 5: Sequestrectomy and Debridement***

Remove necrotic bone and smooth margins with bur under irrigation. Preserve viable bone and avoid excessive resection.

Red flag: Leaving sequestrum unremoved or failing to note extent of debridement creates doubt of incomplete procedure. Every removed fragment must be listed [7].

- ***Step 6: Irrigation and Hemostasis***

Irrigate cavity with saline and betadine; achieve hemostasis with pressure or oxidized cellulose.

Red flag: Unrecorded use of antiseptics or hemostats can invite claims of chemical burns or delayed healing. Specify agents and concentrations used [8].

- ***Step 7: Antibiotic Stewardship***

Administer culture-guided antibiotics for at least 2 - 4 weeks. Record name, dosage, duration, and rationale.

Red flag: Prescribing broad-spectrum antibiotics without documentation of indication or duration violates antimicrobial stewardship norms. In litigation, it reads as irrational prescription [9].

- ***Step 8: Closure and Drain Placement***

Close wound primarily or with drain if indicated. Record drain type and removal date.

Red flag: Drains inserted without documentation of type and date may lead to medicolegal disputes if infection persists [10].

- ***Step 9: Postoperative Care and Follow-Up***

Review within 48 hours for pain, swelling, and drainage. Reassess radiographically after 2 weeks. Continue follow-up monthly for 3 months.

Red flag: Lack of follow-up record after infection surgery equals abandonment of care - indefensible even if healing occurs [11].

- ***Step10:Long-TermRehabilitationandLegalDocumentation***

If bone loss occurs, record functional limitation and reconstructive plan. Maintain full record including consent, cultures, imaging, and antibiotic log for minimum 10 years.

Red flag: Absence of treatment chronology - onset, surgery, cultures, medications, and outcomes - dismantles defense completely [12].

Legal Defensibility and Documentation Anchors

Every osteomyelitis file must include:

- Imaging (OPG/CBCT) and culture reports
- Consent with chronicity and recurrence clause
- Anesthesia and asepsis records
- Operative note describing debridement extent
- Antibiotic rationale and drug details
- Follow-up with photographs or radiographs

- Long-term rehabilitation or referral note

These records reflect professionalism, anticipation, and continuity of care.

Case Study

A 60-year-old diabetic woman developed chronic osteomyelitis after tooth extraction. The dentist prescribed antibiotics empirically and performed debridement without culture or consent for repeat procedures. Recurrence led to mandibulectomy. The court held negligence for absence of diagnostic imaging, microbiological confirmation, and written informed consent acknowledging chronic nature of disease.

Case Learnings

1. Empirical therapy without diagnostic evidence is indefensible.
2. Consent must acknowledge possibility of recurrence and prolonged therapy.
3. Antibiotic records must show duration, dose, and rationale.
4. Culture reports and imaging are your legal spine in infection cases.
5. Recurrence without recordkeeping looks like failure, even if biologically inevitable.

Quick Checklist

- Medical history and systemic control recorded
- Imaging (OPG/CBCT) obtained and filed
- Culture and sensitivity report documented
- Consent includes chronicity clause
- Asepsis and anesthesia recorded
- Debridement and specimen details written
- Antibiotic regimen justified and logged
- Drain and closure documented
- Follow-up and radiographs recorded
- All records preserved minimum 10 years

References

1. *Topazian RG, Goldberg MH, Hupp JR. Oral and Maxillofacial Infections. 5th ed. Elsevier; 2021.*
2. *Baltensperger M, Eyrich G. Osteomyelitis of the Jaws. Springer; 2009.*
3. *National Medical Commission (India). Informed Consent and Chronic Disease Protocols. 2021.*
4. *Ministry of Health and Family Welfare, India. Diagnostic and Laboratory Documentation Guidelines. 2020.*
5. *Malamed SF. Medical Emergencies in the Dental Office. 8th ed. Elsevier; 2020.*
6. *Baltensperger M et al. Microbiology of chronic osteomyelitis of the jaws. J Oral Maxillofac Surg. 2004;62(4):449 - 455.*
7. *Dental Council of India. Surgical Documentation and Specimen Handling Standards. 2022.*
8. *Peterson LJ et al. Contemporary Oral and Maxillofacial Surgery. 7th ed. Elsevier; 2022.*
9. *World Health Organization. Antimicrobial Stewardship: Practical Guide. Geneva; 2019.*
10. *General Dental Council (UK). Intraoperative Device and Drain Recording Standards. 2013.*
11. *Dental Protection Limited. Infection Control and Legal Risk Management. 2021.*
12. *Ministry of Health and Family Welfare, India. Long-Term Record Retention Guidelines. 2020.*

CHAPTER 40

Pathological Lesions of the Jaw - Biopsy Techniques, Specimen Protocols, and Legal Safeguards

Every biopsy is a promise - to find the truth and to document how that truth was reached. The diagnostic act may take five minutes, but its consequences last a lifetime. Courts rarely question the scalpel's sharpness; they question the trail - what was consented, what was labeled, what was sent, and when. This chapter brings together the clinical precision and procedural defensibility needed for handling jaw pathologies safely and lawfully.

Purpose and Indications

Biopsy establishes definitive diagnosis for cysts, tumors, granulomatous lesions, or non-healing ulcers of the jaws. It guides further management - surgical, medical, or oncologic. From a legal standpoint, a biopsy file is the single most important evidence of diagnostic diligence and patient communication [1].

Preparation and Preoperative Evaluation

Record complete medical history, including bleeding tendencies, infections, and medications. Obtain radiographs or CBCT to define lesion boundaries. Explain to the patient the nature of procedure, potential bleeding, scarring, and the need for histopathological evaluation. Obtain written consent for biopsy and specimen use in diagnosis.

Red flag: Performing a biopsy without documented imaging, indication, or written consent violates diagnostic standards and patient rights [2].

- ***Step 1: Type and Site Selection***

Determine whether incisional (sample) or excisional (complete) biopsy is appropriate. Select representative, viable, non-necrotic area.

Red flag: Taking tissue from necrotic or ulcerated surface without recording rationale may yield false diagnosis - a legal as well as clinical misstep [3].

- ***Step 2: Asepsis and Anesthesia***

Use sterile field and instruments. Administer local anesthesia around, not into, the lesion to avoid histological distortion. Record anesthetic type, dose, and batch.

Red flag: Absence of asepsis record or infiltration directly into lesion creates doubt of procedural contamination or diagnostic compromise [4].

- ***Step 3: Incision and Tissue Harvesting***

Make elliptical incision deep enough to include underlying connective tissue or bone if required. Use sharp scalpel, minimal cautery. Handle tissue gently with forceps at margins.

Red flag: Damaging tissue by crushing or cautery, without noting reason, renders sample unfit and invites blame for "diagnostic error." Documentation of technique protects against misinterpretation [5].

- ***Step 4: Specimen Orientation and Labeling***

Mark orientation (superior/inferior or medial/lateral) with suture or ink if relevant. Place immediately in 10% neutral buffered formalin in adequate volume (at least 10× tissue volume). Label container with patient name, site, date, and clinician's signature.

Red flag: Mislabeling or unlabeled containers are the most common sources of medico-legal exposure. Even if pathology lab errs, absence of clinician's signature transfers liability to operator [6].

- ***Step 5: Documentation and Laboratory Referral***

Complete histopathology requisition form with patient details, clinical findings, radiographic impression, and differential diagnosis. Attach preoperative imaging and consent.

Red flag: Sending tissue without requisition form or incomplete details violates medical record rules and creates gaps that are indefensible in audit [7].

- ***Step 6: Hemostasis and Wound Closure***

Achieve hemostasis by pressure, cautery, or sutures. Record method used and suture material. Provide sterile dressing if indicated.

Red flag: Unrecorded postoperative bleeding after biopsy is treated as procedural negligence if no hemostasis method was logged [8].

- ***Step 7: Postoperative Care and Instructions***

Advise cold compress, soft diet, and antiseptic rinses. Provide written instructions and schedule review after 48 - 72 hours.

Red flag: Verbal-only postoperative advice nullifies defense in delayed healing or infection complaints [9].

- ***Step 8: Histopathology Report and Communication***

Record date of dispatch and report receipt. Discuss findings with patient, explain next steps, and document the conversation.

Red flag: Failing to communicate report or leaving it unfiled converts clinical diligence into apparent concealment. Every report must have acknowledgment of discussion [10].

- ***Step 9: Long-Term Record Maintenance***

Preserve histopathology report, photographs, and operative notes for at least 10 years. For malignancies, indefinitely.

Red flag: Destroying or losing pathology-related documents constitutes tampering under medico-legal data laws [11].

- ***Step 10: Interdisciplinary Referral***

If malignancy or uncertain diagnosis is confirmed, refer to oral pathology or oncology specialist. Record referral date, institution, and communication details.

Red flag: Non-referral or undocumented referral after diagnosis of cancer constitutes gross negligence by omission [12].

Legal Defensibility and Documentation Anchors

A legally complete biopsy case includes:

- Imaging and preoperative documentation
- Written consent for biopsy and tissue use
- Operative note detailing technique and orientation
- Labeled specimen container and requisition form
- Histopathology report with communication note

- Referral record (if malignant)
- File retention proof (minimum 10 years)

Such thorough documentation transforms an invasive act into a transparent diagnostic process.

Case Study

A 58-year-old man presented with a persistent mandibular swelling. The dentist performed excisional biopsy without imaging or consent. The tissue was misplaced, and histopathology was never done. Months later, carcinoma was diagnosed elsewhere. Court held the clinician negligent for loss of diagnostic opportunity and absence of specimen record, awarding damages for delayed cancer detection.

Case Learnings

1. Every lesion deserves imaging, consent, and labeling before incision.
2. Orientation and formalin adequacy protect diagnostic accuracy.
3. Loss of specimen equals loss of defense - chain of custody must be unbroken.
4. Report communication and referral complete the legal loop.
5. Thorough records preserve both truth and trust.

Quick Checklist

- Imaging and clinical notes prepared
- Written biopsy consent obtained
- Anesthesia and asepsis recorded
- Tissue harvested from viable site
- Orientation marked and container labeled
- Histopathology requisition completed
- Hemostasis achieved and closure documented
- Postoperative instructions written
- Report received, discussed, and recorded
- Referral made and records preserved minimum 10 years

References

1. *Neville BW, Damm DD, Allen CM, Chi AC. Oral and Maxillofacial Pathology. 5th ed. Elsevier; 2022.*
2. *Ministry of Health and Family Welfare, India. Diagnostic and Histopathology Documentation Standards. 2020.*
3. *Slootweg PJ. Oral biopsy techniques and tissue handling. J Dent Res. 2010;89(6):524 - 529.*
4. *Malamed SF. Handbook of Local Anesthesia. 7th ed. Elsevier; 2019.*
5. *Silverman S. Oral cancer: early diagnosis and biopsy considerations. J Am Dent Assoc. 2001;132(Suppl 1):7S - 11S.*
6. *General Dental Council (UK). Clinical Recordkeeping and Labeling Standards. 2013.*
7. *Dental Council of India. Histopathology Specimen Documentation Guidelines. 2022.*
8. *Dental Protection Limited. Biopsy Errors and Legal Consequences. 2021.*
9. *Ministry of Health and Family Welfare, India. Postoperative Instruction and Communication Protocols. 2020.*
10. *National Medical Commission (India). Duty of Disclosure and Diagnostic Communication Standards. 2021.*
11. *General Dental Council (UK). Data Retention and Recordkeeping Regulations. 2013.*
12. *National Medical Commission (India). Referral and Continuity of Care Guidelines. 2021.*

CHAPTER 41

Odontogenic Cysts and Tumors - Surgical Management, Histopathological Documentation, and Legal Safeguards

Odontogenic cysts and tumors live at the border between benign neglect and catastrophic oversight. They grow quietly, discovered too late or removed too casually. What separates careful surgeons from careless ones is not just their technique - it's their documentation: imaging, consent, histopathology, and follow-up. This chapter unites surgical decision-making with legal defensibility for lesions arising from odontogenic tissues.

Purpose and Indications

Management of odontogenic cysts and tumors aims to eradicate pathology, restore function, and prevent recurrence while preserving vital structures. Common entities include radicular cysts, dentigerous cysts, keratocysts, and ameloblastomas. The legal framework demands evidence of proper diagnosis, definitive treatment, and histological confirmation of lesion type [1].

Preparation and Diagnostic Evaluation

Record comprehensive medical and dental history, including duration, pain, and swelling characteristics. Obtain panoramic radiograph and CBCT to define lesion boundaries, cortical expansion, and tooth relation. Plan surgery only after histopathologic confirmation (incisional biopsy if needed).

Red flag: Operating on a cystic lesion without histological diagnosis or imaging constitutes diagnostic negligence. "Clinically appeared benign" is not a defense [2].

- ***Step 1: Informed Consent and Case Discussion***

Explain nature of lesion, surgical plan (enucleation, marsupialization, or resection), possible recurrence, nerve injury risk, and need for long-term follow-up. Obtain written consent with "possible need for repeat procedures" clause.

Red flag: Lack of consent mentioning recurrence or histopathology is indefensible when lesion reappears years later [3].

- ***Step 2: Preoperative Preparation and Asepsis***

Ensure sterile field, appropriate instruments, suction, and hemostatic agents. Administer anesthesia (local or general) with recorded drug name, dose, and batch.

Red flag: Missing anesthesia or asepsis record converts any infection or postoperative complication into presumed negligence [4].

- ***Step 3: Surgical Access and Exposure***

Raise mucoperiosteal flap to expose cyst wall or tumor capsule. Use bone window for access without excessive removal.

Red flag: Overzealous resection or inadequate exposure without rationale note invites scrutiny in nerve or bone loss complications [5].

- ***Step 4: Enucleation or Marsupialization***

Enucleate entire cystic lining or marsupialize large lesions for decompression. Ensure complete removal of epithelial remnants.

Red flag: Incomplete enucleation without mention of technique or reason allows recurrence claims that are legally indefensible [6].

- ***Step 5: Specimen Handling and Histopathology***

Label specimen immediately with patient name, site, and date. Place in formalin and send with requisition form including radiographs and clinical notes.

Red flag: Sending specimen unlabeled or without requisition form is a major medico-legal breach - chain of custody failure equates to evidence tampering [7].

- ***Step 6: Management of Adjacent Teeth and Structures***

Record extraction or preservation of related teeth and nerve management steps.

Red flag: Failure to record rationale for tooth extraction during cyst removal is viewed as over-treatment unless justified in notes [8].

- ***Step 7: Hemostasis, Closure, and Drain Placement***

Achieve hemostasis and close primarily or with drain placement. Document suture type and number.

Red flag: Persistent postoperative bleeding with no closure details implies incomplete surgery or poor technique [9].

- ***Step 8: Postoperative Care and Medication***

Prescribe antibiotics, analgesics, and antiseptic rinses. Provide printed discharge sheet with instructions on swelling, infection, or recurrence symptoms.

Red flag: Verbal-only instructions nullify defense in delayed infection or recurrence cases [10].

- ***Step 9: Follow-Up and Radiographic Monitoring***

Review at one week, one month, and three months. Take follow-up radiograph to confirm bone fill and absence of recurrence.

Red flag: No follow-up imaging record transforms recurrence into apparent missed lesion - legally indefensible even if recurrence is biological [11].

- ***Step 10: Long-Term Recordkeeping and Patient Notification***

Retain operative notes, radiographs, histopathology reports, and follow-up data for at least 10 years. Notify patient in writing of the need for annual review.

Red flag: Absence of written follow-up recommendation implies incomplete care and professional neglect [12].

Legal Defensibility and Documentation Anchors

For cysts and tumors, every complete and defensible record should contain:

- Radiographs/CBCT and preoperative diagnosis
- Written consent with recurrence clause
- Operative note describing access and removal

- Specimen label and histopathology form
- Medication and discharge documentation
- Radiographic follow-up proof
- Annual review advice in writing

This builds an irrefutable chronology of care, communication, and accountability.

Case Study

A 35-year-old patient underwent cyst removal in the mandible. No histopathology report was obtained. The lesion recurred as ameloblastoma after two years, requiring resection. The court held negligence for failure to confirm diagnosis histologically and for inadequate postoperative documentation. Compensation was granted for repeated surgical morbidity.

Case Learnings

1. Never remove a lesion without histopathological confirmation.
2. Consent must include recurrence risk and reoperation possibility.
3. Labeling and requisition documentation are the surgeon's strongest defense.
4. Follow-up imaging and written reminders show continuity of care.
5. The record of caution often outweighs the result of cure.

Quick Checklist

- Radiograph/CBCT and diagnosis documented
- Consent includes recurrence and reoperation clause
- Asepsis and anesthesia recorded
- Cyst or tumor removal technique noted
- Specimen labeled and requisition completed
- Teeth and structure management justified
- Hemostasis and closure recorded

- Written discharge instructions signed
- Follow-up imaging and notes filed
- Records retained minimum 10 years

References

1. *Neville BW, Damm DD, Allen CM, Chi AC. Oral and Maxillofacial Pathology. 5th ed. Elsevier; 2022.*
2. *Shear M, Speight PM. Cysts of the Oral and Maxillofacial Regions. 4th ed. Wiley-Blackwell; 2007.*
3. *National Medical Commission (India). Informed Consent and Chronic Disease Protocols. 2021.*
4. *Ministry of Health and Family Welfare, India. Surgical Documentation and Asepsis Standards. 2020.*
5. *Regezi JA, Sciubba JJ. Oral Pathology: Clinical-Pathologic Correlations. 7th ed. Elsevier; 2022.*
6. *Philipsen HP, Reichart PA. Odontogenic keratocysts and their recurrences. Oral Oncol. 2004;40(4):364 - 372.*
7. *Dental Council of India. Histopathology Specimen Handling Guidelines. 2022.*
8. *General Dental Council (UK). Scope of Treatment and Consent Standards. 2013.*
9. *Dental Protection Limited. Complications in Oral Surgery: Legal Perspective. 2021.*
10. *Ministry of Health and Family Welfare, India. Discharge and Follow-Up Instruction Standards. 2020.*
11. *Pogrel MA. Recurrence patterns in odontogenic cysts and tumors. J Oral Maxillofac Surg. 2010;68(3):470 - 476.*
12. *National Medical Commission (India). Record Retention and Patient Follow-Up Regulations. 2021.*

CHAPTER 42

Jaw Reconstruction and Bone Grafting - Clinical Principles, Donor Site Ethics, and Legal Safeguards

Jaw reconstruction defines the surgeon's craft and character. Technically, it restores bone; ethically, it restores dignity. When grafts fail or deformities persist, patients rarely sue over biology - they sue over silence, missing notes, or unexplained choices. This chapter outlines stepwise clinical conduct and the medico-legal framework for bone grafting and reconstruction in oral and maxillofacial practice.

Purpose and Indications

Jaw reconstruction aims to restore form and function following trauma, cyst/tumor resection, or atrophy. Indications include alveolar ridge defects, continuity loss, and implant site augmentation. From a legal standpoint, the justification for graft type, donor site selection, and informed consent determine defensibility more than the final contour [1].

Preparation and Diagnostic Evaluation

Record preoperative photographs, radiographs, and CBCT to define defect size and quality of remaining bone. Document systemic health (diabetes, vascular disease, smoking), as these affect graft success. Discuss aesthetic and functional expectations.

Red flag: Operating without preoperative imaging or consent describing defect size and graft plan equates to unquantified risk - a frequent legal failure point [2].

- ***Step 1: Treatment Planning and Consent***

Explain graft type (autograft, allograft, xenograft, or alloplastic), donor site, anesthesia, expected outcome, and possible complications (infection, graft loss, scarring, paresthesia). Obtain written consent mentioning "possible partial or total graft failure" and "donor site morbidity."

Red flag: Missing donor-site risk clause or graft-type justification in consent makes postoperative complications legally indefensible [3].

- ***Step 2: Preoperative Asepsis and Anesthesia***

Ensure sterile preparation of both recipient and donor sites. Record anesthesia type, dose, and site. Use prophylactic antibiotics as indicated.

Red flag: Dual-site surgery without asepsis or anesthesia documentation breaches standard of care and infection control laws [4].

- ***Step 3: Recipient Site Preparation***

Reflect mucoperiosteal flap, remove fibrous tissue, and decorticate bone to induce bleeding. Maintain irrigation to prevent necrosis.

Red flag: Excessive decortication or thermal damage without documentation of irrigation and rationale may invite claims of negligence when graft fails [5].

- ***Step 4: Graft Harvesting (Autogenous)***

Harvest bone from iliac crest, symphysis, ramus, or calvarium using sterile technique. Record site, amount, instruments, and hemostasis method. Photograph or diagram donor site.

Red flag: Unrecorded donor-site details or absent consent on donor morbidity exposes surgeon to dual liability - for both sites [6].

- ***Step 5: Graft Placement and Fixation***

Contour and fix graft with screws or membranes ensuring intimate contact and immobility. Record material type, manufacturer, and batch number.

Red flag: Omission of implant or fixation details violates medical device traceability laws and nullifies defense in case of foreign-body reactions [7].

- ***Step 6: Hemostasis and Wound Closure***

Achieve tension-free closure using resorbable sutures. Document suture material and layers closed.

Red flag: Postoperative wound dehiscence without closure record or material specification invites assumptions of improper technique [8].

- ***Step 7: Postoperative Care and Instructions***

Prescribe antibiotics, analgesics, and mouth rinses. Provide printed instructions covering oral hygiene, diet, swelling, and signs of infection.

Red flag: Verbal-only instructions are inadmissible in legal defense; every patient must sign acknowledgment of receiving postoperative guidance [9].

- ***Step 8: Follow-Up and Radiographic Evaluation***

Review at one week, one month, and three months. Record graft integration on radiographs and clinical stability.

Red flag: Lack of follow-up radiographs or clinical notes is legally interpreted as abandonment, even if graft integration appears successful later [10].

- ***Step 9: Management of Complications***

In case of infection, graft exposure, or non-integration, record onset, site, management steps, and discussion with patient.

Red flag: Absence of complication documentation or late disclosure creates presumption of concealment - the single most damaging factor in litigation [11].

- ***Step 10: Long-Term Rehabilitation and Record Retention***

After integration, document implant placement or prosthetic phase with photographs. Maintain all operative, radiographic, and consent records for at least 10 years.

Red flag: Missing donor site notes, histologic proof, or graft source traceability are violations under medical material regulations [12].

Legal Defensibility and Documentation Anchors

A defensible reconstruction record must include:

- Imaging and preoperative planning documentation
- Written consent with donor-site and graft-failure clauses
- Asepsis and anesthesia log
- Donor and recipient site details
- Fixation hardware specifications
- Postoperative instruction sheet and patient acknowledgment

- Follow-up radiographs and complication records
- Long-term retention of case documents

Such transparency not only satisfies the law but also reinforces patient confidence.

Case Study

A 45-year-old woman underwent iliac crest graft for mandibular continuity defect. Graft failed with infection and donor site scar. The consent form mentioned "bone graft" but not donor site or possible failure. Surgeon had no operative photos or implant batch record. The court ruled partial negligence, citing inadequate disclosure and documentation gaps despite technical adequacy.

Case Learnings

1. Consent must name graft type and donor site explicitly.
2. Every graft source and fixation material must have batch traceability.
3. Photographic documentation of donor and recipient sites supports both science and law.
4. Early communication of graft failure prevents litigation.
5. A well-written record defends where results cannot.

Quick Checklist

- Preoperative imaging and defect documentation done
- Consent includes graft type and donor-site clause
- Asepsis and anesthesia recorded
- Recipient site prepared and irrigated
- Donor site details documented
- Fixation material type and batch logged
- Hemostasis and layered closure achieved
- Written postoperative instructions signed
- Follow-up radiographs reviewed and filed
- All records stored minimum 10 years

References

1. *Fonseca RJ et al. Oral and Maxillofacial Surgery. 3rd ed. Elsevier; 2022.*
2. *National Medical Commission (India). Documentation Standards in Reconstructive Surgery. 2021.*
3. *Ministry of Health and Family Welfare, India. Informed Consent and Donor Site Ethics. 2020.*
4. *Dental Council of India. Dual-Site Surgery Asepsis Guidelines. 2022.*
5. *Pogrel MA. Bone grafting in oral surgery: clinical and medico-legal aspects. J Oral Maxillofac Surg. 2010;68(6):1347 - 1355.*
6. *General Dental Council (UK). Donor Site Consent and Recordkeeping Standards. 2013.*
7. *World Health Organization. Traceability of Surgical Implants and Biomaterials. Geneva; 2018.*
8. *Dental Protection Limited. Graft Failures and Risk Documentation. 2021.*
9. *Ministry of Health and Family Welfare, India. Patient Communication and Discharge Instruction Protocols. 2020.*
10. *Dental Council of India. Follow-Up and Clinical Audit in Surgical Reconstruction. 2022.*
11. *National Medical Commission (India). Adverse Event Disclosure and Legal Accountability. 2021.*
12. *Government of India. Medical Device Rules and Record Retention Requirements. 2019.*

CHAPTER 43

Implantology - Surgical Protocols, Peri-Implant Complications, and Legal Defensibility

Dental implants sit at the crossroad of surgery, prosthetics, and law. When they succeed, they're invisible; when they fail, they're evidence. Most implant disputes do not arise from infection or bone loss-they arise from unrecorded expectations, missing consent, or poor traceability. This chapter lays out the clinical discipline and documentation backbone every implant surgeon must follow to stay scientifically sound and legally safe.

Purpose and Indications

Implant placement replaces missing teeth and restores function and esthetics. Indications include single-tooth loss, edentulous ridges, or full-arch rehabilitation. Medico-legally, implants are elective and demand higher standards of consent, imaging, and patient communication than routine surgery [1].

Preparation and Diagnostic Evaluation

Record full medical and dental history, systemic conditions, smoking habits, and medications affecting bone metabolism (bisphosphonates, steroids, antidiabetics). Obtain CBCT for 3D assessment of bone height, width, and anatomical proximity to nerves or sinuses.

Red flag: Placing an implant without 3D imaging or risk discussion violates global implant safety norms. Courts interpret it as failure to plan [2].

- ***Step 1: Informed Consent and Patient Education***

Explain procedure, cost, duration, and long-term maintenance needs. Document risks-implant failure, nerve injury, sinus perforation, infection, peri-implantitis, and need for revision. Obtain signed consent mentioning "elective procedure" and "no guaranteed success rate."

Red flag: No written acknowledgment that implant is elective equals consent deficiency. "Doctor promised permanence" statements become uncontested evidence if no disclaimers exist [3].

- ***Step 2: Treatment Planning and Imaging Documentation***

Perform diagnostic wax-up or digital planning. Record implant brand, size, and torque guidelines. Include printed CBCT images and planning screenshots in file.

Red flag: Lack of planning record implies improvisation-indefensible if anatomical damage or implant failure occurs [4].

- ***Step 3: Asepsis and Anesthesia***

Prepare sterile surgical field. Record anesthesia type, concentration, and quantity. Maintain sterile draping, gloves, and irrigation.

Red flag: Absence of asepsis log transforms postoperative infection into presumed negligence. Infection control records are mandatory [5].

- ***Step 4: Flap Design and Osteotomy Preparation***

Design crestal or flapless incision ensuring adequate access. Drill sequentially under continuous saline irrigation, maintaining manufacturer's speed and torque limits.

Red flag: Overheating due to lack of irrigation or unrecorded drill speed creates indefensible implant necrosis. Operative notes must mention irrigation use [6].

- ***Step 5: Implant Placement and Primary Stability***

Insert implant with controlled torque (document N·cm value). Record implant brand, model, lot, and batch number.

Red flag: Missing implant identification stickers or batch logs breaches medical device regulations. Without them, surgeon assumes product liability [7].

- ***Step 6: Soft Tissue Management and Suturing***

Adapt soft tissue for tension-free closure. Record suture material and number. Photograph site post-closure.

Red flag: No photographic or descriptive record invites dispute over implant position or surgical method [8].

- ***Step 7: Postoperative Instructions and Medication***

Prescribe antibiotics, analgesics, and antiseptic rinses. Provide printed instructions detailing oral hygiene, diet, and re-entry schedule.

Redflag: Verbal discharge advice carries no weight in implant complaints-signed instruction acknowledgment is essential [9].

- ***Step 8: Prosthetic Phase and Documentation***

Record impression date, abutment type, torque value, and prosthesis design. Keep manufacturer's torque charts attached.

Red flag: Absence of prosthetic torque record converts screw loosening or abutment failure into presumed mechanical negligence [10].

- ***Step 9: Maintenance and Recall Schedule***

Document follow-up at one week, one month, six months, and annually. Record peri-implant tissue health, probing depths, and radiographs.

Red flag: No long-term maintenance record shifts full liability of late failure onto the operator. Recall logs protect against time-delayed claims [11].

- ***Step 10: Complication Management and Legal Disclosure***

In cases of peri-implantitis, fracture, or nerve injury, record event time, treatment steps, and communication with patient. Provide written disclosure and referral if needed.

Red flag: Concealing implant loss or silently replacing it without documentation constitutes deliberate suppression-grounds for disciplinary action [12].

Legal Defensibility and Documentation Anchors

A defensible implant case includes:

- CBCT and diagnostic plan filed
- Written consent stating elective nature and risks
- Implant batch sticker and torque log
- Asepsis, anesthesia, and irrigation records
- Postoperative instructions signed
- Prosthetic phase documentation
- Maintenance and recall entries
- Complication disclosures filed

This creates a continuous chain of proof-planning to outcome-unbreakable under scrutiny.

Case Study

A 52-year-old man developed paresthesia after mandibular implant placement. CBCT had not been done; consent lacked mention of nerve risk. Implant brand and lot number were unrecorded. The dentist argued technical skill but lost the case on absence of imaging, consent, and traceability documents.

Case Learnings

1. Every implant procedure is elective-higher consent standards apply.
2. Batch labels and torque logs are legal evidence of diligence.
3. Imaging and documented planning outweigh verbal assurance.
4. Transparent disclosure after complication builds defense.
5. Legal protection in implantology begins before the first drill.

Quick Checklist

- CBCT and digital planning attached
- Consent includes elective and risk clauses
- Asepsis and anesthesia recorded
- Sequential drilling with irrigation logged
- Implant batch sticker and torque recorded
- Soft tissue closure documented
- Written discharge instructions signed
- Prosthetic torque values recorded
- Maintenance reviews documented
- Complication disclosure filed and stored 10 years

References

1. *Misch CE. Contemporary Implant Dentistry. 4th ed. Elsevier; 2021.*
2. *Bornstein MM. CBCT for implant planning: consensus statements. Clin Oral Implants Res. 2014;25(11):1248 - 1256.*
3. *General Dental Council (UK). Consent and Patient Communication Standards. 2013.*
4. *Ministry of Health and Family Welfare, India. Digital Imaging and Diagnostic Documentation Norms. 2020.*
5. *Dental Council of India. Asepsis and Surgical Recordkeeping Guidelines. 2022.*
6. *Sakka S, Baroudi K. Guidelines for implant drilling protocols. Int J Oral Maxillofac Surg. 2012;41(3):350 - 357.*
7. *Government of India. Medical Device Traceability Rules. 2019.*
8. *Dental Protection Limited. Implant Litigation and Clinical Risk Management. 2021.*
9. *Ministry of Health and Family Welfare, India. Patient Discharge Communication Standards. 2020.*
10. *Goodacre CJ et al. Mechanical complications in implant prosthodontics. J Prosthet Dent. 2003;90(2):121 - 132.*
11. *Renvert S, Polyzois I. Maintenance of dental implants: clinical evidence and protocols. Periodontol 2000. 2015;68(1):254 - 266.*
12. *National Medical Commission (India). Adverse Event Disclosure and Legal Accountability. 2021.*

CHAPTER 44

Maxillofacial Infections and Cellulitis - Emergency Management, Antibiotic Protocols, and Legal Reporting Duties

Infections of the face and jaws turn ordinary discomfort into systemic threat faster than most surgeons expect. When airway, vision, or trismus enter the picture, timing and documentation become life-saving acts. The surgeon's technical response saves the patient; the written record saves the surgeon. This chapter aligns clinical urgency with legal precision in the diagnosis and management of maxillofacial infections and cellulitis.

Purpose and Indications

The goal in managing maxillofacial infections is to control infection, secure airway, and prevent systemic spread. Indications include swelling, fever, dysphagia, trismus, or respiratory distress. The medico-legal duty is to recognize severity, document escalation decisions, and justify antibiotic use in line with stewardship norms [1].

Preparation and Initial Evaluation

Record history of dental pain, trauma, prior antibiotics, and systemic illnesses. Document swelling site, trismus grade, and airway status. Record vitals, especially temperature, pulse, and oxygen saturation.

Red flag: Failing to record airway status before anesthesia or drainage is indefensible. "Not documented" reads as "not checked" in court [2].

- ***Step 1: Risk Stratification and Consent***

Classify infection as localized (periapical, buccal) or deep-space (submandibular, submental, parapharyngeal). Obtain informed consent mentioning "risk of airway obstruction, hospitalization, and possible tracheostomy."

Red flag: No mention of airway risk in consent voids legal defense if patient deteriorates postoperatively [3].

- ***Step 2: Imaging and Laboratory Tests***

Order panoramic radiograph or CT scan for space involvement and pus tracking. Record CBC, CRP, and blood sugar.

Red flag: Incision and drainage without imaging or lab baseline implies unverified severity-indefensible if infection spreads systemically [4].

- ***Step 3: Airway and Resuscitation Preparedness***

Keep airway tray, suction, and emergency equipment ready. Record airway assessment before sedation.

Red flag: Lack of airway preparation record during deep-space abscess drainage is viewed as procedural recklessness [5].

- ***Step 4: Incision and Drainage***

Make dependent incision with blunt dissection to break loculi. Collect pus for culture and sensitivity. Insert drain for 48 - 72 hours. Record quantity and appearance of discharge.

Red flag: Performing drainage without recording pus culture or drain details equates to blind treatment-medico-legally indefensible [6].

- ***Step 5: Empirical and Culture-Guided Antibiotic Therapy***

Start broad-spectrum antibiotics (amoxicillin-clavulanate or clindamycin; add metronidazole if anaerobes suspected). Adjust per culture report. Record drug name, dose, route, and rationale.

Red flag: Continuing empirical antibiotics beyond 72 hours without justification violates stewardship guidelines and attracts censure [7].

- ***Step 6: Pain Control and Supportive Care***

Administer NSAIDs and maintain hydration. Record temperature and swelling reduction daily.

Red flag: No progress notes for 48 hours implies neglect-even if patient clinically improves. Courts rely on records, not memory [8].

- ***Step 7: Hospitalization and Referral***

If infection extends to parapharyngeal, retropharyngeal, or mediastinal spaces, transfer immediately to tertiary care. Record date, facility name, and communication.

Red flag: Delayed referral or undocumented transfer in spreading infection cases is a frequent cause of disciplinary action [9].

- ***Step 8: Postoperative Instructions and Discharge***

Provide written sheet detailing warm saline rinses, medication course, and red flags (breathing difficulty, fever, neck stiffness). Obtain patient signature.

Red flag: Verbal-only advice fails during dispute-written discharge is the only admissible defense [10].

- ***Step 9: Follow-Up and Review***

Schedule reviews on day two and day five. Record healing, drain removal, and laboratory improvement. Attach culture reports.

Red flag: Missing follow-up entries suggest abandonment, even if infection resolved spontaneously [11].

- ***Step 10: Legal Documentation and Reporting***

Maintain complete record: consent, airway assessment, operative note, culture report, antibiotic log, and discharge summary. Report fatal or near-fatal infections to public health authority if sepsis develops.

Red flag: Non-reporting of life-threatening infection under clinical establishment rules is a legal violation under national health regulations [12].

Legal Defensibility and Documentation Anchors

A defendable infection case includes:

- Airway and vitals documentation
- Written consent with airway risk clause
- Imaging and lab investigations filed
- Pus culture and antibiotic log

- Progress and referral records
- Signed discharge instructions
- Case file retention for 10 years

This trail reflects vigilance, communication, and compliance-your legal shield in sepsis-related claims.

Case Study

A 33-year-old male presented with submandibular swelling and fever. The dentist performed drainage without airway assessment or pus culture. The patient developed respiratory distress and required emergency tracheostomy. Court held the dentist negligent for inadequate risk assessment and absence of airway documentation, despite correct surgical technique.

Case Learnings

1. Infections evolve fast-records must evolve faster.
2. Airway status is the first and last legal safeguard.
3. Pus culture and antibiotic documentation prove diligence.
4. Written discharge and follow-up preserve continuity.
5. Every infection case is part medicine, part legal affidavit.

Quick Checklist

- Airway and vitals recorded
- Consent includes airway and tracheostomy risk
- Imaging and labs completed
- Pus culture collected and recorded
- Antibiotic choice and duration justified
- Drain type and placement noted
- Written discharge and patient signature obtained
- Follow-up entries with improvement noted
- Referral or hospitalization documented
- All records retained for 10 years

References

1. *Peterson LJ et al. Contemporary Oral and Maxillofacial Surgery. 7th ed. Elsevier; 2022.*
2. *Malamed SF. Medical Emergencies in the Dental Office. 8th ed. Elsevier; 2020.*
3. *National Medical Commission (India). Informed Consent Standards in Emergency Oral Surgery. 2021.*
4. *Ministry of Health and Family Welfare, India. Clinical Imaging and Documentation Protocols. 2020.*
5. *Dental Council of India. Airway Management Preparedness in Oral Surgery. 2022.*
6. *Flynn TR. Oral and maxillofacial infections: principles and treatment. Oral Maxillofac Surg Clin North Am. 2011;23(3):421 - 440.*
7. *World Health Organization. Antimicrobial Stewardship in Dental Practice. Geneva; 2019.*
8. *Dental Protection Limited. Infection Progress Notes and Legal Compliance. 2021.*
9. *National Medical Commission (India). Referral Obligations and Escalation of Care. 2021.*
10. *Ministry of Health and Family Welfare, India. Patient Discharge Documentation Standards. 2020.*
11. *General Dental Council (UK). Follow-Up and Recordkeeping Requirements. 2013.*
12. *Government of India. Clinical Establishment (Regulation and Reporting) Act. 2010.*

CHAPTER 45

Facial Space Infections - Surgical Anatomy, Drainage Protocols, and Legal Defensibility in Airway-Threatening Conditions

Facial space infections are where oral surgery stops being elective and becomes life-saving. They move fast, distort anatomy, and choke airways before paperwork catches up. In these moments, it's not enough to drain the abscess - the surgeon must document judgment. This chapter bridges anatomy, emergency decision-making, and the legal responsibility that comes with managing space infections.

Purpose and Indications

Facial space infections arise when odontogenic or traumatic infections spread beyond the alveolus into fascial planes. Common spaces include buccal, canine, submandibular, submental, and parapharyngeal. Indications for surgical drainage include trismus, dysphagia, dyspnea, or rapid swelling. The medicolegal objective is to prove early recognition, airway safety, and justified escalation [1].

Preparation and Initial Assessment

Record swelling location, temperature, trismus, airway patency, and swallowing difficulty. Photograph swelling and note onset time. Obtain CBC, CRP, and imaging (CT neck or contrast OPG) to map spread.

Red flag: Managing space infections without airway documentation or imaging constitutes procedural negligence. Every airway note is a legal life jacket [2].

- ***Step 1: Airway and Consent Protocol***

Assess and record Mallampati score, tongue elevation, and mouth opening.

Obtain written consent including "possible airway compromise, need for tracheostomy, hospitalization, and referral."

Red flag: No written consent mentioning airway risk invalidates legal protection if airway emergency occurs during or after drainage [3].

- ***Step 2: Localization and Incision Planning***

Identify involved spaces and mark dependent incision points following facial aesthetic and drainage safety lines (Hilton's method).

Red flag: Incision placed without recording rationale or anatomical line of safety is indefensible if neurovascular injury or scarring follows [4].

- ***Step 3: Asepsis and Anesthesia***

Prepare surgical field under sterile conditions. Administer local anesthesia away from infection site to avoid intravascular spread. Document drug, dose, and batch.

Red flag: Infiltrating directly into infected tissue without note of necessity is legally interpreted as careless technique [5].

- ***Step 4: Blunt Dissection and Drainage***

Insert hemostat or sinus forceps, break loculi gently, and establish dependent drainage. Collect pus for culture and sensitivity.

Red flag: Drainage without culture report is indefensible if infection recurs - "no lab, no defense" [6].

- ***Step 5: Drain Placement and Fixation***

Insert corrugated rubber or Penrose drain, secure with suture, and record drain type, site, and fixation method.

Red flag: Unrecorded drain size or retention duration is a major medico-legal gap in post-surgical infection cases [7].

- ***Step 6: Antibiotic and Supportive Therapy***

Start empirical IV antibiotics covering anaerobes and aerobes (ampicillin-sulbactam, clindamycin, or metronidazole combinations). Adjust per culture report. Record route, dose, duration, and response.

Red flag: Continuation of empirical antibiotics beyond 72 hours without update or culture justification violates antibiotic stewardship standards [8].

- ***Step 7: Pain and Airway Monitoring***

Document daily airway assessment, pain score, temperature, and trismus.

Red flag: Missing progress notes in hospitalized infection patients is treated as patient neglect even if recovery occurs [9].

- ***Step 8: Referral and Interdisciplinary Collaboration***

If parapharyngeal or retropharyngeal involvement suspected, consult ENT or critical care team. Document communication and referral date.

Red flag: Verbal referral without written note converts collaboration into absence - indefensible when infection spreads [10].

- ***Step 9: Discharge and Written Instructions***

Once afebrile and swelling subsides, remove drains, irrigate wounds, and issue written discharge form specifying hygiene, nutrition, and warning signs (breathing difficulty, trismus, fever).

Red flag: Verbal-only discharge instructions fail to prove patient education and legal closure [11].

- ***Step 10: Record Retention and Audit Compliance***

Retain complete case file: consent, airway chart, imaging, operative note, drain record, antibiotic log, and discharge summary.

Red flag: Missing airway chart or culture report in audit triggers regulatory penalty under clinical establishment laws [12].

Legal Defensibility and Documentation Anchors

A legally defendable facial space infection case includes:

- Airway assessment and risk note
- Imaging and lab results
- Written consent with tracheostomy clause
- Drainage technique and culture record
- Daily airway and vitals documentation
- Referral and interdisciplinary notes
- Signed discharge summary
- File retention for minimum 10 years

This structured record establishes the chain of clinical judgment and communication required for defensible emergency practice.

Case Study

A 41-year-old male with Ludwig's angina underwent submandibular drainage without airway evaluation or consent for possible tracheostomy. Postoperatively, airway obstruction led to emergency intubation and ICU admission. Court held the dentist negligent for failure to anticipate airway risk and lack of informed consent, despite technically correct drainage.

Case Learnings

1. Airway comes before incision - always documented, never assumed.
2. Every drainage requires culture, consent, and photographic proof.
3. Verbal referrals vanish in court; written records remain.
4. Patient education through written discharge notes limits liability.
5. The safest surgeon is the one with the most transparent file.

Quick Checklist

- Airway and vitals recorded at admission
- Consent includes tracheostomy and airway risk
- Imaging and labs completed
- Dependent incision with rationale documented
- Culture and sensitivity recorded
- Drain size and fixation noted
- Daily airway and temperature monitoring charted
- Interdisciplinary referrals documented
- Written discharge instructions issued and signed
- Records archived for minimum 10 years

References

1. *Flynn TR. Principles and surgical management of fascial space infections. Oral Maxillofac Surg Clin North Am. 2011;23(3):421 - 440.*
2. *Peterson LJ et al. Contemporary Oral and Maxillofacial Surgery. 7th ed. Elsevier; 2022.*
3. *National Medical Commission (India). Informed Consent Standards for Surgical Emergencies. 2021.*
4. *Stanley RE. Hilton's method revisited: surgical safety in drainage of deep-space infections. Br J Oral Maxillofac Surg. 2014;52(3):205 - 209.*
5. *Malamed SF. Medical Emergencies in the Dental Office. 8th ed. Elsevier; 2020.*
6. *Ministry of Health and Family Welfare, India. Infection Control and Documentation Protocols. 2020.*
7. *Dental Council of India. Surgical Drain Documentation Standards. 2022.*
8. *World Health Organization. Antibiotic Stewardship in Clinical Dentistry. Geneva; 2019.*
9. *Dental Protection Limited. Hospital Infection Case Documentation Failures. 2021.*
10. *National Medical Commission (India). Referral and Interdepartmental Coordination Protocols. 2021.*
11. *Ministry of Health and Family Welfare, India. Discharge Documentation Guidelines. 2020.*
12. *Government of India. Clinical Establishments (Standards and Regulation) Rules. 2010.*

CHAPTER 46

Osteoradionecrosis and Medication-Related Osteonecrosis of the Jaw (MRONJ) - Prevention, Management, and Legal Implications

Osteonecrosis exposes the quiet fault lines between medicine and dentistry. It develops slowly, often after treatment elsewhere, but the blame lands squarely on the last operator. When the bone dies, the law comes alive. This chapter clarifies preventive steps, surgical conduct, and recordkeeping that separate inevitable complications from avoidable malpractice.

Purpose and Indications

Osteoradionecrosis (ORN) follows radiation-induced vascular compromise; MRONJ arises from antiresorptive or antiangiogenic medications such as bisphosphonates, denosumab, or bevacizumab. Both present as exposed, non-healing bone persisting beyond eight weeks. The aim is to prevent occurrence through screening, coordination, and meticulous documentation of risk communication [1].

Preparation and Risk Assessment

Take detailed medical and oncologic history-radiation dose, field, duration, and last exposure. For MRONJ, record all antiresorptive drugs with start date, dosage, and indication. Obtain physician clearance before extractions or implants.

Red flag: Performing dental surgery without verifying oncologic or medication history is indefensible; courts treat it as "failure to anticipate known risk" [2].

- ***Step 1: Pre-Treatment Evaluation and Consent***

Identify high-risk zones (posterior mandible, irradiated fields). Obtain written consent that explicitly mentions "risk of bone necrosis, delayed healing, and need for future surgery."

Red flag: Absence of radiation or drug-related risk clause in consent makes even minor necrosis claims legally indefensible [3].

- ***Step 2: Pre-Therapy Dental Clearance (For Cancer Patients)***

Before radiation or bisphosphonate therapy, eliminate potential infection foci-non-restorable teeth, periapical lesions, and periodontal pockets. Document extractions and healing status.

Red flag: Failing to provide or document pre-therapy dental clearance shifts later necrosis liability to dentist when preventive opportunity was missed [4].

- ***Step 3: Asepsis and Surgical Minimalism***

If extraction is unavoidable, use atraumatic technique, smooth bone, irrigate with saline, and achieve primary closure.

Red flag: Aggressive bone removal or flap elevation in irradiated/mronj-risk bone without written justification implies procedural recklessness [5].

- ***Step 4: Antibiotic and Antiseptic Protocols***

Administer prophylactic antibiotics and 0.12% chlorhexidine rinses. Continue antiseptic care for two weeks post-procedure.

Red flag: Infection following procedure without antibiotic documentation appears as preventable negligence [6].

- ***Step 5: Medical Coordination and Communication***

Communicate with treating oncologist or physician regarding "drug holiday" or modification. Record date, name, and advice received.

Red flag: No documentation of physician communication during MRONJ management equals failure of multidisciplinary duty [7].

- ***Step 6: Diagnosis of Established ORN/MRONJ***

Confirm diagnosis clinically (exposed bone >8 weeks) and radiographically (sequestrum, sclerosis). Stage disease per AAOMS criteria and note stage in record.

Red flag: Treating without staging or imaging documentation is seen as random, non-protocol-based practice [8].

- ***Step 7: Conservative Management and Monitoring***

Start chlorhexidine rinses, antibiotics, analgesics, and regular irrigation. Record symptom relief and tissue changes at each visit.

Red flag: No follow-up notes in chronic necrosis equals "abandonment of care" in medico-legal review [9].

- ***Step 8: Surgical Debridement or Resection (Advanced Stages)***

Excise necrotic bone conservatively; obtain culture and histopathology. Record tissue removed, instrument sterilization, and closure method.

Red flag: Performing resection without histopathology report nullifies legal defense if recurrence or progression occurs [10].

- ***Step 9: Patient Education and Documentation***

Provide printed instructions-soft diet, oral hygiene, no trauma, and immediate reporting of pain or exposure. Obtain signature acknowledging understanding.

Red flag: Verbal instructions leave no proof of education-signed documentation alone supports the surgeon's diligence [11].

- ***Step 10: Long-Term Follow-Up and Reporting***

Schedule reviews every four weeks initially, then biannually. Maintain record for at least ten years. For MRONJ, report adverse drug events to pharmacovigilance authority.

Red flag: Omission of mandatory reporting for drug-related osteonecrosis breaches national pharmacovigilance laws [12].

Legal Defensibility and Documentation Anchors

A defendable osteonecrosis case includes:

- Medical, radiation, and drug history with clearance proof
- Written consent mentioning necrosis risk
- Pre-therapy dental clearance documentation
- Surgical records and antibiotic log

- Physician communication records
- Stage-wise diagnosis and management notes
- Signed patient education sheet
- Follow-up and pharmacovigilance reporting

This evidentiary chain demonstrates anticipation, collaboration, and continuity of care.

Case Study

A 70-year-old woman on oral bisphosphonates developed mandibular bone exposure after extraction. The dentist had neither verified medication history nor documented consent. Court ruled negligence for "failure to obtain relevant medical history and risk disclosure," emphasizing that bisphosphonate-related necrosis was a known, preventable complication.

Case Learnings

1. Every patient on antiresorptives or radiation requires written clearance.
2. Consent must name the drug class and risk explicitly.
3. Documentation of physician communication equals shared accountability.
4. Histopathology and staging records are the foundation of defense.
5. Preventive counseling, if recorded, is the most powerful legal shield.

Quick Checklist

- Medical and radiation history documented
- Physician clearance obtained and filed
- Consent includes necrosis and recurrence risk
- Aseptic, atraumatic technique used
- Antibiotic and antiseptic protocol logged
- Multidisciplinary communication documented
- Stage of ORN/MRONJ recorded
- Histopathology report filed (if surgery done)

- Patient education sheet signed
- Follow-up and pharmacovigilance report completed

References

1. *Ruggiero SL et al. American Association of Oral and Maxillofacial Surgeons (AAOMS) Position Paper on Medication-Related Osteonecrosis of the Jaw. J Oral Maxillofac Surg. 2022;80(5):920 - 943.*
2. *National Medical Commission (India). Clinical History and Drug Documentation Standards. 2021.*
3. *Ministry of Health and Family Welfare, India. Informed Consent and High-Risk Procedure Guidelines. 2020.*
4. *Marx RE. Osteoradionecrosis: a new concept of its pathophysiology. J Oral Maxillofac Surg. 1983;41(5):283 - 288.*
5. *Dental Council of India. Surgical Asepsis and Tissue Handling Protocols. 2022.*
6. *World Health Organization. Antimicrobial Prophylaxis Guidelines in Surgery. Geneva; 2018.*
7. *Dental Protection Limited. Interprofessional Communication and Risk Sharing. 2021.*
8. *Beumer J III, Harrison R, Sanders B. Osteoradionecrosis of the jaws. J Prosthet Dent. 1984;52(6):852 - 858.*
9. *General Dental Council (UK). Recordkeeping in Chronic Care Cases. 2013.*
10. *Ministry of Health and Family Welfare, India. Histopathology and Surgical Record Guidelines. 2020.*
11. *National Medical Commission (India). Patient Education and Consent Documentation Norms. 2021.*
12. *Government of India. Pharmacovigilance Programme of India (PvPI) Reporting Standards. 2020.*

CHAPTER 47

Maxillofacial Trauma Rehabilitation - Occlusion Restoration, Functional Recovery, and Medico-Legal Continuity of Care

Rehabilitation after maxillofacial trauma is the long road where surgery ends but responsibility continues. Plates may heal bone, but it is the follow-up, physiotherapy, and communication that heal trust. Courts often see litigation not from fractures themselves but from the silence that follows them - missing records, poor occlusal follow-up, or unaddressed functional loss. This chapter builds a structure for post-trauma recovery that is both clinically restorative and legally complete.

Purpose and Indications

Rehabilitation of maxillofacial trauma seeks to restore occlusion, symmetry, mastication, speech, and psychological well-being after surgical fixation or conservative management. It includes physical therapy, secondary correction, and prosthetic restoration. Legally, rehabilitation continues until the patient's function is documented as stable - not just "discharged." [1]

Preparation and Postoperative Baseline

After initial fixation, record occlusion, mouth opening, and facial symmetry. Take postoperative radiographs and photographs. Record any residual paresthesia or trismus.

Red flag: Failing to document baseline function post-fixation means future deterioration cannot be distinguished from surgical error - a fatal gap in defense [2].

- ***Step 1: Early Mobilization and Functional Assessment***

Begin gentle jaw exercises once stability allows. Record range of motion, pain score, and patient compliance.

Red flag: No physiotherapy record implies neglect. "Patient advised exercises" without written instruction is legally meaningless [3].

- ***Step 2: Occlusal Verification and Adjustment***

Check occlusion at one, four, and eight weeks post-surgery. Adjust elastics or occlusal contacts if deviation persists.

Red flag: Postoperative malocclusion complaints are indefensible if no periodic occlusion notes exist. "Not checked" becomes "not done." [4]

- ***Step 3: Implant, Plate, or Hardware Review***

Inspect intraoral plates or wires for loosening, exposure, or infection. Record hardware status and removal timeline.

Red flag: Absence of hardware audit or removal documentation nullifies traceability - a key legal protection if infection or fracture recurs [5].

- ***Step 4: Soft Tissue and Scar Management***

Massage scars and prescribe physiotherapy for mobility. Record texture, tenderness, and aesthetic recovery.

Red flag: Neglecting to note scar management gives grounds for cosmetic litigation - especially in facial disfigurement claims [6].

- ***Step 5: Nutritional and Psychological Counseling***

Advise high-protein, soft diet and refer for counseling if trauma affects speech or self-image. Document referral and summary.

Red flag: Failure to acknowledge psychosocial impact or offer referral may be seen as incomplete rehabilitation care [7].

- ***Step 6: Secondary Corrections or Revision Surgery***

If deformity or malocclusion persists, plan revision after bone healing (3 - 6 months). Obtain new consent and radiographs.

Red flag: Performing secondary correction without new imaging or consent is legally treated as unauthorized procedure [8].

- ***Step 7: Prosthetic or Implant Rehabilitation***

For missing teeth or bone, plan implants or prosthetics only after bone healing confirmation by radiograph or CT. Record planning and patient discussion.

Red flag: Initiating implants before bone consolidation without documented justification is indefensible if failure occurs [9].

- ***Step 8: Long-Term Follow-Up and Records***

Schedule annual reviews for two years. Record function, sensation, occlusion, and any residual discomfort. Retain photos and radiographs.

Red flag: Discharging patient without recorded long-term plan breaks continuity - legally equivalent to abandonment of care [10].

- ***Step 9: Medico-Legal Continuity of Care***

Maintain full chain of documentation from trauma management through rehabilitation - consent, imaging, physiotherapy, hardware log, and follow-up. This complete “rehabilitation dossier” establishes that care did not stop with fixation.

Red flag: Missing any link (physiotherapy or hardware removal) opens breach in defense; incomplete continuity equals incomplete care [11].

- ***Step 10: Final Outcome Documentation and Patient Communication***

At discharge, document occlusal status, mouth opening, and patient satisfaction. Obtain signed acknowledgment that treatment objectives have been met or explained.

Red flag: Verbal discharge without written closure or patient acknowledgment makes the case legally open-ended - inviting later disputes [12].

Legal Defensibility and Documentation Anchors

To protect both patient and practitioner, a maxillofacial rehabilitation file must include:

- Post-fixation baseline records and radiographs
- Physiotherapy and occlusion progress notes
- Hardware audit and removal records

- Scar and soft tissue management documentation
- Counseling and secondary correction records
- Signed discharge and satisfaction note
- Two-year follow-up proof

This timeline of recovery proves continuity, care, and closure - the legal trilogy of defensible rehabilitation.

Case Study

A 28-year-old man with mandibular fracture fixation complained of restricted mouth opening a year later. The dentist produced no physiotherapy or follow-up record. Though surgery had been successful, the absence of rehabilitation documentation led the court to infer inadequate postoperative management, ruling in favor of the patient.

Case Learnings

1. Trauma management does not end with fixation - documentation must continue through function.
2. Physiotherapy logs are as vital as radiographs in defense.
3. Scar and aesthetic notes protect against cosmetic litigation.
4. Written discharge with satisfaction acknowledgment closes legal exposure.
5. Courts trust continuity more than perfection.

Quick Checklist

- Post-fixation baseline occlusion and photos recorded
- Physiotherapy and jaw mobility documented
- Occlusal checks at defined intervals
- Hardware audit and removal record kept
- Scar and soft tissue evaluation noted
- Nutritional and psychological counseling recorded
- Secondary corrections consented and planned

- Two-year follow-up schedule documented
- Final discharge note with patient acknowledgment
- Records archived minimum 10 years

References

1. *Fonseca RJ et al. Oral and Maxillofacial Surgery. 3rd ed. Elsevier; 2022.*
2. *Ministry of Health and Family Welfare, India. Postoperative Documentation Standards in Trauma Care. 2020.*
3. *Ellis E. Functional rehabilitation after maxillofacial trauma. J Oral Maxillofac Surg. 2010;68(6):1449 - 1456.*
4. *Dental Council of India. Occlusal Verification and Recordkeeping Guidelines. 2022.*
5. *National Medical Commission (India). Implant and Hardware Traceability Standards. 2021.*
6. *Dental Protection Limited. Cosmetic and Functional Complications in Facial Trauma. 2021.*
7. *Ministry of Health and Family Welfare, India. Mental Health and Counseling Documentation Protocols. 2020.*
8. *General Dental Council (UK). Consent for Secondary and Revision Procedures. 2013.*
9. *Misch CE. Contemporary Implant Dentistry. 4th ed. Elsevier; 2021.*
10. *National Medical Commission (India). Long-Term Follow-Up and Continuity of Care Regulations. 2021.*
11. *Dental Council of India. Comprehensive Case Record Guidelines for Surgical Rehabilitation. 2022.*
12. *Ministry of Health and Family Welfare, India. Discharge and Patient Satisfaction Recordkeeping Standards. 2020.*

CHAPTER 48

Temporomandibular Joint Disorders and Ankylosis - Clinical Management, Surgical Decisions, and Legal Documentation Essentials

Temporomandibular disorders (TMD) and ankylosis test both diagnostic judgment and documentation discipline. Symptoms evolve slowly-pain, deviation, clicks, stiffness-but the accusations come fast: "You made it worse." When joints lock or fail to open, every note, consent, and radiograph becomes evidence of prudence. This chapter ties anatomy, therapy, and legal foresight into one defendable pathway.

Purpose and Indications

TMDs cover a spectrum of myofascial pain, internal derangement, arthritis, and ankylosis. Indications for intervention include chronic pain, restricted movement, or structural deformity. The legal focus lies on demonstrating comprehensive diagnosis, conservative management before surgery, and transparent patient communication [1].

Preparation and Diagnostic Evaluation

Record detailed history: pain duration, clicking, locking, bruxism, trauma, stress, and previous dental treatment. Note maximum mouth opening and deviation on opening. Take radiographs or CBCT; for ankylosis, CT or MRI is mandatory to confirm bony fusion and joint morphology.

Red flag: Starting invasive therapy without imaging or movement documentation is indefensible; "clinical impression" alone cannot justify surgery [2].

- ***Step 1: Differential Diagnosis and Consent***

Identify whether pain is muscular, intra-articular, or structural. Discuss possible outcomes, recurrence, and need for physiotherapy. Obtain written consent mentioning "joint stiffness, residual limitation, and recurrence risk."

Red flag: Consent that mentions "TMJ procedure" without specifying limitations or recurrence renders post-surgical stiffness indefensible [3].

- ***Step 2: Conservative Management***

Begin with soft diet, heat therapy, NSAIDs, physiotherapy, and occlusal splints. Record each modality and review after four weeks.

Red flag: Proceeding to arthrocentesis or surgery without written proof of failed conservative care is a major legal breach; courts demand documented stepwise escalation [4].

- ***Step 3: Arthrocentesis or Arthroscopy (When Indicated)***

Perform under aseptic conditions using sterile saline lavage (100 - 200 mL). Record needle entry points, solution volume, and complications.

Red flag: Absent operative record or omitted joint side notation turns minor arthrocentesis into indefensible "unverified procedure" [5].

- ***Step 4: Open Joint Surgery or Ankylosis Release***

If fibrosis or bony fusion confirmed, perform gap arthroplasty or interpositional arthroplasty using temporalis fascia or alloplastic material. Record incision, amount of bone removed, and interpositional material with batch details.

Red flag: Absence of operative note specifying gap size or material batch number violates implant traceability and reconstruction standards [6].

- ***Step 5: Intraoperative Documentation and Asepsis***

Maintain photographic or diagrammatic record. Document anesthesia type, drugs, vitals, and aseptic protocol.

Red flag: Postoperative infection or facial nerve injury without asepsis record suggests negligence by omission [7].

- ***Step 6: Postoperative Care and Physiotherapy***

Initiate mouth-opening exercises within 24 - 48 hours. Record range of motion and compliance daily for one week, then weekly for a month.

Red flag: No physiotherapy record implies failure of postoperative care; immobility becomes malpractice rather than outcome [8].

- ***Step 7: Pain and Function Monitoring***

Assess pain (VAS scale) and opening range at each visit. Record improvement or relapse.

Red flag: Lack of objective progress notes makes even successful recovery appear undocumented; "no chart, no defense" [9].

- ***Step 8: Complication Management***

If relapse, infection, or deviation occurs, record onset, probable cause, and corrective plan. Obtain fresh consent for any revision surgery.

Red flag: Performing revision without new consent constitutes unauthorized procedure, regardless of intent [10].

- ***Step 9: Long-Term Review and Counseling***

Schedule periodic reviews for one year to ensure function and prevent fibrosis. Document patient education regarding jaw exercises and stress reduction.

Red flag: Failure to issue written long-term exercise plan equals incomplete rehabilitation and legal noncompliance [11].

- ***Step 10: Record Retention and Case Summary***

Compile all notes-diagnosis, imaging, consent, physiotherapy charts, operative report, and follow-up. Retain for minimum 10 years.

Red flag: Missing physiotherapy or follow-up logs undermines the entire defense, even when surgery was textbook-perfect [12].

Legal Defensibility and Documentation Anchors

A defendable TMJ/ankylosis record contains:

- Diagnostic imaging and mouth-opening documentation
- Written consent with recurrence and limitation clauses
- Conservative management record before intervention
- Operative note with joint side, approach, and material traceability
- Physiotherapy and progress documentation
- Long-term review schedule and patient education sheet

This documentation proves anticipation, skill, and continuous care - the three legal shields of joint surgery.

Case Study

A 26-year-old woman underwent TMJ gap arthroplasty for unilateral ankylosis. Postoperatively, she developed restricted opening and facial nerve weakness. The surgeon produced no physiotherapy logs or preoperative consent mentioning possible nerve injury. Court concluded negligence for inadequate disclosure and lack of postoperative documentation, awarding compensation despite technical success.

Case Learnings

1. Diagnosis without documentation is assumption, not evidence.
2. Stepwise conservative-to-surgical escalation must be provable.
3. Every TMJ record must include imaging, physiotherapy, and consent.
4. Traceability of grafts or materials is non-negotiable.
5. Written education and compliance tracking protect both care and credibility.

Quick Checklist

- Detailed history and imaging recorded
- Consent includes recurrence and limitation clause
- Conservative therapy duration noted
- Arthrocentesis/arthroplasty details recorded
- Material and graft traceability documented
- Asepsis and anesthesia log maintained
- Postoperative physiotherapy logged daily
- Pain and movement chart maintained
- Revision consent (if any) filed
- Records retained for minimum 10 years

References

1. *Dimitroulis G. Management of temporomandibular joint disorders: a clinical and legal overview. Aust Dent J. 2018;63(Suppl 1):S65 - S71.*
2. *National Medical Commission (India). Diagnostic Imaging Standards in TMJ Disorders. 2021.*
3. *General Dental Council (UK). Informed Consent and Risk Disclosure Standards. 2013.*
4. *Okeson JP. Management of Temporomandibular Disorders and Occlusion. 8th ed. Elsevier; 2020.*
5. *Nitzan DW. Arthrocentesis: clinical indications and outcomes. J Oral Maxillofac Surg. 2006;64(9):1440 - 1444.*
6. *Dental Council of India. Traceability Guidelines for Alloplastic and Autogenous Materials. 2022.*
7. *Ministry of Health and Family Welfare, India. Asepsis and Operative Documentation Regulations. 2020.*
8. *Kaban LB et al. Surgical management of TMJ ankylosis in children and adults. J Oral Maxillofac Surg. 2009;67(9):1966 - 1978.*
9. *Dental Protection Limited. Physiotherapy Documentation and Legal Accountability. 2021.*
10. *National Medical Commission (India). Consent and Revision Surgery Guidelines. 2021.*
11. *Ministry of Health and Family Welfare, India. Rehabilitation Documentation Standards. 2020.*
12. *General Dental Council (UK). Recordkeeping and Case Retention Regulations. 2013.*

CHAPTER 49

Facial Aesthetic and Orthognathic Surgery - Preoperative Assessment, Patient Expectations, and Legal Safeguards

Facial aesthetic and orthognathic surgeries balance between art and accountability. Patients come seeking transformation, not survival; expectations are personal, emotional, and legally sensitive. Success is measured as much in satisfaction as in symmetry. A single missing consent clause or absent preoperative photograph can convert artistry into liability. This chapter defines the documentation architecture and ethical guardrails for aesthetic and corrective jaw surgeries.

Purpose and Indications

Facial aesthetic and orthognathic procedures aim to correct deformities, asymmetry, or malocclusion while improving facial balance and function. Indications include skeletal discrepancies, occlusal disharmony, or cosmetic dissatisfaction. The legal emphasis lies on comprehensive counseling, photographic documentation, and transparency about limitations and potential relapse [1].

Preparation and Diagnostic Evaluation

Take full facial photographs (frontal, profile, and oblique), lateral cephalogram, panoramic radiograph, and 3D imaging if required. Record occlusion, facial measurements, and psychological readiness.

Red flag: Performing surgery without preoperative imaging or photographs removes the possibility of proving baseline anatomy - an immediate legal vulnerability [2].

- ***Step 1: Informed Consent and Psychological Screening***

Discuss the procedure, aesthetic expectations, healing time, complications (paresthesia, relapse, asymmetry, scarring), and realistic outcomes. Include signed consent mentioning "results may vary," "no guaranteed symmetry," and "possible need for revision."

Red flag: Generic consent lacking "no guarantee" clause invalidates defense in dissatisfaction or cosmetic failure claims [3].

- ***Step 2: Orthodontic and Surgical Planning***

Coordinate with orthodontist for pre-surgical alignment and postoperative stabilization. Document joint consultation notes and treatment sequence.

Red flag: Absence of multidisciplinary planning record in orthognathic cases equates to negligence of coordination; courts view it as fragmented care [4].

- ***Step 3: Preoperative Mock-Up and Simulation***

Prepare digital or manual mock-ups showing anticipated facial changes. Share with patient and record acknowledgment of discussion.

Red flag: Verbal explanations without written or visual documentation of expected results lead to "unmet expectation" litigation - among the most common aesthetic disputes [5].

- ***Step 4: Anesthesia and Surgical Field Preparation***

Record anesthesia type, airway plan, blood loss estimation, and asepsis measures. Photograph draped field and note assistant names.

Red flag: Postoperative infection or nerve injury without asepsis log or operative record implies procedural negligence [6].

- ***Step 5: Osteotomy and Fixation***

Describe incision approach, osteotomy type (Le Fort, sagittal split, genioplasty), fixation method, and hardware details (manufacturer, batch, screw count).

Red flag: Missing hardware traceability violates implant regulations; without batch data, manufacturer and surgeon liability blur into each other [7].

- ***Step 6: Intraoperative Verification***

Record occlusion, midline alignment, and facial symmetry before closure. Photograph intraoperative positioning if feasible.

Red flag: No intraoperative verification record weakens defense in asymmetry or malocclusion disputes [8].

- ***Step 7: Wound Closure and Hemostasis***

Document closure layers, suture material, and estimated blood loss.

Red flag: Postoperative bleeding or hematoma without closure note appears as incomplete or careless surgery [9].

- ***Step 8: Postoperative Instructions and Care***

Provide printed sheet detailing swelling timeline, diet, oral hygiene, and appearance expectations. Schedule regular follow-up.

Red flag: Lack of written discharge advice leads to claims of neglect in prolonged swelling or sensory loss cases [10].

- ***Step 9: Follow-Up and Result Documentation***

Record weekly progress for six weeks, then at three, six, and twelve months. Photograph healing and occlusal stability. Compare with baseline images.

Red flag: Absence of serial photos or measurements makes it impossible to defend against subjective dissatisfaction claims [11].

- ***Step 10: Revision Planning and Final Disclosure***

If residual deformity or relapse occurs, document cause (biologic, mechanical, patient noncompliance) and discuss revision options with written consent.

Red flag: Performing revision without updated consent or explanation constitutes unauthorized intervention under legal scrutiny [12].

Legal Defensibility and Documentation Anchors

A defensible aesthetic/orthognathic case file must include:

- Preoperative photographs and imaging
- Psychological and orthodontic consultation records
- Mock-up/simulation discussion and acknowledgment
- Written consent with "no guarantee" clause

- Surgical notes and implant traceability
- Serial photographic follow-ups
- Revision consent (if applicable)

These records prove informed choice, shared responsibility, and continuous care.

Case Study

A 25-year-old woman underwent bimaxillary orthognathic surgery for jaw asymmetry. Post-surgery, she alleged worsened appearance and numbness. The surgeon lacked preoperative photographs, mock-up consent, or traceability logs. Despite technically correct surgery, the court ruled partial negligence for inadequate counseling and documentation gaps.

Case Learnings

1. Every aesthetic or corrective jaw surgery begins with consent and ends with proof of discussion.
2. Baseline photographs and simulations are non-negotiable.
3. Coordination and documentation define professionalism more than results.
4. "No guarantee" and "possible revision" clauses protect integrity, not just legality.
5. Photographs, not words, close disputes.

Quick Checklist

- Baseline photographs and 3D imaging completed
- Orthodontic and psychological evaluation recorded
- Mock-up and simulation discussed and signed
- Written consent with "no guarantee" clause obtained
- Asepsis, anesthesia, and fixation documented
- Hardware batch details recorded
- Postoperative instructions signed

- Follow-up photographs archived
- Revision consent filed (if applicable)
- Records retained minimum 10 years

References

1. *Bell WH, Guerrero CA. Distraction Osteogenesis of the Facial Skeleton. BC Decker; 2007.*
2. *Ministry of Health and Family Welfare, India. Imaging and Preoperative Documentation Standards. 2020.*
3. *General Dental Council (UK). Informed Consent in Cosmetic and Elective Surgery. 2013.*
4. *National Medical Commission (India). Multidisciplinary Documentation Requirements. 2021.*
5. *Baker DC, Shaw WW. The art and responsibility of facial aesthetic surgery. Plast Reconstr Surg. 1989;84(1):5 - 15.*
6. *Dental Council of India. Aseptic and Operative Field Documentation Guidelines. 2022.*
7. *Government of India. Medical Device Traceability Rules. 2019.*
8. *Dental Protection Limited. Aesthetic and Orthognathic Surgery Litigation Cases. 2021.*
9. *Ministry of Health and Family Welfare, India. Operative Note and Hemostasis Standards. 2020.*
10. *National Medical Commission (India). Postoperative Counseling and Patient Communication. 2021.*
11. *Dental Council of India. Serial Photography and Recordkeeping in Cosmetic Procedures. 2022.*
12. *General Dental Council (UK). Revision Surgery and Updated Consent Regulations. 2013.*

CHAPTER 50

Facial Nerve Injuries and Parotid Surgery - Prevention, Repair, and Legal Accountability

Facial nerve injury is among the most feared complications in oral and maxillofacial surgery. One wrong plane of dissection can erase expression, confidence, and trust in seconds. Patients rarely forgive loss of smile symmetry, and courts rarely forgive missing documentation. This chapter explains how clinical precision, foresight, and written clarity transform a potential catastrophe into a defensible event.

Purpose and Indications

Facial nerve management during parotid, TMJ, or trauma surgery focuses on preserving function while treating pathology such as tumors, cysts, or fractures. Indications include benign and malignant parotid lesions, trauma with nerve transection, or decompression for neuropathies. The legal obligation extends beyond the operation-to demonstrate anticipation, consent, intraoperative vigilance, and transparent follow-up [1].

Preparation and Preoperative Evaluation

Perform baseline facial nerve examination-raise eyebrows, close eyes, smile, puff cheeks-and record symmetry. Document results with photographs or video. Obtain imaging (MRI, CT) to define lesion proximity to the nerve.

Red flag: Operating without baseline nerve documentation removes all ability to prove pre-existing weakness or surgical care; the default assumption is iatrogenic injury [2].

- ***Step 1: Informed Consent and Counseling***

Discuss potential outcomes including transient paresis, permanent paralysis, facial asymmetry, salivary fistula, Frey's syndrome, and need for secondary repair. Obtain written consent mentioning "temporary or permanent facial weakness possible."

Red flag: Omission of facial nerve risk clause in consent is indefensible in any subsequent facial paralysis claim [3].

- ***Step 2: Surgical Planning and Exposure***

Plan incision (Blair's, modified facelift, or preauricular) to protect branches. Mark landmarks-tragal pointer, posterior belly of digastric, tympanomastoid suture.

Red flag: Lack of recorded surgical plan or marking diagram invalidates defense in nerve transection disputes, even if technique was correct [4].

- ***Step 3: Asepsis and Anesthesia***

Ensure sterile preparation, nerve monitoring equipment readiness, and anesthetic record (agent, dose, side).

Red flag: Postoperative infection or nerve injury without asepsis or anesthesia documentation implies poor operative conduct [5].

- ***Step 4: Identification and Dissection***

Identify main trunk near stylomastoid foramen using nerve stimulator. Dissect under magnification. Avoid traction or cautery near branches. Record identification landmarks and intraoperative findings.

Red flag: Absent operative note of nerve identification is equivalent to "blind dissection" in legal evaluation [6].

- ***Step 5: Tumor or Lesion Removal***

Excise lesion preserving branches when possible; if nerve sacrifice required, document extent, rationale, and patient's prior consent for possible grafting.

Red flag: Removing lesion with unconsented nerve sacrifice constitutes unauthorized procedure and malpractice under consent law [7].

- ***Step 6: Nerve Repair or Grafting***

If transection occurs, perform immediate microsurgical repair or cable graft (great auricular/sural nerve). Record gap length, technique, magnification, and suture material.

Red flag: Performing repair without documentation of timing and graft source breaches surgical traceability standards [8].

- ***Step 7: Hemostasis and Closure***

Ensure hemostasis, drain placement, and layered closure. Record drain type, site, and removal schedule.

Red flag: Postoperative hematoma or infection without drain record implies incomplete closure documentation [9].

- ***Step 8: Postoperative Nerve Monitoring and Care***

Assess facial movement daily-eye closure, smile, and forehead wrinkles. Record progress and use eye protection if lagophthalmos present.

Red flag: No postoperative nerve assessment or charting converts transient neuropraxia into presumed permanent negligence [10].

- ***Step 9: Physiotherapy and Secondary Repair***

Initiate physiotherapy by day 7 if paresis persists. Record referral and progress. For unresolved paralysis beyond 6 months, consider nerve grafting or muscle transfer. Document referral discussions.

Red flag: Absence of documented referral or rehabilitation plan after nerve injury is legally equated to abandonment of care [11].

- ***Step 10: Long-Term Documentation and Reporting***

Photograph recovery stages, record EMG or nerve conduction results, and maintain file for 10 years. Report any permanent disability to the relevant medical board if applicable.

Red flag: Non-reporting of permanent facial paralysis under disability notification law is a statutory violation [12].

Legal Defensibility and Documentation Anchors

A defendable facial nerve or parotid case includes:

- Baseline nerve function record with photographs/videos
- Imaging correlating lesion to nerve path
- Written consent including nerve injury risk
- Operative note with landmarks and nerve identification details

- Graft or repair record with traceability
- Postoperative nerve monitoring log
- Physiotherapy and referral documentation
- Disability reporting (if applicable)

This structured record converts high-risk surgery into a legally transparent event.

Case Study

A 45-year-old woman underwent superficial parotidectomy for pleomorphic adenoma. Postoperatively, she developed facial nerve palsy. The surgeon had no preoperative facial symmetry record or consent mentioning nerve risk. Despite correct technique, the court ruled negligence for "failure to disclose risk and baseline documentation," awarding damages for cosmetic disfigurement.

Case Learnings

1. Always photograph or video-record preoperative facial function.
2. Written consent must specifically mention facial nerve risk.
3. Every operative note must list identification landmarks.
4. Early physiotherapy and documentation show continuity of care.
5. Transparency before and after surgery defends honesty, not perfection.

Quick Checklist

- Baseline nerve exam and photos recorded
- Consent includes facial nerve and asymmetry risk
- Imaging defines lesion-nerve proximity
- Asepsis and anesthesia records maintained
- Nerve identification landmarks noted
- Graft or repair documented with details
- Drain placement and closure logged
- Postoperative nerve function monitored

- Rehabilitation and referral records filed
- Records archived minimum 10 years

References

1. *Bailey BJ, Johnson JT, Newlands SD. Head and Neck Surgery: Otolaryngology. 6th ed. Wolters Kluwer; 2021.*
2. *National Medical Commission (India). Preoperative Functional Documentation Guidelines. 2021.*
3. *General Dental Council (UK). Surgical Consent and Risk Communication Standards. 2013.*
4. *Dulguerov P, Marchal F, Gysin C. Anatomical landmarks for parotid surgery. Arch Otolaryngol Head Neck Surg. 1999;125(3):308 - 314.*
5. *Ministry of Health and Family Welfare, India. Operative Asepsis and Anesthesia Documentation Protocol. 2020.*
6. *Dental Protection Limited. Facial Nerve Litigation and Prevention Strategies. 2021.*
7. *National Medical Commission (India). Consent for Nerve Sacrifice and High-Risk Procedures. 2021.*
8. *Kahn JB, Lanzino G. Facial nerve repair: technique and timing. Neurosurg Clin N Am. 2018;29(2):267 - 273.*
9. *Ministry of Health and Family Welfare, India. Drainage and Hemostasis Recordkeeping Rules. 2020.*
10. *Gillenwater AM, Lewin JS. Postoperative care of the facial nerve patient. Otolaryngol Clin North Am. 2016;49(2):423 - 436.*
11. *Dental Council of India. Rehabilitation and Referral in Facial Nerve Injury. 2022.*
12. *Government of India. Persons with Disabilities Act (Medical Reporting Obligations). 2016.*

CHAPTER 51

Head and Neck Tumors - Biopsy, Margins, Reconstruction, and Legal Chain of Custody

Tumor surgery tests the surgeon's conscience as much as skill. Every incision removes disease but also evidence. Courts do not retry cancer-they retrace paperwork: who biopsied, who labeled, who consented, and who informed. A technically flawless surgery without a documented chain of custody or consent reads as a legal amputation of accountability. This chapter unites oncologic precision with medico-legal discipline.

Purpose and Indications

Head and neck tumor management includes diagnostic biopsy, wide local excision, neck dissection, and reconstruction. Indications range from benign neoplasms to squamous cell carcinoma. Medico-legally, the primary duties are accurate diagnosis, histopathology confirmation, traceable specimen handling, and documented informed consent for both excision and possible disfigurement [1].

Preparation and Diagnostic Workup

Record detailed history-tobacco use, duration, ulceration, dysphagia, bleeding, or lymphadenopathy. Perform intraoral and neck examination with diagrammatic notes. Obtain imaging (CT, MRI, or PET-CT).

Red flag: Performing excision before histopathologic confirmation of malignancy is indefensible - every tumor deserves diagnosis before scalpel [2].

- ***Step 1: Biopsy and Specimen Handling***

Perform incisional biopsy avoiding necrotic tissue and vital structures.

Immediately place specimen in 10% formalin and label with patient name, site, and date. Complete requisition form signed by both surgeon and pathologist.

Red flag: Unlabeled or mismatched specimen jars constitute a breach of evidence chain - legally equivalent to data tampering [3].

- ***Step 2: Informed Consent for Definitive Surgery***

Discuss diagnosis, extent of resection, possible bone involvement, lymph node dissection, and cosmetic/functional consequences. Include written consent mentioning "risk of disfigurement, speech and swallowing difficulty, and possible recurrence."

Red flag: Generic consent for "tumor removal" without mention of functional loss or reconstructive intent invalidates defense during disfigurement litigation [4].

- ***Step 3: Multidisciplinary Planning***

Coordinate with oncologist, pathologist, and anesthetist. Document tumor board or multidisciplinary meeting notes.

Red flag: Absence of multidisciplinary discussion record is interpreted as unilateral decision-making, often cited in negligence claims for incomplete clearance [5].

- ***Step 4: Asepsis, Anesthesia, and Marking***

Record asepsis protocol, anesthesia details, and surgical markings for margins and vital structures.

Red flag: Postoperative infection or margin error without operative record reflects absence of standardized protocol [6].

- ***Step 5: Resection and Margins***

Excise tumor with 1 - 2 cm clinical margins (as per site). Label margins separately and send in individual formalin containers with orientation (superior, inferior, deep).

Red flag: Sending a single specimen without labeled margins erases traceability; this is treated as gross negligence in oncologic documentation [7].

- ***Step 6: Frozen Section and Intraoperative Confirmation***

When available, request frozen section to confirm margin status. Record results in operative notes.

Red flag: Proceeding without margin confirmation where facilities exist shows deviation from standard of care [8].

- ***Step 7: Reconstruction and Closure***

Plan primary closure, local flap, or free flap as indicated. Record flap type, donor site, microvascular status, and implant materials with batch details.

Red flag: Missing graft or flap documentation breaks traceability; in legal audits, every flap must have a name, date, and record [9].

- ***Step 8: Postoperative Monitoring and Reporting***

Document vitals, flap color, drainage, and nerve function daily. Record all complications (hematoma, infection, flap failure) with management steps.

Red flag: No daily postoperative note for oncology patients equals "no care rendered" - defensibility collapses regardless of outcome [10].

- ***Step 9: Histopathology Correlation and Communication***

Record receipt and result of histopathology report. Note margin status (clear/involved) and staging (TNM). Communicate findings to patient and oncology team with date and signature.

Red flag: Absence of communication record or staging note is legally interpreted as failure to disclose disease status [11].

- ***Step 10: Follow-Up and Continuity***

Schedule follow-ups at one month, three months, and quarterly for two years. Record recurrence status and rehabilitation (speech, swallowing, esthetics). Retain all reports for 10 years.

Red flag: Missing follow-up notes post-oncologic surgery implies abandonment - courts consider it as professional neglect even in remission [12].

Legal Defensibility and Documentation Anchors

A defendable head and neck oncology record includes:

- Biopsy and specimen labeling with requisition proof
- Written consent specifying disfigurement and recurrence risk
- Multidisciplinary planning notes
- Labeled margin specimens and operative diagram

- Frozen section record (if applicable)
- Reconstruction details with graft/flap traceability
- Postoperative monitoring logs
- Histopathology report with patient communication record
- Long-term follow-up documentation

This record builds a seamless legal chain - from biopsy to recovery - that can withstand scrutiny line by line.

Case Study

A 56-year-old man underwent tongue carcinoma excision. Margins were unlabelled and no frozen section requested. Recurrence occurred within six months. The court found negligence due to lack of margin documentation and absence of tumor board record, despite otherwise competent surgery.

Case Learnings

1. The scalpel may cure, but only documentation proves it.
2. Label every margin as though it will be questioned later - because it will.
3. Multidisciplinary planning notes are the shield against unilateral blame.
4. Communicate histopathology results formally and document it.
5. The chain of custody is the legal backbone of oncology.

Quick Checklist

- Detailed history and imaging recorded
- Biopsy performed and specimen labeled
- Written consent includes disfigurement and recurrence risks
- Multidisciplinary notes attached
- Asepsis, anesthesia, and marking recorded
- Margins labeled and oriented
- Frozen section result documented (if done)

- Reconstruction and graft details filed
- Histopathology and staging communicated
- Follow-up notes retained 10 years

References

1. *Shah JP, Patel SG, Singh B. Head and Neck Surgery and Oncology. 5th ed. Elsevier; 2020.*
2. *National Medical Commission (India). Preoperative Diagnostic Documentation Standards. 2021.*
3. *Ministry of Health and Family Welfare, India. Specimen Handling and Chain of Custody Rules. 2020.*
4. *General Dental Council (UK). Consent and Cosmetic Disfigurement Disclosure Standards. 2013.*
5. *National Cancer Grid (India). Multidisciplinary Tumor Board Guidelines. 2021.*
6. *Dental Council of India. Surgical Asepsis and Operative Planning Documentation. 2022.*
7. *American Joint Committee on Cancer. AJCC Cancer Staging Manual. 8th ed. Springer; 2017.*
8. *Ministry of Health and Family Welfare, India. Frozen Section and Oncologic Margin Protocols. 2020.*
9. *Dental Protection Limited. Oncologic Flap Reconstruction Litigation Review. 2021.*
10. *National Medical Commission (India). Postoperative Monitoring Documentation Standards. 2021.*
11. *Government of India. Patient Information and Communication Guidelines. 2020.*
12. *Dental Council of India. Follow-Up and Continuity of Oncologic Care Standards. 2022.*

SECTION 6

Oral Pathology, Radiology, and Diagnostic Sciences

Diagnosis is where dentistry begins and where every courtroom question eventually returns. Before any handpiece spins or flap is raised, a clinician must first see — clearly, completely, and in writing. This section sharpens that vision, teaching not only how to interpret disease but how to prove you recognized it in time.

It starts with the foundations of radiographic documentation — exposure accuracy, labeling, and archiving — because a film or digital image is not just a clinical tool; it is sworn evidence. The following chapters move through oral pathology, mucosal lesions, cysts, tumors, and early cancer detection, teaching a structured way to describe findings, select biopsy sites, and preserve specimens with a documented chain of custody.

You'll learn how to recognize radiolucencies and opacities without ambiguity, to use cautious language that informs without misleading, and to refer decisively when malignancy cannot be ruled out. The section insists that every report bears your signature, date, and impression — because a diagnosis without identity has no credibility.

The medicolegal link is constant: a missed shadow becomes a missed chance, and a missing note becomes negligence. Through examples and case reflections, you'll see how radiologic oversight, misfiled pathology reports, or uncommunicated results often weigh heavier than technical errors.

By its close, this section restores the dignity of diagnosis. It reminds you that the most powerful act in dentistry isn't cutting or curing — it's noticing early and recording honestly. In the end, seeing well and writing well are the same skill viewed through different lenses.

CHAPTER 52

Oral Pathology and Biopsy Protocols - Diagnostic Accuracy, Sample Preservation, and Legal Integrity of Reports

Diagnosis begins with tissue. A single biopsy can define life expectancy, treatment plan, or lawsuit. Courts never ask if you cut well-they ask if you labeled well, fixed well, and informed well. Oral pathology work demands surgical precision in the mouth and clerical precision on paper. This chapter lays out the scientific and legal anatomy of biopsy collection, preservation, reporting, and documentation.

Purpose and Indications

Biopsy serves to confirm diagnosis in oral mucosal lesions, cysts, tumors, and unexplained swellings. Indications include persistent ulcerations, leukoplakia, erythroplakia, or radiolucent lesions. The legal objective is verifiable specimen identity, integrity of transport, and documented communication of results to patient and referring clinician [1].

Preparation and Clinical Evaluation

Record lesion size, site, color, texture, and duration. Photograph before biopsy. Obtain medical history (anticoagulants, diabetes, immunosuppression) and written consent mentioning "diagnostic purpose, minor bleeding, pain, and possible repeat procedure."

Red flag: Performing biopsy without photographic evidence or consent removes all proof of preoperative condition - legally indefensible if lesion worsens [2].

- ***Step 1: Site Selection and Technique Choice***

Choose representative, viable tissue from lesion edge including normal margin. Use incisional or excisional approach depending on size and suspicion level.

Red flag: Sampling necrotic or non-representative area leads to false negatives; legally termed "diagnostic negligence" if misdiagnosis follows [3].

- ***Step 2: Asepsis and Local Anesthesia***

Maintain sterile field; infiltrate anesthetic at least 5 mm away from lesion to avoid artifact. Record drug, dose, and site.

Red flag: Tissue artifact from direct infiltration without note of technique implies careless handling; patient can claim "poor sample collection" [4].

- ***Step 3: Tissue Handling and Fixation***

Transfer specimen immediately to 10% neutral buffered formalin, volume at least 10 times tissue size. Label jar with patient name, site, date, and operator initials.

Red flag: Any unlabeled, leaking, or formalin-deficient jar violates bio-specimen transport rules-courts classify it as evidence contamination [5].

- ***Step 4: Requisition Form and Chain of Custody***

Complete requisition with patient demographics, clinical findings, provisional diagnosis, and sketch of biopsy site. Both surgeon and pathologist must sign.

Red flag: Absence of requisition form or missing signature breaks the chain of custody, invalidating report credibility in litigation [6].

- ***Step 5: Transport and Laboratory Communication***

Deliver specimen within 24 hours; maintain record of dispatch time and receiver signature.

Red flag: Delay in transport without reason allows opposing counsel to allege "sample degradation" leading to false results [7].

- ***Step 6: Pathology Report Review and Interpretation***

Upon receipt, read report carefully, confirm diagnosis with clinical findings, and record correlation note in file. If incongruent, request re-evaluation or second opinion.

Red flag: Accepting inconclusive report without follow-up action constitutes professional negligence under diagnostic accountability norms [8].

- ***Step 7: Patient Communication and Documentation***

Explain result, prognosis, and next steps in writing. Obtain signature acknowledging receipt of report and discussion.

Red flag: Verbal disclosure alone leaves patient free to claim "never informed of diagnosis" - courts prioritize written proof [9].

- ***Step 8: Record Retention and Report Authentication***

Store histopathology report, requisition, and specimen ID in record for at least 10 years. Maintain scanned copies of labeling and report acknowledgment.

Red flag: Missing biopsy ID or digital backup breaks continuity; legally treated as poor record management under clinical establishment regulations [10].

- ***Step 9: Error Reporting and Correction***

If labeling or transcription error discovered, issue immediate correction letter co-signed by both clinician and pathologist, preserving original copy.

Red flag: Quietly replacing reports or relabeling samples after issue is viewed as deliberate data falsification-criminal offense under medical ethics law [11].

- ***Step 10: Quality Assurance and Audit Readiness***

Participate in periodic audit of biopsy labeling, fixation, and report dispatch. Maintain log of specimen IDs, dispatch dates, and receiving pathologist details.

Red flag: Inability to produce specimen logbook or audit report during legal review equates to documentation failure and institutional negligence [12].

Legal Defensibility and Documentation Anchors

A defensible biopsy case includes:

- Clinical and photographic lesion record
- Written consent with diagnostic disclosure

- Labeled specimen and fixation details
- Signed requisition and transport log
- Correlation note and report acknowledgment
- Error correction record (if any)
- Audit log and report retention for 10 years

Together these form a transparent trail-from suspicion to certainty-that cannot be broken in litigation.

Case Study

A 50-year-old man underwent biopsy of a non-healing tongue ulcer. The specimen jar was unlabeled, and the report indicated benign ulceration. Six months later, carcinoma was diagnosed. The hospital could not trace the original tissue. The court ruled institutional negligence for loss of evidence and absence of labeling record, awarding compensation for delayed diagnosis.

Case Learnings

1. Every biopsy is both a medical act and legal document.
2. Label first, cut second-never reverse the order.
3. Photographs and requisition forms are equal to operative notes.
4. Written communication closes diagnostic loops.
5. Traceability is not optional; it's the core of credibility.

Quick Checklist

- Lesion photographed and charted
- Written consent obtained
- Representative tissue selected
- Aseptic technique and anesthesia recorded
- Specimen fixed and labeled immediately
- Requisition form signed and dispatched
- Report correlated and acknowledged

- Error corrections documented
- Audit log maintained
- All records archived for 10 years

References

1. *Neville BW, Damm DD, Allen CM, Chi AC. Oral and Maxillofacial Pathology. 5th ed. Elsevier; 2022.*
2. *Ministry of Health and Family Welfare, India. Preoperative Consent and Clinical Photography Standards. 2020.*
3. *Speight PM, Takata T. Diagnostic challenges in oral pathology. J Pathol. 2018;244(4):407 - 419.*
4. *Dental Council of India. Biopsy and Tissue Handling Protocols. 2022.*
5. *Government of India. Biomedical Waste and Specimen Transport Regulations. 2016.*
6. *National Medical Commission (India). Chain of Custody in Clinical Specimens. 2021.*
7. *World Health Organization. Laboratory Specimen Collection and Transport Guidelines. Geneva; 2018.*
8. *General Dental Council (UK). Diagnostic Accountability and Second Opinion Standards. 2013.*
9. *Ministry of Health and Family Welfare, India. Patient Communication and Result Disclosure Regulations. 2020.*
10. *Dental Protection Limited. Record Retention and Documentation in Diagnostic Procedures. 2021.*
11. *Government of India. Medical Ethics and Data Integrity Rules. 2019.*
12. *National Accreditation Board for Testing and Calibration Laboratories (NABL). Pathology Quality Assurance Manual. 2020.*

CHAPTER 53

Oral Cancer Screening and Early Detection - Community Protocols, Diagnostic Responsibility, and Legal Duties of Disclosure

Early diagnosis of oral cancer saves lives, but late documentation ends careers. The disease often begins as a white patch or ulcer dismissed in haste. Every missed lesion later reappears in court as "failure to detect." This chapter frames screening and detection not only as a public health duty but as a legal obligation - built on vigilance, communication, and traceable records.

Purpose and Indications

Oral cancer screening aims to identify precancerous or malignant lesions at an early, treatable stage. Indications include tobacco or alcohol use, chronic irritation, persistent ulcers, leukoplakia, erythroplakia, or unexplained swelling. The legal dimension is clear: every examination, however routine, must leave behind a dated, written trail that proves attention was given [1].

Preparation and Risk Assessment

Record tobacco, alcohol, betel nut, or occupational exposures. Document any symptoms - pain, bleeding, altered taste, difficulty swallowing. Record findings even if normal.

Red flag: Failure to record "no abnormality detected" is as risky as missing a lesion - legally interpreted as absence of examination [2].

- ***Step 1: Clinical Examination Protocol***

Inspect lips, buccal mucosa, tongue (dorsal, ventral, lateral), floor of mouth, gingiva, and oropharynx under good illumination. Palpate neck nodes and floor of mouth.

Red flag: Incomplete oral cavity documentation makes the record indefensible if later malignancy appears in an unrecorded site [3].

- ***Step 2: Use of Adjunctive Tools***

Use toluidine blue staining, brush biopsy, autofluorescence, or cytology when indicated. Record indication and results.

Red flag: Employing screening aids without noting reason or result creates a gap where defensive medicine fails - "technology used, not recorded" equals "not used" in audit [4].

- ***Step 3: Patient Counseling and Risk Communication***

Explain findings and risk factors. Advise cessation of tobacco, alcohol, or irritants. Provide written leaflet or note.

Red flag: Verbal counseling without documented advice leads to allegations of "failure to warn" when cancer develops later [5].

- ***Step 4: Referral and Follow-Up for Suspicious Lesions***

Refer all suspicious lesions for biopsy or specialist evaluation. Record referral details, date, and destination.

Red flag: Delayed or undocumented referral is legally equated to diagnostic delay - one of the most common causes of compensation in oral cancer cases [6].

- ***Step 5: Documentation and Coding***

Use standard nomenclature for lesion description (location, size, color, surface, induration). Record photographic evidence with patient consent.

Red flag: Absent lesion coding or photographs leave no proof that early signs were noticed - undermining credibility in "missed diagnosis" claims [7].

- ***Step 6: Biopsy and Confirmation (if performed in clinic)***

Follow standard biopsy and labeling protocols as detailed in the previous chapter. Record communication of report and next steps.

Red flag: Receiving malignant biopsy report without documented patient disclosure breaches duty of care and informed follow-up responsibility [8].

- ***Step 7: Community and Institutional Screening Programs***

During camps or outreach, record participant demographics, findings, referrals, and counseling materials distributed. Maintain signed register.

Red flag: Missing participant logs or follow-up documentation turns well-meaning camps into untraceable events - no proof, no protection [9].

- ***Step 8: Integration with National Health Records***

Submit data to oral cancer registries or regional health authorities as required. Keep copy of submission acknowledgement.

Red flag: Failure to report findings from institutional programs violates public health regulations under disease surveillance mandates [10].

- ***Step 9: Legal Reporting and Communication Duty***

In confirmed malignancy, record written communication to patient and referring doctor within 48 hours. Keep copy of letter or email.

Red flag: Delayed communication or undocumented disclosure invites litigation for "withholding diagnosis," a serious professional offense [11].

- ***Step 10: Periodic Review and Audit***

Audit screening outcomes quarterly: number of cases examined, suspicious lesions found, biopsies performed, and confirmed malignancies.

Red flag: No periodic audit equals unverified quality - unfit for accreditation or defense in medico-legal review [12].

Legal Defensibility and Documentation Anchors

A legally sound oral cancer screening record includes:

- Risk factor documentation
- Complete oral examination record
- Adjunctive test use and results
- Counseling and written advice
- Referral with proof of dispatch
- Biopsy and report communication notes

- Screening camp registers and reports
- Annual audit records

Such comprehensive documentation shows care, continuity, and compliance - the triad of legal protection.

Case Study

A 42-year-old tobacco user visited a dental clinic for scaling. The dentist noticed a white patch but gave no written advice or referral. Two years later, squamous cell carcinoma developed at the same site. The patient alleged delayed diagnosis. Court found negligence for lack of recorded counseling or referral, despite routine visit context.

Case Learnings

1. Every oral exam is a potential cancer screening - documentation proves it.
2. "No abnormality" must be written, not assumed.
3. Written counseling transforms advice into evidence.
4. Early referral and proof of dispatch carry more legal weight than treatment.
5. Screening without records is not screening - it's exposure.

Quick Checklist

- Risk factors recorded
- Full oral cavity and neck examined
- Adjunctive screening tests logged
- Written counseling and advice given
- Referral with proof documented
- Biopsy and communication recorded
- Screening camp register maintained
- Data submitted to registry (if required)
- Quarterly audit performed
- Records archived 10 years

References

1. *Warnakulasuriya S. Global epidemiology of oral and oropharyngeal cancer. Oral Oncol. 2020;102:104557.*
2. *Ministry of Health and Family Welfare, India. Clinical Examination Documentation Protocols. 2020.*
3. *Neville BW et al. Oral and Maxillofacial Pathology. 5th ed. Elsevier; 2022.*
4. *Lingen MW et al. Adjunctive diagnostic technologies for oral cancer detection. J Am Dent Assoc. 2017;148(9):663 - 672.*
5. *National Medical Commission (India). Patient Counseling and Risk Communication Guidelines. 2021.*
6. *Dental Protection Limited. Delayed Diagnosis and Referral Claims in Oral Oncology. 2021.*
7. *World Health Organization. Standardized Recording and Reporting of Oral Lesions. Geneva; 2018.*
8. *General Dental Council (UK). Disclosure and Communication of Diagnostic Results Standards. 2013.*
9. *Government of India. National Programme for Prevention and Control of Cancer, Diabetes, CVD and Stroke (NPCDCS). 2022.*
10. *Ministry of Health and Family Welfare, India. Disease Surveillance and Reporting Obligations. 2020.*
11. *National Medical Commission (India). Legal Duty of Disclosure in Malignant Diagnoses. 2021.*
12. *Dental Council of India. Audit and Quality Assurance Standards in Screening Programs. 2022.*

CHAPTER 54

Oral and Maxillofacial Radiology - Imaging Protocols, Interpretation Errors, and Legal Documentation Standards

A radiograph is both a diagnostic map and a legal record. It outlives the patient, the surgeon, and every spoken word. Courts don't argue over what was seen-they examine what was recorded, reported, and retained. In oral and maxillofacial practice, imaging carries a unique burden: clarity, interpretation, and traceability. This chapter establishes the standards of radiologic diligence and the medico-legal consequences of every missed shadow.

Purpose and Indications

Oral radiology provides anatomical, pathological, and surgical insight for diagnosis, planning, and postoperative evaluation. Indications include trauma, cysts, tumors, impactions, bone pathologies, and implant assessment. The legal imperative: every image must be justified, interpreted, dated, and stored-nothing "routine" about radiation [1].

Preparation and Imaging Justification

Record indication for every radiograph-symptom, site, and suspected pathology. Confirm pregnancy status for females of reproductive age. Note exposure parameters (kVp, mA, time).

Red flag: Taking or repeating radiographs without indication or consent breaches radiation safety law and constitutes medico-legal overexposure [2].

- ***Step 1: Informed Consent and Radiation Safety***

Explain purpose, minimal radiation risk, and necessity. Use lead apron and thyroid collar. Obtain verbal or written consent for high-dose imaging (CBCT, CT).

Red flag: Missing consent for CBCT or repeated radiographs violates radiation protection regulations and is indefensible if complications arise [3].

- ***Step 2: Equipment Calibration and Operator Competence***

Ensure machine calibration every 6 - 12 months by certified physicist. Maintain calibration log and operator radiation safety certificate.

Red flag: Equipment without calibration record invalidates all imaging evidence in legal proceedings; courts disregard unverified images [4].

- ***Step 3: Image Acquisition Protocol***

Use appropriate field size and exposure settings to minimize dose. Record patient ID, date, and site on image.

Red flag: Anonymous or mislabeled images have zero evidentiary value-equivalent to unverified data [5].

- ***Step 4: Image Interpretation and Reporting***

Interpret every radiograph systematically-location, size, border, relation to teeth or structures, and possible differential diagnoses. Sign and date report.

Red flag: Taking radiographs without written interpretation makes any later claim of "missed lesion" indefensible; "seen but undocumented" equals "not seen" [6].

- ***Step 5: Double Reading and Peer Review (When Doubtful)***

For ambiguous or suspicious findings, seek second opinion or radiologist review. Record reason and communication.

Red flag: Failure to consult when findings unclear constitutes diagnostic negligence; law expects escalation of doubt [7].

- ***Step 6: Communication of Findings to Patient and Clinician***

Convey results verbally and in writing; provide copy of report. Record acknowledgment in file.

Red flag: Not communicating significant findings-especially pathologic lesions-violates duty of disclosure; omission equals concealment [8].

- ***Step 7: Data Storage and Backup***

Archive all radiographs (digital or analog) with patient ID, date, and indication. Maintain digital backups for minimum 10 years; store CBCT/CT files in DICOM format.

Red flag: Lost or corrupted radiographic data without backup constitutes breach of medical record retention laws [9].

- ***Step 8: Error Reporting and Correction***

If misinterpretation discovered later, issue addendum report with date, reason, and re-interpretation. Retain original report; do not overwrite.

Red flag: Altering or deleting prior report without annotation is treated as record manipulation - a punishable ethical breach [10].

- ***Step 9: Radiation Protection Compliance***

Display radiation warning signs, maintain dosimeter logs, and record cumulative exposure for staff. Retain safety audit certificates.

Red flag: Absence of radiation safety officer's records or dosimeter logs during inspection is regulatory violation under Atomic Energy Act [11].

- ***Step 10: Legal Readiness and Expert Testimony***

In litigation, radiographs are admissible only if authentic, traceable, and interpreted by qualified personnel. Maintain credentials and registration proof of reporting practitioner.

Red flag: Reports signed by unqualified personnel or unsigned altogether are inadmissible as expert evidence [12].

Legal Defensibility and Documentation Anchors

A defendable radiology record includes:

- Justified indication and exposure record
- Consent and radiation safety compliance proof
- Labeled, dated, and authenticated image
- Written interpretation and communication note
- Peer review or second opinion record (if any)

- Secure storage and backup logs
- Radiation audit and calibration certificates

This complete chain demonstrates prudence, compliance, and accountability - three pillars of radiologic legality.

Case Study

A 48-year-old patient later diagnosed with mandibular cyst sued for delayed detection. The earlier radiograph had shown the lesion faintly, but the dentist had neither reported it nor documented any interpretation. Court found negligence for "failure to diagnose from existing evidence" and "absence of written radiographic report," awarding damages despite technical competence.

Case Learnings

1. Radiographs without written reports are silent witnesses - they defend no one.
2. Every exposure must have reason, record, and report.
3. Consent protects intent; labeling protects identity.
4. Peer review of doubt strengthens legal defense.
5. Calibration and safety records are the invisible proof of professional diligence.

Quick Checklist

- Indication for imaging recorded
- Consent (especially for CBCT/CT) obtained
- Machine calibration and safety logs maintained
- Image labeled with patient ID and date
- Interpretation written, signed, and dated
- Communication to patient/clinician recorded
- Second opinion documented if needed
- Data stored and backed up securely
- Radiation audit and dosimeter logs filed

- Records archived minimum 10 years

References

1. *White SC, Pharoah MJ. Oral Radiology: Principles and Interpretation. 9th ed. Elsevier; 2023.*
2. *Government of India. Atomic Energy (Radiation Protection) Rules. 2004.*
3. *Ministry of Health and Family Welfare, India. Diagnostic Imaging Consent Standards. 2020.*
4. *Atomic Energy Regulatory Board (AERB). Equipment Calibration and Radiation Safety Guidelines. 2022.*
5. *Dental Council of India. Radiographic Identification and Labeling Standards. 2022.*
6. *Dental Protection Limited. Missed Lesion Litigation in Dental Radiology. 2021.*
7. *National Medical Commission (India). Second Opinion and Escalation of Diagnostic Doubt Guidelines. 2021.*
8. *General Dental Council (UK). Communication of Significant Findings in Radiology. 2013.*
9. *Ministry of Health and Family Welfare, India. Medical Record Retention and Archival Rules. 2020.*
10. *Government of India. Medical Data Integrity and Amendments Regulation. 2019.*
11. *Atomic Energy Regulatory Board (AERB). Radiation Worker Safety and Dosimetry Manual. 2022.*
12. *National Medical Commission (India). Radiologic Reporting and Expert Testimony Standards. 2021.*

SECTION 7

Prosthodontics, Forensics, and Ethical Governance

When the cutting is done and the healing holds, dentistry turns to rebuilding — not just form and function, but trust. This closing section gathers the professions' higher ground: restoration, identification, and integrity. It speaks to how a clinician closes loops — with craftsmanship, conscience, and clear documentation.

It opens with prosthodontics, where the science of replacement meets the art of realism. Each restoration, denture, or maxillofacial prosthesis becomes a signed declaration of competence. The details that matter — occlusion charts, shade notes, lab communications, and patient approvals — are presented not as formalities but as defensive signatures. A crown or bridge can fail; a well-kept record cannot.

Next comes forensic odontology — where the same clinical habits serve justice. Bite marks, dental records, and identification protocols show how your daily documentation might one day speak in your absence. This chapter grounds forensic participation in chain-of-evidence ethics and courtroom clarity.

Then the section widens: medical negligence, insurance disputes, billing transparency, and the legal expectations of financial honesty. The reader learns to balance commerce with conscience, keeping every transaction traceable and every claim verifiable.

Finally, ethics steps forward — not as philosophy but as routine behavior. Disclosure, boundaries, and truth-telling become tools as essential as scalers or mirrors. The book closes with what follows every clinical act: reflection. How you testify, how you explain, and how you carry professional accountability define not only your defense but your dignity.

By the end, this section completes the circle — from sterilization to ethics, from instruments to integrity. Dentistry begins with precision of hand; it ends with precision of character.

CHAPTER 55

Oral and Maxillofacial Prosthetics - Rehabilitation, Documentation, and Legal Obligations of Functional Outcome

Maxillofacial prosthetics is not just about replacing what is lost - it is about restoring the patient's ability to eat, speak, and meet their reflection without shame. Every prosthesis becomes part of the person's identity, and when it fails, the patient often seeks justice, not just repair. This chapter outlines how a prosthodontist can merge artistry with defensibility: detailed documentation, informed consent, and follow-up that proves care did not stop at delivery.

Purpose and Indications

Maxillofacial prosthetics restores function and appearance following trauma, tumor resection, congenital defects, or disease. Indications include obturators, facial prostheses, speech aids, and implant-retained appliances. The legal dimension demands documented functional assessment, written communication of expectations, and traceable fabrication steps for every prosthesis provided [1].

Preparation and Case Evaluation

Record medical and surgical history, residual defect type, radiographs, tissue condition, and psychological readiness. Photograph pre-prosthetic condition. Discuss limitations (retention, maintenance, life span).

Red flag: Delivering prosthesis without pre-treatment photos or written limitation note leaves practitioner defenseless if patient later alleges disfigurement or poor function [2].

- ***Step 1: Informed Consent and Expectation Setting***

Explain design, materials, esthetic limitations, adjustment needs, and potential for mechanical or biological complications. Obtain signed consent stating "prosthesis is artificial, requires maintenance, and may not fully restore appearance or function."

Red flag: Absence of explicit expectation-management clause makes dissatisfaction legally indefensible - perfection is assumed when limitation is undocumented [3].

- ***Step 2: Impression and Jaw Relation Records***

Take primary and final impressions under asepsis. Note materials, batch numbers, and date. Record jaw relation with photographs.

Red flag: Missing impression material record or date breaks traceability; contaminated or unidentified impressions compromise medico-legal credibility [4].

- ***Step 3: Laboratory Communication and Fabrication Record***

Send prescription form to lab specifying design, material, shade, and instructions. Maintain signed lab receipt and final fabrication log.

Red flag: No lab form or fabrication record converts mechanical failure into presumed clinical negligence [5].

- ***Step 4: Try-In and Verification***

Conduct esthetic and functional try-in with patient consent for adjustments. Record acceptance with signature.

Red flag: Delivering final prosthesis without documented try-in acceptance nullifies defense in dissatisfaction or speech impairment complaints [6].

- ***Step 5: Delivery and Patient Education***

Fit prosthesis, evaluate comfort, phonetics, and occlusion. Provide written care instructions: hygiene, removal, and storage.

Red flag: Verbal instruction alone invalidates claims of patient negligence - written proof of education is essential for defense [7].

- ***Step 6: Follow-Up and Adjustment Records***

Schedule review at one week, one month, and six months. Record adjustments, relines, or repairs.

Red flag: Absence of follow-up entries implies abandonment of prosthetic maintenance - legally classified as incomplete rehabilitation [8].

- ***Step 7: Material and Device Traceability***

Keep records of manufacturer, batch, and lot numbers for all components, especially in implant-retained prostheses.

Red flag: Lost or undocumented batch data breaches medical device traceability law and shifts liability entirely onto the operator [9].

- ***Step 8: Complication Management and Disclosure***

Record fractures, ulcerations, or implant loosening. Document communication of problem and corrective action plan.

Red flag: Silent repairs or replacements without written disclosure count as concealment - a severe ethical and legal breach [10].

- ***Step 9: Psychological and Social Reintegration***

Record counseling or referral for patients with visible facial defects. Note discussions on prosthesis wear time and camouflage.

Red flag: Ignoring psychosocial adjustment needs may be interpreted as incomplete rehabilitation or emotional negligence in court [11].

- ***Step 10: Record Retention and Certification***

Maintain complete file - consent, design forms, lab receipts, photos, and follow-ups - for at least 10 years. Provide patient with prosthesis identification card (name, date, material).

Red flag: Missing fabrication proof or ID card creates doubt of authenticity in product liability or allergic reaction cases [12].

Legal Defensibility and Documentation Anchors

A defendable prosthetic rehabilitation file must include:

- Pre-treatment photographs and evaluation
- Written consent with limitation and maintenance clauses
- Impression, material, and lab records with batch data
- Try-in acceptance note
- Delivery and patient education sheet
- Adjustment and complication records

- Psychological counseling note (if relevant)
- Prosthesis identification card and 10-year record archive

This framework proves diligence, transparency, and patient engagement-core to both ethics and law.

Case Study

A 55-year-old man received obturator prosthesis after maxillectomy. Two months later, it fractured. The patient alleged poor design. The dentist produced lab forms, batch details, try-in acceptance, and signed care instructions. Court dismissed the claim, citing adequate disclosure and documented maintenance education.

Case Learnings

1. Every prosthesis is a contract - clarity protects both parties.
2. Written limitation and maintenance clauses preempt most disputes.
3. Laboratory and batch traceability make mechanical failures defendable.
4. Signed patient education notes carry more legal weight than testimony.
5. Rehabilitation without records is charity, not practice.

Quick Checklist

- Pre-treatment evaluation and photos recorded
- Consent includes limitations and maintenance clause
- Impression and material batch logged
- Lab form and fabrication record signed
- Try-in acceptance documented
- Written care instructions provided
- Follow-up adjustments recorded
- Batch and component traceability maintained
- Complications disclosed and noted
- Records retained minimum 10 years

References

1. *Beumer J III, Curtis TA, Marunick MT. Maxillofacial Rehabilitation: Prosthodontic and Surgical Considerations. 4th ed. Quintessence; 2020.*
2. *Ministry of Health and Family Welfare, India. Pre-Rehabilitation Documentation Protocols. 2020.*
3. *General Dental Council (UK). Consent and Expectation Management in Prosthodontics. 2013.*
4. *Dental Council of India. Impression Material Safety and Traceability Standards. 2022.*
5. *World Health Organization. Medical Device Communication and Documentation in Dentistry. Geneva; 2018.*
6. *Dental Protection Limited. Legal Review of Prosthetic Dissatisfaction Claims. 2021.*
7. *National Medical Commission (India). Patient Education and Maintenance Responsibility Guidelines. 2021.*
8. *Ministry of Health and Family Welfare, India. Rehabilitation Follow-Up Documentation Standards. 2020.*
9. *Government of India. Medical Device Rules. 2019.*
10. *National Medical Commission (India). Adverse Event Disclosure Norms. 2021.*
11. *Dental Council of India. Psychosocial Rehabilitation and Counseling Protocols. 2022.*
12. *Ministry of Health and Family Welfare, India. Record Retention and Identification Card Standards. 2020.*

CHAPTER 56

Forensic Odontology - Identification, Evidence Handling, and Legal Testimony Standards

Forensic odontology is where dentistry leaves the clinic and enters the courtroom. Here, impressions, restorations, and bite marks are not treatment-they are testimony. The credibility of the odontologist depends not on dramatic opinions but on disciplined procedure. Every tooth, photograph, and cast is a legal artifact; once misplaced, the truth itself is lost. This chapter defines the forensic workflow that protects both justice and the clinician from error or accusation.

Purpose and Indications

Forensic odontology applies dental science to human identification, age estimation, bite mark analysis, and examination of dental evidence in civil or criminal investigations. Indications include disaster victim identification (DVI), assault cases, malpractice investigations, and mass casualties. Legally, every action must preserve chain of custody and maintain objectivity-findings must serve fact, not narrative [1].

Preparation and Authorization

Work only upon written request from legal or investigative authority. Verify identity of deceased or patient, case number, and jurisdiction. Record the date, officer in charge, and evidence condition before handling.

Red flag: Conducting forensic analysis without authorization or documentation converts findings into inadmissible evidence, discrediting the expert and violating legal procedure [2].

- ***Step 1: Scene and Evidence Documentation***

Photograph remains or evidence before manipulation using scale and case

ID. Record GPS coordinates, lighting, and orientation. Maintain digital and printed copies.

Red flag: Absence of pre-handling photographs invalidates the integrity of all subsequent records; "no image, no proof" [3].

- ***Step 2: Collection and Labeling of Dental Evidence***

Collect dental fragments, prostheses, or radiographs using sterile technique. Label each item with case number, description, and handler initials. Seal in tamper-proof bag with signature across seal.

Red flag: Unlabeled or unsealed dental specimens break chain of custody-rendering even accurate analysis inadmissible [4].

- ***Step 3: Postmortem Examination and Charting***

Document all teeth, restorations, prostheses, anomalies, and pathologies. Use standard forensic odontogram (Federation Dentaire Internationale system).

Red flag: Incomplete charting or use of non-standard notation confuses court interpretation-rejected under evidentiary standards [5].

- ***Step 4: Antemortem Data Collection***

Retrieve dental records, radiographs, and prosthetic details from treating dentist. Verify authenticity through signature and clinic seal.

Red flag: Presenting unauthenticated records violates evidence reliability standards; courts require verification from source [6].

- ***Step 5: Comparison and Analysis***

Perform dental, radiographic, and morphological comparison between antemortem and postmortem data. Document points of concordance and discrepancy with photographic overlays.

Red flag: Reporting opinion without visual correlation or annotated evidence is interpreted as speculative and non-expert [7].

- ***Step 6: Bite Mark Analysis (When Applicable)***

Photograph bite mark with scale at multiple angles. Make silicone impressions of suspect dentition. Compare using transparent overlays or 3D scans. Record methodology and limitations.

Red flag: Expressing certainty without noting limitations in bite mark comparison violates forensic reporting ethics and has been repeatedly challenged in court [8].

- ***Step 7: DNA Sampling and Preservation***

If required, extract pulpal tissue, dentin, or saliva under sterile conditions. Label and store in approved DNA evidence tube. Record chain-of-custody transfer to forensic lab.

Red flag: DNA sample collected or transported without logged handover invalidates biological evidence by law [9].

- ***Step 8: Reporting and Opinion Formation***

Prepare written report including background, methods, observations, and conclusions based on evidence only. Avoid suggestive or speculative statements. Sign with credentials, date, and registration number.

Red flag: Subjective or conclusive statements beyond data interpretation ("match confirmed beyond doubt") are inadmissible unless validated statistically [10].

- ***Step 9: Court Presentation and Testimony***

Submit report through proper legal channel. Present findings neutrally, using photographs and diagrams. Respond only to questions within expertise.

Red flag: Introducing new opinions or data in court not included in written report violates evidentiary law and undermines credibility [11].

- ***Step 10: Record Retention and Confidentiality***

Retain duplicate records, photographs, and chain-of-custody logs for minimum 10 years. Do not disclose information outside court or investigation.

Red flag: Public or social media disclosure of forensic details breaches confidentiality laws and professional ethics [12].

Legal Defensibility and Documentation Anchors

A defendable forensic record includes:

- Written authorization and case ID
- Pre-handling photographs and documentation
- Properly labeled and sealed evidence
- Standard odontogram and authenticated antemortem data
- Methodical comparison with annotated proof

- Chain-of-custody logs
- Objective report signed and dated
- Retention and confidentiality compliance

This structure demonstrates impartiality, procedural integrity, and professional competence-essential in both justice and self-defense.

Case Study

A forensic odontologist identified a disaster victim using partial dentures. However, no photographic proof of pre-analysis condition or seal logs existed. Despite correct identification, the court rejected the report, ruling "procedural violation of evidence handling," nullifying weeks of work.

Case Learnings

1. Accuracy without procedure has no legal value.
2. Every sample handled must carry its signature of custody.
3. Bite mark certainty is obsolete; limitations must be stated.
4. Photographic and chain-of-custody proof outweigh opinion.
5. The best forensic report sounds factual, not dramatic.

Quick Checklist

- Official authorization and case ID verified
- Scene and specimen photographed with scale
- Evidence labeled, sealed, and logged
- Postmortem charting completed using FDI system
- Antemortem records verified and authenticated
- Comparison documented with overlays and photos
- DNA samples logged and transferred securely
- Report factual, signed, and dated
- Confidentiality maintained
- Records archived minimum 10 years

References

1. *Pretty IA, Sweet D. Forensic Odontology: A Review. Forensic Sci Int. 2001;120(2-3):173 - 182.*
2. *Ministry of Home Affairs, India. Forensic Evidence Handling Protocols. 2020.*
3. *International Criminal Police Organization (INTERPOL). DVI Guide: Disaster Victim Identification. 2021.*
4. *National Medical Commission (India). Chain of Custody Documentation Standards. 2021.*
5. *Dental Council of India. Forensic Odontogram and Recordkeeping Guidelines. 2022.*
6. *World Health Organization. Guidelines for Forensic Evidence Authentication. Geneva; 2019.*
7. *Dorion RBJ. Bitemark Evidence: A Color Atlas and Text. CRC Press; 2011.*
8. *National Academy of Sciences (USA). Strengthening Forensic Science in the United States. 2009.*
9. *Government of India. DNA Technology (Use and Application) Regulation Bill. 2019.*
10. *General Dental Council (UK). Expert Witness and Forensic Reporting Standards. 2013.*
11. *Ministry of Law and Justice, India. Indian Evidence Act (Sections 45 - 51). 2020 Amendment.*
12. *Dental Protection Limited. Confidentiality and Legal Conduct in Forensic Testimony. 2021.*

CHAPTER 57

Medical Negligence in Dental Practice - Legal Framework, Documentation Defense, and Risk Management Strategies

Negligence is not about harm alone-it is about proof of preventable harm. In dentistry, even minor injuries can become legal landmarks when notes are missing, consent is vague, or communication fails. This chapter defines what negligence means in law, how to prevent it in practice, and how to defend one's conduct when judgment is questioned. The aim is not fear-it is foresight.

Purpose and Definition

Medical negligence arises when a professional duty of care is breached, leading to damage that could have been avoided with reasonable skill. The core legal tests remain *duty, breach, causation, and damage*. Dentistry's risks lie in documentation gaps-when charts, not care, fail to protect the clinician [1].

Preparation and Awareness

Understand that every act in the dental chair is both clinical and contractual. Keep updated with consumer protection law, clinical establishment regulations, and professional conduct rules.

Red flag: Claiming ignorance of patient rights or documentation norms does not exempt liability; law expects competence, not perfection [2].

- ***Step 1: Establishing Duty of Care***

Once a patient registers, duty begins. Record demographic details, diagnosis, and treatment plan. Display registration, fee structure, and consent policy publicly.

Red flag: Absence of clinic registration or displayed credentials implies unqualified service and weakens legal standing from the start [3].

- ***Step 2: Informed Consent and Risk Disclosure***

Obtain procedure-specific written consent, explaining benefits, alternatives, risks, and complications. Provide copy to patient.

Red flag: Generic consent ("I agree to dental treatment") is legally void; each procedure must have its own consent form [4].

- ***Step 3: Standard of Care and Clinical Protocols***

Follow accepted professional norms and guidelines-sterilization, anesthesia monitoring, and evidence-based practice.

Red flag: Deviation from guidelines without justification is treated as "reckless indifference," not discretion [5].

- ***Step 4: Communication and Documentation***

Record every interaction-diagnosis, advice, refusal of treatment, or missed appointments. Use progress notes with date, time, and signature.

Red flag: Missing entries imply absence of action; courts view blank spaces as silence against the dentist [6].

- ***Step 5: Emergency Preparedness***

Maintain emergency drugs, oxygen, and staff trained in basic life support. Record drills and equipment expiry checks.

Red flag: Patient collapse without documented readiness is considered gross negligence, regardless of underlying cause [7].

- ***Step 6: Confidentiality and Record Retention***

Preserve patient data securely; share only with consent or by law. Retain records for 10 years (adults) and until majority for minors.

Red flag: Lost or destroyed files during litigation period imply concealment and attract presumption of guilt [8].

- ***Step 7: Communication After Complication***

If an adverse event occurs, inform the patient promptly, record discussion, and outline next steps.

Red flag: Concealment or delayed disclosure converts minor complications into legal violations of honesty and ethics [9].

- ***Step 8: Referral and Continuity of Care***

When beyond one's expertise, refer in writing to appropriate specialist or facility. Record reason and communication.

Red flag: Failure to refer or undocumented referral is interpreted as abandonment of care-among the most common negligence verdicts [10].

- ***Step 9: Complaint Response and Defense Preparation***

Respond calmly to complaints; provide documented chronology and copies of records. Seek legal counsel before replying to legal notices.

Red flag: Emotional or defensive written replies without review can self-incriminate; always respond factually, not sentimentally [11].

- ***Step 10: Institutional and Insurance Safeguards***

Maintain professional indemnity insurance and clinic compliance certificates (biomedical waste, radiation safety, sterilization). Conduct annual medico-legal audits.

Red flag: Practicing without insurance or compliance records makes even baseless claims financially ruinous [12].

Legal Defensibility and Documentation Anchors

A defensible dental record system includes:

- Registration and patient intake data
- Procedure-specific consent forms
- Progress and communication notes
- Emergency preparedness log
- Referral and follow-up documentation
- Complication disclosure records
- Retained and indexed archives
- Compliance and insurance proof

Together, these form a visible pattern of vigilance-the difference between negligence and professional judgment.

Case Study

A 34-year-old patient developed paresthesia after lower molar extraction. The dentist had explained risk verbally but had no written consent or preoperative radiograph. Despite acceptable technique, the consumer court ruled negligence for "failure of disclosure and documentation," awarding compensation.

Case Learnings

1. Law protects skill supported by records, not memory.
2. Every consent must match the specific act performed.
3. Timely, honest communication prevents escalation.
4. Referral and recordkeeping are shields against shared blame.
5. Negligence is often proven not by error, but by absence of evidence.

Quick Checklist

- Clinic registration and credentials displayed
- Procedure-specific consent signed
- Progress and communication notes maintained
- Emergency drugs and drills documented
- Referral and follow-up records filed
- Complication disclosures recorded
- Records archived minimum 10 years
- Confidentiality maintained
- Professional indemnity active
- Annual compliance audits performed

References

1. *Indian Penal Code, 1860 - Section 304A (Death by Negligence).*
2. *Consumer Protection Act, 2019 - Chapter VI, Medical Services.*
3. *Clinical Establishments (Registration and Regulation) Act, 2010.*
4. *General Dental Council (UK). Consent and Risk Disclosure Principles. 2013.*
5. *National Medical Commission (India). Standard Treatment and Clinical Protocols. 2021.*
6. *Dental Council of India. Clinical Documentation Standards. 2022.*
7. *Ministry of Health and Family Welfare, India. Emergency Preparedness and Safety in Dental Practice. 2020.*
8. *Government of India. Digital Health Data Management Policy. 2021.*
9. *Dental Protection Limited. Managing Adverse Events and Patient Communication. 2021.*
10. *National Medical Commission (India). Referral Obligations and Escalation Guidelines. 2021.*
11. *Ministry of Law and Justice, India. Civil Procedure and Evidence Disclosure Acts. 2020.*
12. *Insurance Regulatory and Development Authority of India (IRDAI). Professional Indemnity Policy Guidelines. 2020.*

CHAPTER 58

Documentation Templates and Case Audit Framework - From Recordkeeping to Legal Readiness

Good documentation does not begin with handwriting-it begins with anticipation. Every line in a patient record speaks for the clinician when silence follows a complaint. A neat, complete, time-stamped note is the simplest and strongest evidence of integrity. This chapter brings together the structure, rhythm, and legal purpose of documentation in modern dental practice, showing how each entry transforms from routine record to courtroom defense.

Purpose and Scope

Clinical documentation ensures continuity of care, audit readiness, and medico-legal defense. Templates standardize how findings, procedures, and communications are captured. A well-structured file protects both patient rights and practitioner accountability. Legally, any undocumented action is assumed never to have occurred [1].

Preparation and Record Framework

Use standardized forms: history, consent, operative notes, anesthesia records, and follow-up sheets. Assign each patient a unique ID and maintain both physical and digital backups.

Red flag: Missing patient ID or unsigned record invalidates every entry; the law recognizes only authenticated documentation [2].

- ***Step 1: Patient Registration and Demographics***

Collect complete personal details, contact numbers, identification proof, and emergency contact. Obtain signature verifying accuracy.

Red flag: Anonymous or incomplete registration weakens traceability-vital for court summons, insurance, or communication [3].

- ***Step 2: Medical and Dental History Template***

Record systemic diseases, medications, allergies, previous surgeries, and bleeding history. Include question on tobacco and alcohol use.

Red flag: Undocumented comorbidities expose clinician to liability for "failure to elicit and record risk factors" in any adverse event [4].

- ***Step 3: Clinical Examination and Charting***

Record extraoral and intraoral findings, probing depths, mobility, restorations, and radiographic interpretation. Date, sign, and store diagrammatic chart.

Red flag: Lack of pre-treatment chart nullifies later defense against "iatrogenic damage" claims [5].

- ***Step 4: Diagnosis and Treatment Planning Template***

Note provisional and final diagnoses with investigations advised. Record alternatives discussed, costs, and patient's chosen option.

Red flag: No written treatment plan implies absence of informed choice-one of the most common litigation grounds [6].

- ***Step 5: Procedure Documentation and Chairside Notes***

Record anesthetic agent, batch number, dosage, procedure steps, instruments used, and complications. Take pre-, intra-, and post-operative photos when possible.

Red flag: Missing intraoperative note or photo allows assumption of unrecorded deviation from protocol [7].

- ***Step 6: Consent and Communication Records***

Attach signed, dated consent with specific procedure name and risks explained. Keep copy of pre- and post-discussion notes.

Red flag: Verbal consent is legally invisible; courts only accept written and signed acknowledgment [8].

- ***Step 7: Postoperative Instructions and Follow-Up Record***

Provide printed instructions with signature of both patient and assistant. Record revisit schedule, telephonic follow-ups, and advice given.

Red flag: Absence of discharge advice record shifts blame entirely to operator for any postoperative complication [9].

- ***Step 8: Complication and Adverse Event Log***

Maintain separate register for complications-nature, management, outcome, and date of disclosure.

Red flag: Unlogged complications suggest concealment and raise suspicion of malpractice [10].

- ***Step 9: Audit and Quality Review Template***

Audit 10% of records quarterly for completeness, consent validity, and complication documentation. Sign audit summary and corrective action plan.

Red flag: Clinics without periodic audits fail statutory quality requirements; absence of self-review is seen as institutional indifference [11].

- ***Step 10: Record Retention, Backup, and Disposal***

Retain all files minimum 10 years; for minors, until 3 years after reaching adulthood. Use encrypted storage for digital records and authorized destruction with certificate after expiry.

Red flag: Loss or premature destruction of record during litigation window constitutes obstruction of justice [12].

Legal Defensibility and Documentation Anchors

A legally defensible documentation system must include:

- Unique patient ID with registration verification
- Standardized history and examination templates
- Procedure-specific consent and operative note
- Photographs and imaging records
- Complication and communication logs
- Signed postoperative instructions
- Audit reports and retention certificates
- Data backup and controlled access logs

Together they form the backbone of legal readiness-transparent, time-bound, and tamper-proof.

Case Study

A 37-year-old woman alleged improper crown fit leading to chronic pain. The dentist produced history, charting, anesthesia records, intraoperative photos, consent form, and signed follow-up sheet showing patient satisfaction before complaint. The consumer court dismissed the case, citing "complete and authenticated documentation."

Case Learnings

1. Every record speaks louder than recollection.
2. Templates create consistency, consistency builds credibility.
3. Signed consent and photographs neutralize most disputes.
4. Audits prevent negligence before it matures into litigation.
5. Organized records reflect professional ethics beyond compliance.

Quick Checklist

- Unique ID and registration verified
- History and charting templates completed
- Treatment plan and cost options noted
- Procedure and anesthesia details recorded
- Consent signed and stored
- Postoperative instructions acknowledged
- Complications logged and reviewed
- Quarterly audits performed
- Digital and paper backups secured
- Retention certificate filed after 10 years

References

1. *Ministry of Health and Family Welfare, India. Medical Records and Documentation Rules. 2020.*
2. *Dental Council of India. Standardized Clinical Recordkeeping Protocols. 2022.*
3. *National Medical Commission (India). Patient Registration and Traceability Guidelines. 2021.*
4. *General Dental Council (UK). Recording of Medical History and Risk Assessment Standards. 2013.*
5. *Dental Protection Limited. Recordkeeping and Litigation in Dental Practice. 2021.*
6. *Consumer Protection Act, 2019 (India). Section on Medical Services Documentation.*
7. *National Medical Commission (India). Operative Note and Procedural Documentation Standards. 2021.*
8. *Ministry of Law and Justice, India. Legal Validity of Written Consent in Healthcare. 2020.*
9. *Dental Council of India. Discharge and Postoperative Instruction Protocols. 2022.*
10. *Government of India. Adverse Event Reporting and Transparency Regulation. 2020.*
11. *National Accreditation Board for Hospitals and Healthcare Providers (NABH). Dental Clinic Audit Guidelines. 2021.*
12. *Ministry of Health and Family Welfare, India. Record Retention and Disposal Rules. 2020.*

CHAPTER 59

Ethical Decision-Making and Professional Conduct - Boundaries, Disclosure, and Accountability in Dental Practice

Skill earns trust; conduct sustains it. A dentist's actions are judged not only by outcomes but by intent and transparency. Ethics in dentistry begins where manuals end-at moments of hesitation, disclosure, or temptation. This chapter converts abstract ethics into clear, documentable behavior that protects patient dignity and professional honor.

Purpose and Relevance

Ethical decision-making governs honesty in diagnosis, respect in consent, confidentiality in recordkeeping, and integrity in billing. The legal and moral frameworks often overlap; both demand traceable fairness. Every clinical choice carries two outcomes-clinical success and ethical consequence [1].

Preparation and Awareness

Understand core principles: autonomy, beneficence, non-maleficence, justice, and veracity. Incorporate them into each case note, not just lectures.

Red flag: Ethical breaches rarely appear sudden-they begin with skipped disclosures and undocumented intentions [2].

- ***Step 1: Respect for Autonomy and Informed Consent***

Ensure patients participate in decision-making. Provide alternatives and time to decide without coercion. Record written acknowledgment.

Red flag: Rushed consent before procedure is ethically void-consent without comprehension is deception [3].

- ***Step 2: Beneficence and Non-Maleficence***

Choose procedures that maximize benefit and minimize harm, even when profit or convenience tempt otherwise. Document justification for every clinical choice.

Red flag: Performing high-risk or costly procedures without recorded indication invites claims of over-treatment and ethical exploitation [4].

- ***Step 3: Honesty in Diagnosis and Communication***

Disclose uncertainty or diagnostic limits openly. Offer referral when unsure.

Red flag: Concealing doubt violates veracity; false confidence recorded nowhere still becomes negligence in retrospect [5].

- ***Step 4: Confidentiality and Data Protection***

Secure patient records physically and digitally. Release information only with written consent or legal order.

Red flag: Sharing case details or images on social media without consent constitutes ethical misconduct and privacy violation [6].

- ***Step 5: Fair Financial Practices***

Provide transparent cost estimates and receipts. Avoid dual pricing or misleading discount schemes.

Red flag: Hidden charges or verbal fee changes without documentation are viewed as unethical and can trigger consumer litigation [7].

- ***Step 6: Collegial Respect and Referral Conduct***

Acknowledge colleagues' work, avoid defamation, and provide clear referral notes. Maintain professional courtesy in shared cases.

Red flag: Criticizing previous treatment without factual documentation or patient benefit breaches ethical boundaries [8].

- ***Step 7: Managing Conflicts of Interest***

Disclose financial ties with suppliers, companies, or laboratories if influencing patient care.

Red flag: Receiving benefits from manufacturers or laboratories without disclosure can be treated as inducement under anti-corruption codes [9].

- ***Step 8: Handling Patient Dissatisfaction***

Listen objectively, document complaint, and propose resolution. If unresolved, provide referral for second opinion.

Red flag: Arguing or ignoring complaints without record shows arrogance in court and ethics boards alike [10].

- ***Step 9: Continuing Professional Development (CPD)***

Attend periodic CME, skill updates, and ethics workshops. Maintain certificates in clinic file.

Red flag: Outdated skills are silent ethical failures-law now equates non-updation with incompetence [11].

- ***Step 10: Accountability and Self-Audit***

Review case logs monthly for communication gaps, consent errors, or delays. Discuss ethical dilemmas with peers rather than hiding them.

Red flag: Absence of ethical audit log implies indifference to professional responsibility, exposing clinician to disciplinary review [12].

Legal Defensibility and Ethical Anchors

An ethically strong record includes:

- Written consent with comprehension proof
- Clear justification for clinical choices
- Transparent billing and communication logs
- Secure data storage and controlled sharing
- Documented complaints and resolutions
- Ongoing CPD and self-audit records

Such records reflect intent-the invisible layer of legality that decides most judgments.

Case Study

A 45-year-old patient alleged unnecessary root canal therapy for a vital tooth. The dentist produced case notes showing documented vitality test, X-ray, written consent, and patient counseling note on alternatives. Court found no ethical or procedural lapse, citing clear disclosure and documentation of intent.

Case Learnings

1. Ethics is not ideology-it is traceable conduct.
2. Disclosure converts judgment into trust.
3. Every bill, note, or email is a mirror of values.
4. Silence after an error is always louder in court.
5. Updating skill and recording doubt are both marks of maturity.

Quick Checklist

- Consent and comprehension verified
- Treatment justified and documented
- Uncertainty disclosed and referred
- Confidentiality maintained
- Transparent billing and receipts issued
- Professional conduct toward peers upheld
- Conflicts of interest declared
- Complaints documented and resolved
- CPD participation recorded
- Ethical self-audit completed quarterly

References

1. *Beauchamp TL, Childress JF. Principles of Biomedical Ethics. 8th ed. Oxford University Press; 2019.*
2. *General Dental Council (UK). Standards for the Dental Team. 2013.*
3. *Ministry of Health and Family Welfare, India. Informed Consent and Patient Autonomy Guidelines. 2020.*
4. *National Medical Commission (India). Ethical Regulation for Over-Treatment and Commercial Bias. 2021.*
5. *Dental Protection Limited. Ethical Communication and Diagnostic Disclosure in Dentistry. 2021.*
6. *Government of India. Digital Personal Data Protection Act. 2023.*
7. *Consumer Protection Act, 2019 - Misleading Trade Practices Section.*
8. *Dental Council of India. Code of Ethics and Collegial Conduct. 2022.*
9. *Central Vigilance Commission (India). Conflict of Interest and Professional Disclosure Manual. 2020.*
10. *Ministry of Law and Justice, India. Mediation and Grievance Redressal Framework. 2022.*
11. *National Medical Commission (India). Continuing Professional Development and Competency Norms. 2021.*
12. *Dental Council of India. Professional Ethics and Self-Audit Guidelines. 2022.*

CHAPTER 60

Dental Insurance, Billing, and Medico-Legal Implications - Financial Transparency, Fraud Prevention, and Audit Preparedness

In dentistry, the line between service and business is fine - and law watches where the money moves. Billing errors, false claims, or unrecorded discounts can turn a thriving clinic into a criminal file. This chapter lays out the framework of ethical billing, insurance coordination, and financial documentation so that every rupee and every receipt can defend itself in audit or court.

Purpose and Relevance

Billing and insurance documentation protect both patient and practitioner. Transparency builds trust; accuracy prevents litigation. Every financial entry - from estimate to receipt - is a legal record that must align with clinical notes and consent forms [1].

Preparation and System Setup

Maintain separate modules for treatment records, billing, and insurance communication. Use digital software with time-stamped entries. Back up data monthly.

Red flag: Manual billing without backups or invoice numbering allows manipulation suspicion - auditors treat missing bills as evidence tampering [2].

- ***Step 1: Treatment Estimate and Pre-Authorization***

Provide detailed written estimate before treatment. For insured patients, submit pre-authorization with clinical notes, radiographs, and cost breakdown.

Red flag: Starting procedure without pre-authorization violates insurer guidelines and can void coverage, exposing dentist to reimbursement disputes [3].

- ***Step 2: Informed Financial Consent***

Obtain signed patient acknowledgment of estimated cost, possible variations, and non-covered services.

Red flag: Absence of written financial consent turns fee disagreements into legal claims of "hidden cost" or "unfair trade practice" [4].

- ***Step 3: Billing Transparency and Receipts***

Issue computer-generated receipts with tax identification number, patient ID, and treatment code. Maintain copies electronically and physically.

Red flag: Handwritten or missing receipts imply underreporting or tax evasion during audits [5].

- ***Step 4: Insurance Claim Documentation***

Submit itemized bill, clinical notes, operative photos, radiographs, and consent copies to insurer. Keep acknowledgment slip.

Red flag: Fabricated or exaggerated procedure claims constitute insurance fraud punishable under criminal law [6].

- ***Step 5: Coordination with Insurance Providers***

Document every email, message, or call with insurer. Retain pre-authorization numbers and approval letters in file.

Red flag: Missing correspondence records weaken defense in denied-claim disputes; verbal promises hold no legal weight [7].

- ***Step 6: Refunds, Discounts, and Adjustments***

Record any refunds or discounts on the same invoice with reason and signature. Avoid off-record cash adjustments.

Red flag: Hidden cash settlements or unlogged refunds are red flags in financial forensics - treated as concealment [8].

- ***Step 7: Tax and Regulatory Compliance***

Maintain GST registration, invoices, and reconciliation reports. File returns timely and store certificates for seven years minimum.

Red flag: Failure to reconcile tax returns with patient receipts is considered deliberate misrepresentation under revenue law [9].

- ***Step 8: Handling Overcharging or Billing Complaints***

Acknowledge complaint in writing, review treatment and cost, and respond within seven working days. Keep audit note of resolution.

Red flag: Ignoring or deleting billing complaints implies unethical intent - legally equivalent to concealment [10].

- ***Step 9: Insurance Audit and Verification Preparedness***

Keep segregated folders for each insurance claim: pre-authorization, treatment notes, photos, receipts, and correspondence.

Red flag: Mixed or incomplete claim files fail audit traceability; missing supporting documents void legitimate claims [11].

- ***Step 10: Annual Financial Ethics Review***

Conduct yearly review of billing, refund, and claim files. Ensure parity between clinical charts and invoices.

Red flag: Clinics without annual financial audits are unprotected against both tax and medico-legal scrutiny [12].

Legal Defensibility and Documentation Anchors

A defensible billing and insurance system includes:

- Pre-treatment estimate and authorization
- Written financial consent
- Digital, numbered receipts and tax logs
- Complete claim documentation with evidence
- Refunds and discounts recorded transparently
- Insurance communication logs
- Annual financial audit reports

Such documentation demonstrates integrity and foresight - the true markers of lawful practice.

Case Study

A 39-year-old insured patient accused a clinic of double billing - one receipt for insurer and another discounted for cash. The clinic produced time-stamped digital invoices, pre-authorization letters, and bank receipts matching entries. The insurance audit cleared the dentist of wrongdoing and fined the patient for false allegation.

Case Learnings

1. Financial transparency is both ethical and protective.
2. Every invoice must mirror the clinical record.
3. Pre-authorization and written estimates close 90% of disputes.
4. Never adjust off the record - honesty survives audit.
5. Digital time stamps are modern truth witnesses.

Quick Checklist

- Treatment estimate and pre-authorization done
- Signed financial consent obtained
- Receipts issued with ID and tax number
- Claims submitted with supporting documents
- Insurance communication logged
- Refunds and discounts recorded on invoice
- Tax filings matched to patient receipts
- Billing complaints resolved in writing
- Audit files organized by insurer and year
- Annual financial ethics review completed

References

1. *Insurance Regulatory and Development Authority of India (IRDAI). Health Insurance Claims Guidelines. 2020.*
2. *Ministry of Finance, India. Digital Financial Recordkeeping and Tax Compliance Rules. 2021.*
3. *RDAI. Pre-Authorization and Cashless Claim Procedure Manual. 2020.*
4. *Consumer Protection Act, 2019 - Misleading Pricing and Unfair Trade Practices Section.*
5. *Goods and Services Tax Act, 2017 - Dental Healthcare Billing Requirements.*
6. *Ministry of Law and Justice, India. Insurance Fraud and Misrepresentation Provisions (IPC Sec. 420).*
7. *IRDAI. Communication and Audit Retention Policy. 2021.*
8. *National Medical Commission (India). Financial Ethics in Healthcare Services. 2021.*
9. *Central Board of Direct Taxes (CBDT). Medical and Healthcare Taxation Compliance Manual. 2022.*
10. *Consumer Protection (E-Commerce and Billing) Rules, 2020.*
11. *Dental Council of India. Insurance Documentation and Audit Standards. 2022.*
12. *NABH. Annual Audit and Billing Transparency Guidelines. 2021.*

CHAPTER 61

Death in Dental Practice - Legal Obligations, Reporting, and Defensive Documentation

Death inside or shortly after a dental procedure is rare, but when it occurs, it changes the clinic forever. Even if the cause is medical and unforeseeable, suspicion will begin with the records. This chapter outlines how to act, report, and document in the aftermath of a patient death-calmly, lawfully, and with respect for both the family and the evidence.

Purpose and Scope

The goal is not avoidance of blame but preservation of truth. A documented, transparent sequence of actions protects the dentist, staff, and family from chaos and conjecture. Legal compliance demands immediate reporting, preserved evidence, and an unbroken paper trail from incident to investigation [1].

Preparation and Emergency Readiness

Every dental setup must maintain an updated emergency response plan-staff roles, ambulance contacts, crash cart inventory, and escalation protocol.

Red flag: Lack of written emergency plan or BLS training log implies institutional negligence even before death occurs [2].

- ***Step 1: Immediate Medical Response***

Stop all treatment, assess airway, breathing, and circulation. Initiate basic life support, call for ambulance, and document exact time of collapse and resuscitation attempts.

Red flag: No time-stamped CPR or EMS call record creates doubt whether aid was timely-first and fatal legal question [3].

- ***Step 2: Notification of Authorities***

Inform local police and health department immediately. Do not remove body or alter instruments until authorities arrive. Record name, designation, and time of officer contacted.

Red flag: Delayed or informal reporting constitutes concealment under criminal law, even if death was natural [4].

- ***Step 3: Communication with Family***

Inform family in person or via documented call, clearly stating clinical facts and resuscitation efforts. Avoid speculation. Record names and relation of those informed.

Red flag: Casual or evasive communication deepens suspicion-families remember tone more than words [5].

- ***Step 4: Preservation of Records and Evidence***

Seal dental chair, instruments, anesthetic vials, and syringes in presence of witness. Store used materials in labeled bags with signatures.

Red flag: Cleaning or disposing of instruments before inspection is destruction of evidence, punishable under criminal procedure [6].

- ***Step 5: Post-Event Documentation***

Prepare a detailed incident report-timeline, drugs administered, staff involved, vitals, interventions, and time of death declaration. All staff must sign individually.

Red flag: Missing or unsigned event report converts procedural clarity into collective blame [7].

- ***Step 6: Cooperation with Forensic Investigation***

Provide patient file, radiographs, consent forms, anesthesia logs, and CCTV footage if available. Do not alter or add entries post-event.

Red flag: Post-incident edits, even to "clarify," are considered tampering; courts reject all such modified records [8].

- ***Step 7: Institutional and Regulatory Reporting***

Submit mandatory notification to dental council, health authority, and insurance provider. Obtain acknowledgment copies.

Red flag: Failing to inform professional body violates ethics regulations and forfeits indemnity coverage [9].

- ***Step 8: Autopsy and Postmortem Coordination***

Cooperate with authorized forensic expert. Provide drug and anesthetic samples, treatment records, and informed consent forms.

Red flag: Refusing to release records or interfering with postmortem process obstructs justice and amplifies liability [10].

- ***Step 9: Counseling and Support for Staff and Family***

Arrange psychological counseling and written debriefing for staff. Meet family with empathy, not defensiveness.

Red flag: Avoidance or absence of empathy fuels litigation-documentation of humane behavior matters legally and ethically [11].

- ***Step 10: Post-Incident Review and Preventive Audit***

Conduct internal mortality audit within 72 hours. Review system errors, update protocols, and file corrective action report.

Red flag: No follow-up audit implies indifference to prevention and weakens future defense during tribunal hearings [12].

Legal Defensibility and Documentation Anchors

A defensible death-in-practice file includes:

- Written emergency plan and BLS certification logs
- Time-stamped incident record and EMS call
- Witness-signed preservation of evidence
- Complete treatment and anesthesia notes
- Police and health authority acknowledgment letters
- Family communication record
- Autopsy coordination proof
- Mortality audit and corrective report

Such a file demonstrates integrity under investigation-proof of diligence, not guilt.

Case Study

A 52-year-old hypertensive patient collapsed after local anesthesia injection. The clinic performed CPR and called emergency services within five minutes. The dentist documented time-stamped efforts, police notification, and preserved all drugs and syringes. Postmortem showed cardiac arrest unrelated to anesthesia. The inquiry concluded "no negligence," praising thorough documentation.

Case Learnings

1. In emergencies, documentation must run parallel to action.
2. Early police and health authority notification builds credibility.
3. Every time stamp-call, injection, CPR-is a lifeline in court.
4. Transparent behavior reduces family anger and legal aggression.
5. A post-event audit is not self-incrimination-it's maturity.

Quick Checklist

- Emergency plan and BLS log available
- Collapse time and CPR efforts recorded
- Police and health department notified
- Family informed with record
- All instruments sealed and labeled
- Incident report signed by staff
- Forensic cooperation documented
- Regulatory bodies informed
- Psychological support arranged
- Mortality audit completed within 72 hours

References

1. *Ministry of Health and Family Welfare, India. Death Reporting and Medical Incident Documentation Rules. 2020.*
2. *National Medical Commission (India). Emergency Preparedness and BLS Requirements. 2021.*
3. *American Heart Association. Basic Life Support Guidelines. 2020.*
4. *Indian Penal Code, 1860 - Section 201: Destruction of Evidence.*
5. *Dental Protection Limited. Communicating with Families After Adverse Events. 2021.*
6. *Ministry of Law and Justice, India. Criminal Procedure Code, Section 174: Police Inquest.*
7. *NABH. Incident Reporting and Root Cause Analysis Framework. 2021.*
8. *Government of India. Medical Record Integrity and Post-Event Documentation Regulation. 2019.*
9. *Dental Council of India. Ethical Obligations and Reporting Requirements. 2022.*
10. *World Health Organization. Guidelines on Death Investigation and Autopsy Cooperation. 2017.*
11. *National Medical Commission (India). Healthcare Staff Counseling Post-Adverse Event. 2021.*
12. *Ministry of Health and Family Welfare, India. Mortality Audit and Risk Prevention Protocols. 2020.*

CHAPTER 62

The Dentist in Court - Expert Testimony, Cross-Examination, and Defensive Communication Skills

A dentist in a courtroom is no longer a clinician; they are a witness of record. The same calm that guides a root canal must now guide words. How testimony is given often matters more than what is said. This chapter explains how to prepare, present, and protect oneself during legal proceedings-without fear, exaggeration, or evasion.

Purpose and Context

Court appearances arise from civil, consumer, or criminal cases involving alleged negligence, injury, or expert opinion. The aim is to present factual, consistent, and verifiable statements supported by records. The courtroom rewards honesty and penalizes memory. The best defense is precision backed by documentation [1].

Preparation and Familiarization

Review the full case file-records, radiographs, consent forms, communications-before appearing. Discuss with legal counsel to understand sequence and expectations.

Red flag: Entering court without reviewing case notes leads to inconsistencies; opposing counsel will exploit every hesitation [2].

- ***Step 1: Understanding Your Role***

Clarify whether you are a treating dentist, an expert witness, or a fact witness. Stick strictly to that role in testimony.

Red flag: Offering unsolicited opinions beyond role or expertise invites cross-examination traps and undermines credibility [3].

- ***Step 2: Pre-Testimony Briefing and Language Discipline***

Rehearse factual narration-chronology of treatment, discussions, and records. Avoid jargon; speak in plain, clinical terms.

Red flag: Ambiguous or speculative phrases ("I think," "maybe," "probably") weaken testimony and suggest uncertainty [4].

- ***Step 3: Documentation Synchronization***

Ensure every statement aligns with what is written in the file. Carry certified copies only-never original records.

Red flag: Contradictions between verbal testimony and written notes are treated as fabrication, not forgetfulness [5].

- ***Step 4: Demeanor and Communication***

Maintain composure, answer directly, and pause before responding. Address the judge, not the lawyer. Keep tone factual, never defensive.

Red flag: Overexplaining or emotional defense implies guilt; restraint is interpreted as confidence [6].

- ***Step 5: Cross-Examination Handling***

Listen fully, then answer only the question asked. Refer to records if unsure. Admit lack of recollection rather than speculating.

Red flag: Arguing with opposing counsel converts witness into participant; professionalism dissolves instantly [7].

- ***Step 6: Avoiding Speculative or Hypothetical Traps***

When asked "What if you had done differently?", state clearly: "I can only comment on what was clinically indicated and recorded at that time."

Red flag: Entertaining hypothetical answers creates self-contradiction that lawyers can quote out of context [8].

- ***Step 7: Integrity Under Pressure***

If a mistake is pointed out, acknowledge it factually and explain corrective steps taken. Courts respect candor.

Red flag: Denying obvious evidence appears deceptive; honesty softens even adverse findings [9].

- ***Step 8: Presentation of Expert Opinion (if applicable)***

Base expert conclusions on accepted literature, guidelines, and documents provided. State margin of uncertainty where relevant.

Red flag: Giving opinion without citing source or standard protocols renders testimony speculative and inadmissible [10].

- ***Step 9: Post-Testimony Conduct***

Do not discuss case details outside court or with media. Submit any clarifications in writing through legal counsel.

Red flag: Public or social media comments after testimony are contempt of court under disclosure law [11].

- ***Step 10: Emotional and Professional Debriefing***

Court proceedings are draining; document experience privately and review lessons with counsel for future preparedness.

Red flag: Avoid discussing ongoing cases with peers; gossip becomes discoverable evidence in some jurisdictions [12].

Legal Defensibility and Communication Anchors

A defendable court appearance rests on:

- Complete review of all patient and procedural records
- Factual, non-speculative testimony
- Consistency between documentation and speech
- Calm demeanor and concise answers
- Integrity under cross-examination
- Respect for process and confidentiality

A dentist who stays within facts wins credibility, even without winning the case.

Case Study

A 42-year-old patient sued for alleged nerve injury after implant placement. The dentist appeared as the treating clinician. During cross-examination, he referred to radiographs, consent notes, and documented discussions. His composure and factual recall aligned perfectly with written evidence. The court dismissed negligence, noting "clarity, consistency, and truthful restraint."

Case Learnings

1. Truth delivered calmly is stronger than perfect defense delivered nervously.
2. Every answer must return to documented fact.
3. Silence and pause are defensive tools, not weakness.
4. Admitting limits shows professionalism, not incompetence.
5. The court respects integrity more than infallibility.

Quick Checklist

- Review all documentation before hearing
- Clarify role (treating or expert)
- Keep certified copies only
- Speak in factual, plain language
- Avoid speculation or emotion
- Maintain consistent statements
- Handle cross-examination with restraint
- Admit errors honestly if present
- Observe post-testimony confidentiality
- Document lessons for internal record

References

1. *Ministry of Law and Justice, India. Civil and Criminal Procedure Codes - Expert Witness Provisions. 2020.*
2. *Dental Protection Limited. Preparing for Court and Giving Evidence: Dentist's Guide. 2021.*
3. *Indian Evidence Act, 1872 - Sections 45 - 51: Expert Testimony Rules.*
4. *General Dental Council (UK). Professional Conduct During Legal Proceedings. 2013.*
5. *National Medical Commission (India). Documentation Synchronization for Legal Defense. 2021.*
6. *Ministry of Law and Justice, India. Witness Conduct and Communication Ethics. 2020.*
7. *Bar Council of India. Cross-Examination Procedures and Witness Decorum. 2019.*
8. *Government of India. Law of Evidence - Hypothetical Examination Regulations. 2020.*
9. *Dental Council of India. Ethical Conduct and Admission of Error Standards. 2022.*
10. *National Medical Commission (India). Expert Opinion and Evidence-Based Testimony Guidelines. 2021.*
11. *Ministry of Information and Broadcasting, India. Public Commentary and Trial Disclosure Act. 2020.*
12. *Dental Protection Limited. Managing Stress and Professional Reputation After Litigation. 2021.*

APPENDIX 1

Guideline Concordance Table - Linking Clinical Protocols with Legal Requirements

Dentistry today stands on two foundations - evidence-based clinical science and rule-based legal compliance. This concordance table aligns the most frequently applied dental procedures with their corresponding professional guidelines and statutory obligations. It allows the clinician to verify at a glance whether a clinical act also meets the legal test of due diligence.

Purpose and Use

This appendix helps cross-reference every procedural step with the regulatory or ethical framework that governs it. It prevents omission of mandatory documentation and ensures that care remains both clinically sound and legally defensible. Each entry pairs the "what to do" of science with the "how to prove" of law.

Format of Use

Read horizontally. The left column identifies the domain or procedure. The right column lists the parallel legal or regulatory anchors that must be followed or documented. Keep printed copy near treatment records for quick verification.

- ***Sterilization and Infection Control***

Clinical reference: CDC Dental Infection Prevention Guidelines 2021; DCI Sterilization Standards 2022

Legal correspondence: Biomedical Waste Management Rules 2016; Clinical Establishments Act 2010 - Schedule on Infection Control

- ***Local Anesthesia and Pharmacovigilance***

Clinical reference: AHA Basic Anesthetic Safety Update 2020

Legal correspondence: Drugs and Cosmetics Act 1940 - Labeling and Storage Regulation; NMC Drug Safety Guidelines 2021

- ***Consent and Communication***

Clinical reference: AAPD and ADA Informed Consent Recommendations 2020

Legal correspondence: Consumer Protection Act 2019; Ministry of Health and Family Welfare Consent and Disclosure Rules 2020

- ***Radiography and Imaging***

Clinical reference: IAEA Radiation Safety Manual; White & Pharoah Oral Radiology 2023

Legal correspondence: Atomic Energy (Radiation Protection) Rules 2004; AERB Safety Code for Dental Radiology 2022

- ***Prescription and Drug Use***

Clinical reference: WHO Guide to Good Prescribing 2018

Legal correspondence: Narcotic Drugs and Psychotropic Substances Act 1985; Drugs and Cosmetics Rules 1945 (Schedule H and X)

- ***Exodontia and Oral Surgery***

Clinical reference: Contemporary Oral and Maxillofacial Surgery, Peterson 2022

Legal correspondence: NMC Surgical Documentation Guidelines 2021; Dental Council of India Operative Record Norms 2022

- ***Emergency Management and BLS***

Clinical reference: AHA Basic Life Support Algorithm 2020

Legal correspondence: NMC Emergency Preparedness Directive 2021; Occupational Safety and Health Act - Clinic Safety Schedule 2018

- ***Pediatric and Special Needs Dentistry***

Clinical reference: AAPD Behavior Guidance 2022

Legal correspondence: POCSO Act 2012; Rights of Persons with Disabilities Act 2016; Child Consent Documentation Rules 2021

- ***Prosthodontics and Implantology***

Clinical reference: ITI Treatment Guide Vol. 12; Beumer Maxillofacial Rehabilitation 2020

Legal correspondence: Medical Device Rules 2019 - Traceability and Batch Record Requirement; Consumer Protection Act 2019 - Quality and Warranty Clauses

- ***Oral Pathology and Biopsy***

Clinical reference: Neville Oral and Maxillofacial Pathology 2022

Legal correspondence: Biomedical Waste Rules 2016; NMC Chain of Custody and Specimen Handling Protocol 2021

- ***Oncology and Head - Neck Surgery***

Clinical reference: Shah JP Head and Neck Surgery and Oncology 2020

Legal correspondence: National Cancer Grid Guidelines 2021; MOHFW Specimen Margin and Labeling Regulation 2020

- ***Radiology, Prosthetics, and Forensic Odontology***

Clinical reference: IADR Forensic Odontology Manual 2021

Legal correspondence: Indian Evidence Act Sections 45 - 51; DNA Technology Regulation Bill 2019; INTERPOL DVI Guide 2021

- ***Billing, Insurance, and Finance***

Clinical reference: IRDAI Health Insurance Guidelines 2020

Legal correspondence: GST Act 2017; Income Tax Rules 2022; Consumer Protection Rules 2020

- ***Medical Negligence and Legal Defense***

Clinical reference: Dental Protection Limited - Litigation Risk Framework 2021

Legal correspondence: IPC Section 304A; Consumer Protection Act 2019; Clinical Establishments Act 2010

- ***Record Retention and Digital Data***

Clinical reference: NABH Medical Record Manual 2021

Legal correspondence: Digital Personal Data Protection Act 2023; MOHFW Record Retention Rules 2020

- ***Death in Practice and Reporting***

Clinical reference: WHO Death Investigation Guidelines 2017

Legal correspondence: Criminal Procedure Code Section 174; NMC Mortality Audit Protocol 2021; DCI Ethical Notification Standards 2022

- ***Court and Testimony Conduct***

Clinical reference: Dental Protection Limited - Courtroom Preparedness Manual 2021

Legal correspondence: Indian Evidence Act 1872; Ministry of Law and Justice Witness Conduct Regulations 2020

Practical Use Example

A dentist planning surgical extraction consults both Peterson's Oral Surgery (clinical guidance) and NMC Surgical Documentation Guidelines (legal requirement) before beginning. This ensures asepsis, anesthesia, consent, and operative note structure meet national compliance standards. The concordance system thus acts as a pre-procedural checklist and post-procedural audit sheet.

Key Message

Every act in dentistry sits under a twin lens - science and statute. To heal responsibly is to document defensibly. Clinical brilliance is respected; legal conformity is required.

References

1. *National Medical Commission (India). Integrative Clinical - Legal Compliance Guide. 2022.*
2. *Ministry of Health and Family Welfare, India. Clinical Establishments (Compliance and Documentation) Act. 2010.*
3. *Dental Council of India. Regulatory Handbook for Practicing Dentists. 2022.*
4. *World Health Organization. Patient Safety and Health Law Integration Report. 2019.*
5. *General Dental Council (UK). Professional Standards Framework. 2013.*

APPENDIX 2

Legal Lexicon - Practical Definitions and Interpretations for Dental Professionals

Every dentist practices within a legal vocabulary, whether or not they realize it. The meaning of one word in a record can shift the direction of a case. This lexicon lists the essential legal terms every dental professional must understand and apply precisely in notes, consent forms, and communication. It converts legal language into usable, clinic-level sense.

Purpose and Relevance

Dentistry uses ordinary words-negligence, consent, assault, evidence-but law uses them differently. Knowing these meanings prevents casual writing from becoming damaging testimony. Each term below has both a legal and a dental context, written for direct use in documentation or medico-legal explanation.

Act of Omission

Failure to perform an act that a reasonable dentist would have done under similar circumstances.

Example: Not recording a medical allergy before anesthesia.

Legal interpretation: Treated as negligence if omission directly caused harm.

Act of Commission

Performing an act that a reasonable dentist would not have done.

Example: Extracting wrong tooth despite correct diagnosis sheet.

Legal interpretation: Active negligence or reckless conduct.

Adverse Event

An unintended injury or complication arising during or after a dental procedure, not necessarily due to negligence.

Legal use: Must be documented transparently to avoid accusation of concealment.

Assault in Dentistry

Any procedure done without valid consent, even if beneficial.

Example: Extracting retained root without prior discussion.

Legal outcome: Considered assault or battery under consent law.

Autonomy

Patient's right to make informed decisions regarding care.

Legal implication: Every refusal or acceptance must be documented with understanding confirmed.

Breach of Duty

Failure to meet the standard of care expected from a qualified dentist.

Legal test: Did the act fall below that of an ordinarily prudent practitioner?

Burden of Proof

Responsibility to prove or disprove an allegation.

In civil dental cases, burden rests on patient (complainant), but poor records can shift it to the dentist.

Chain of Custody

Continuous documentation of specimen or evidence handling-from collection to report.

Legal relevance: Any break invalidates the evidence.

Compensation

Monetary award to patient for proven negligence or service deficiency.

Legal basis: Granted under Consumer Protection Act or civil law.

Consent (Informed)

Voluntary agreement after full disclosure of procedure, risks, benefits, and alternatives.

Essential elements: capacity, comprehension, and documentation.

Invalid if obtained by misrepresentation, coercion, or omission.

Contributory Negligence

When patient's own actions contribute to harm.

Example: Ignoring postoperative instructions leading to infection.

Effect: Reduces compensation liability of dentist.

Defamation

False statement that damages reputation of another dentist or institution.

Common setting: Criticizing previous treatment without evidence.

Duty of Care

Obligation to act in the patient's best interest according to professional standards.

Begins at first consultation and continues until proper referral or discharge.

Error of Judgment

Reasonable clinical decision that turns out wrong despite due diligence.

Legal interpretation: Not negligence if supported by accepted practice.

Expert Witness

A qualified professional providing opinion based on expertise and evidence, not emotion.

Role: To assist court in understanding technical facts.

Gross Negligence

Extreme departure from standard of care showing reckless disregard for patient safety.

Example: Administering wrong drug concentration knowingly.

Inquest

Official inquiry into cause of death under police or magistrate authority.

Dental context: Required if death occurs during or after dental treatment.

Liability (Civil vs. Criminal)

Civil liability: Compensation for harm caused by negligence.

Criminal liability: Punishment for reckless or willful act causing injury or death.

Malpractice

Professional misconduct due to ignorance, neglect, or lack of skill.

Proof requires duty, breach, causation, and damage.

Material Risk

Any risk significant enough that a reasonable patient would want to know it before consent.

Example: Risk of nerve injury in mandibular implant.

Negligence (Professional)

Failure to exercise reasonable care, skill, or knowledge expected from peers.

Judged using Bolam Test (reasonable doctor rule).

Res Ipsa Loquitur

"Thing speaks for itself." Legal presumption of negligence when outcome is self-explanatory (e.g., extraction of wrong tooth).

Burden shifts to dentist to prove absence of negligence.

Standard of Care

Minimum level of skill, knowledge, and documentation expected from an average qualified dentist.

Dynamic-changes with advances and national guidelines.

Vicarious Liability

Legal responsibility of employer for acts of employees done during employment.

Example: Assistant's error during procedure without supervision.

Volenti Non Fit Injuria

Doctrine meaning "to one who consents, no injury is done."

Applies only when consent was truly informed and documented.

Wrongful Death

Death resulting from negligent or unlawful act during treatment.

Investigated under IPC Section 304A.

Practical Use Note

When drafting or reviewing consent or operative notes, use legal terms precisely:

- Informed consent obtained" instead of "consent taken.
- Adverse event managed and documented" instead of "complication handled.

Precision in words prevents distortion in judgment.

Key Message

The language of law is literal. In records, one misplaced word can reverse years of good work. Write what the law can read, not what habit dictates.

References

1. *Indian Penal Code, 1860 - Relevant Sections 304A, 319 - 338.*
2. *Consumer Protection Act, 2019 - Medical Services and Compensation Clauses.*
3. *Ministry of Health and Family Welfare, India. Consent and Legal Terminology Handbook. 2021.*
4. *Dental Council of India. Ethical and Legal Definitions for Dental Practice. 2022.*
5. *Black's Law Dictionary, 11th Edition. Thomson Reuters; 2019.*

APPENDIX 3

Comparative Framework - International Standards vs. Indian Legal Expectations in Dental Practice

Global dentistry shares the same anatomy but not the same accountability. Clinical protocols may look similar across continents, yet their legal interpretations differ by jurisdiction. This appendix maps how leading international frameworks align-or diverge-from Indian medico-legal expectations. Understanding these parallels helps the clinician adapt global best practices within local law, ensuring both competence and compliance.

Purpose and Utility

Many Indian dentists train or read from international textbooks but practice under Indian law. This comparative framework clarifies what can be adopted directly, what must be adapted, and what requires additional documentation to satisfy Indian regulators.

1. Consent and Autonomy

International standard: Patient autonomy is absolute; verbal consent may suffice for minor procedures (ADA, GDC, AAPD).

Indian expectation: Only written and signed consent is legally recognized, with guardian consent mandatory for minors.

Purpose and Definition Always document written consent, even for scaling or X-rays, to meet national legal defensibility.

2. Recordkeeping and Retention

International: Minimum five years retention (ADA, NHS).

India: Ten years for adults; minors' records must be kept until three years after reaching adulthood (MOHFW 2020).

Practical takeaway: Extend record retention to 10 years; store digital copies with encryption to comply with Data Protection Act 2023.

3. Infection Control and Sterilization

International: CDC guidelines mandate biological monitoring weekly.

India: DCI standards require chemical and biological indicators per cycle, recorded in sterilization logbook.

Practical takeaway: Implement per-cycle biological monitoring and retain autoclave strip documentation for audit readiness.

4. Anesthesia and Sedation

International: ASA guidelines emphasize monitoring and recovery standards; minor oral sedation may be performed in-clinic.

India: MOHFW mandates medical clearance and physician standby for moderate-to-deep sedation in dental clinics.

Practical takeaway: Always document anesthetic drug batch, dose, and monitoring chart; arrange physician standby when deeper sedation planned.

5. Radiographic Safety

International: ALARA principle enforced by ADA and IAEA; lead aprons and thyroid collars recommended.

India: AERB mandates registration of every dental X-ray unit with periodic inspection and staff dosimeter records.

Practical takeaway: Display AERB license, maintain radiation logbook, and renew registration every five years.

6. Advertising and Professional Promotion

International: Dentists may advertise specialty and services within ethical bounds (GDC, ADA).

India: DCI restricts self-promotion, celebrity endorsements, and comparative claims.

Practical takeaway: Avoid words like "best," "painless," or "guaranteed results" in any public medium; focus on factual credentials.

7. Fee Transparency and Billing

International: Price disclosure encouraged but not legally enforced.

India: Mandatory written cost estimate under Consumer Protection Act 2019.

Practical takeaway: Provide printed estimate before treatment; record acknowledgment to prevent later fee disputes.

8. Litigation Process and Expert Testimony

International: Professional boards or indemnity insurers handle initial investigations.

India: Consumer courts and criminal courts directly accept patient complaints without pre-review.

Practical takeaway: Maintain impeccable documentation; cases may proceed without prior peer evaluation.

9. Malpractice Insurance and Indemnity

International: Professional indemnity mandatory (GDC, ADA).

India: Strongly advised but not compulsory; however, hospitals require proof of coverage.

Practical takeaway: Hold indemnity policy covering civil and criminal liability; renew annually.

10. Documentation of Complications and Disclosure

International: Open disclosure encouraged by hospital ethics boards.

India: Disclosure must be recorded in patient file and preferably in writing to family.

Practical takeaway: Always document adverse events and communication; silence equals concealment.

11. Use of Social Media and Patient Data

International: Restricted by GDPR (EU) and HIPAA (USA).

India: Governed by Digital Personal Data Protection Act 2023.

Practical takeaway: Obtain explicit written consent before using patient photographs or testimonials online.

12. Research and Publication Ethics

International: Governed by IRB approval and Helsinki Declaration.

India: Requires Institutional Ethics Committee (IEC) approval and CTRI registration for trials.

Practical takeaway: Never use patient data in publication without IEC clearance and anonymization.

13. Forensic and Identification Work

International: Guided by INTERPOL and DVI (Disaster Victim Identification) standards.

India: Governed by Indian Evidence Act and National Disaster Management Authority protocols.

Practical takeaway: Maintain photographic, radiographic, and dental chart records securely for forensic identification requests.

14. Death in Dental Practice

International: Hospital coroner investigates; report through health system.

India: Mandatory police inquest and autopsy per CrPC Section 174.

Practical takeaway: Always report immediately to local police; non-reporting is treated as concealment.

15. Continuing Professional Development (CPD)

International: 50 - 100 credit hours required over 5 years (GDC, ADA).

India: DCI mandates 30 credit hours every 5 years.

Practical takeaway: Keep CPD certificates in clinic compliance folder for inspection.

Key Message

International standards teach clinical excellence; Indian law demands visible diligence. The clinician who unites both delivers care that withstands audit, inquiry, and time.

References

1. *American Dental Association (ADA). Principles of Ethics and Code of Professional Conduct. 2022.*
2. *General Dental Council (UK). Standards for the Dental Team. 2013.*
3. *Dental Council of India. Code of Ethics Regulations. 2022.*
4. *Ministry of Health and Family Welfare, India. Clinical Establishments (Registration and Regulation) Act. 2010.*
5. *Atomic Energy Regulatory Board (AERB). Dental Radiology Safety Code. 2022.*
6. *Digital Personal Data Protection Act, 2023.*
7. *Consumer Protection Act, 2019.*
8. *National Medical Commission (India). Legal Accountability Guidelines. 2021.*
9. *INTERPOL Disaster Victim Identification Guide. 2021.*
10. *World Health Organization. Global Health Law and Regulation Framework. 2019.*

APPENDIX 4

Practical Templates and Audit Checklists - Ready-to-Use Formats for Daily Clinical and Legal Compliance

Good documentation habits begin with good templates. These ready-to-use formats are designed to make legal defensibility a built-in habit, not an afterthought. Each form can be printed, adapted to clinic software, or used as a daily audit sheet. They simplify compliance by guiding the dentist through what must be recorded and when.

Purpose and Scope

This appendix provides sample templates for clinical use, medico-legal safety, and internal audit. Each template lists only the essential fields required for traceability, verification, and ethical transparency.

1. Patient Registration and Consent Form

- ***Patient Information***
- Name:
- Age/Sex:
- Address:
- Contact:
- Identification Proof No:
- Emergency Contact:

Medical History Summary

- Known systemic illness:
- Current medications:
- Allergies (drug/latex):
- Past surgeries/hospitalizations:
- ***Proposed Dental Procedure***
- Procedure Name:
- Expected Benefits:
- Common Risks Explained:
- Alternatives Discussed:
- Estimated Cost:
- Operator Name and Signature:
- Date and Time of Explanation:

Consent Declaration

I have understood the nature, benefits, and risks of the above procedure. I have been given the opportunity to ask questions and have received satisfactory answers.

Patient/Guardian Signature:

Date:

Witness Signature:

Red Flag Reminder: Never begin procedure unless this form is fully signed and dated by both patient and dentist.

2. Local Anesthesia and Drug Log

- Patient Name / ID:
- Date:
- Anesthetic Agent and Concentration:
- Batch No. and Expiry:
- Volume Used:
- Injection Site:
- Operator:
- Vital Signs Pre-/Post-Injection:
- Adverse Reaction (if any):
- Action Taken:

Red Flag Reminder: Record every anesthetic batch and dose; absence of entry invalidates later defense in allergy or toxicity cases.

3. Operative Procedure Note

- Patient ID:
- Procedure Performed:
- Date and Time Started/Ended:
- Pre-operative Condition:
- Technique Used:
- Instruments / Materials:
- Findings / Complications:
- Photographs Taken (Yes/No):
- Assistant Name:
- Operator Signature:

Red Flag Reminder: Never alter or add entries after completion-use separate addendum note signed with date.

4. Postoperative Instruction Sheet

- Procedure:
- Immediate Care Instructions Given:
- Dietary Advice:
- Medication Prescribed (Name, Dose, Duration):
- Follow-Up Visit Date:
- Emergency Contact Number Provided:
- Patient/Guardian Signature:
- Assistant Signature (for record of verbal reinforcement):

Red Flag Reminder: Provide printed copy to patient; handwritten verbal advice has no legal weight.

5. Complication and Incident Record

- Patient ID:
- Date / Time of Event:
- Description of Incident:
- Immediate Management:
- Persons Present:
- Communication to Family (Time / Person):
- Outcome / Referral Made:
- Operator Signature:
- Witness Signature:

Red Flag Reminder: All incidents must be entered on same day; omission reads as concealment.

6. Sterilization and Infection Control Log

- Autoclave Cycle Date / Time:
- Load Details (Instruments / Trays):
- Chemical Indicator Result:
- Biological Indicator Result:
- Cycle Validated By (Signature):
- Corrective Action (if failed):

Red Flag Reminder: Keep cycle log and indicator strips for three months minimum for inspection.

7. Radiography Register

- Patient ID:
- Type of Radiograph:
- Exposure Parameters:
- Operator Name:
- Justification for Exposure:
- AERB License Number:
- Dosimeter Reading (if recorded):
- Image Storage Location:

Red Flag Reminder: Missing justification entry violates radiation safety rules; record "diagnostic reason" each time.

8. Emergency and Crash Cart Checklist

- Date Checked:
- Adrenaline 1:1000 Expiry:
- Nitroglycerin Tablets Expiry:
- Oxygen Cylinder Pressure:

- Ambu Bag Functioning:
- Airway Devices Present:
- CPR Board / Suction Checked:
- Checked By:

Red Flag Reminder: Empty oxygen or expired adrenaline is direct proof of institutional negligence.

9. Financial Transparency and Billing Record

- Patient ID:
- Procedure Performed:
- Estimate Given:
- Final Bill Amount:
- Receipt Number:
- Mode of Payment:
- Insurance Pre-Authorization Number (if applicable):
- Refunds / Adjustments Noted:
- Billing Staff Signature:

Red Flag Reminder: Every bill must correspond to one clinical note and one receipt-mismatch suggests dual invoicing.

10. Monthly Clinical - Legal Audit Checklist

- Audit Date:
- Cases Reviewed (10% of total):
- Parameters Verified:
- • Consent Form Present
- • Diagnosis Justified
- • Operative Note Complete

- • Complication Log Maintained
- • Billing Linked to Record
- • Follow-Up Documented
- Deficiencies Found:
- Corrective Action Taken:
- Auditor Name and Signature:

Red Flag Reminder: Store audit sheet in compliance folder; lack of periodic audit counts as systemic negligence.

11. Death or Medical Emergency Reporting Form

- Patient Name / ID:
- Date and Time of Collapse:
- Immediate Action Taken:
- Time EMS / Police Called:
- Drugs Administered:
- Staff Present:
- Family Informed (Time / Name):
- Police Acknowledgment Number:
- Operator Signature:

Red Flag Reminder: Report immediately-any delay becomes obstruction of justice under CrPC Section 174.

12. Guardian Consent for Pediatric / Special Needs Dentistry

- Patient Name / Age:
- Guardian Name and Relation:
- Identification Proof:

- Procedure Name:
- Behavior Management / Restraint Type (if any):
- Duration and Indication:
- Risks and Alternatives Explained:
- Consent Declaration:
- Guardian Signature:
- Witness Signature:

Red Flag Reminder: Never use physical or pharmacologic restraint without this separate consent form.

13. Digital Data and Confidentiality Register

- Patient ID:
- Type of Data Stored (X-ray / Photo / Record):
- Purpose of Storage:
- Consent for Digital Use (Yes/No):
- Encryption / Access Path:
- Date of Backup:
- Deletion Approval (after retention period):

Red Flag Reminder: Digital file without consent trail breaches Data Protection Act 2023.

14. Continuing Professional Development Record

- Program Title:
- Organizer / Accrediting Body:
- Hours Earned:
- Date Completed:
- Certificate Number:

- Filed In (Location):

Red Flag Reminder: Keep physical or scanned copy of all certificates-lack of CPD record can imply outdated competence.

15. Patient Feedback and Grievance Form

- Patient Name:
- Treatment Received:
- Satisfaction Rating:
- Comments / Complaint:
- Acknowledged By (Staff Name):
- Action Taken / Date:
- Follow-Up Communication Record:

Red Flag Reminder: Every complaint deserves an acknowledgment within seven days; silence invites escalation to legal complaint.

Key Message

Templates are not bureaucracy-they are proof of discipline. Each completed form converts intent into evidence. The clinic that documents routinely rarely defends reactively.

References

1. *Dental Council of India. Standard Clinical Documentation Templates. 2022.*
2. *National Medical Commission (India). Medico-Legal Recordkeeping Framework. 2021.*
3. *Ministry of Health and Family Welfare, India. Health Establishment Record Standards. 2020.*
4. *NABH. Audit and Quality Compliance Manual for Dental Clinics. 2021.*
5. *Digital Personal Data Protection Act, 2023.*

How to Use These Appendices

These appendices are not meant for academic reading but for daily use. They serve as your silent checklist before, during, and after each procedure - to make sure every act of care is matched by a record of diligence. Each appendix builds on the chapters that came before, turning principles into action and words into proof.

Purpose

The appendices convert guidelines, definitions, and standards into tools that fit a real-world clinic. They simplify legal literacy so you can focus on treatment without overlooking compliance.

Practical Approach

1. Before a Procedure

Review the *Guideline Concordance Table*. Confirm that what you plan matches both scientific protocol and national regulation. Use it as a pre-treatment compliance map.

Red flag: Ignoring a required consent or regulatory form because "it's routine" leaves a legal gap bigger than any clinical one.

2. During a Procedure

Keep the *Practical Templates* close. Fill forms and logs as you go - not after. Real-time recording preserves accuracy and credibility.

Red flag: Retrospective entries, even correct ones, appear suspicious under cross-examination.

3. After a Procedure

Update your *Audit Checklists* weekly. Tick each element only after verifying physical evidence - signed consent, complete note, photograph filed.

Red flag: Partial audit creates false confidence; incomplete logs are worse than none.

4. When Handling Complications or Legal Queries

Refer to the *Legal Lexicon* first. Use legally precise terms in your response, complaint letter, or court statement.

Red flag: Using vague or emotional language ("mishap," "accident") instead of structured terms ("adverse event," "incident report") weakens defense.

5. When Updating Practice or Training Staff

The *Comparative Framework* helps you harmonize international standards with Indian law. Review it annually to keep protocols updated.

Red flag: Blindly importing foreign consent formats or retention policies may violate national rules.

6. For Teaching and Mentorship

Integrate these appendices into resident or assistant training. Ensure every team member can complete each form without supervision.

Red flag: A system is only as strong as its weakest link - if one person skips a step, the whole chain of custody fails.

Key Message

The appendices are living tools. Print them, annotate them, replace them as laws evolve. What you record today may one day stand between truth and accusation. Consistency is the only real shield in dentistry - not fear, not influence, but disciplined paperwork.

References

1. *Ministry of Health and Family Welfare, India. Clinical Establishments Documentation Standards. 2020.*
2. *Dental Council of India. Ethical and Recordkeeping Framework for Dental Clinics. 2022.*
3. *National Medical Commission (India). Compliance Integration Manual. 2021.*
4. *World Health Organization. Practical Guide to Patient Safety Documentation. 2019.*

INDEX OF KEY LEGAL TERMS AND PROCEDURES

- ***Abandonment of Care*** - Failure to provide follow-up or arrange alternative treatment once a professional relationship has begun.
- ***Accountability Log*** - A running record of all critical clinical decisions, signed and dated, proving diligence during complex or prolonged cases.
- ***Adverse Event Reporting*** - Immediate written record of any intra-operative or postoperative complication, signed by attending staff. Essential for *Oral Surgery* and *Anesthesia Failures*.
- ***Batch Number Documentation*** - Recording the lot and expiry details of materials such as grafts, membranes, implants, or cements. Mandatory for traceability and infection-control defense.
- ***Bleeding Documentation*** - Entry describing nature, duration, and management of postoperative hemorrhage. Serves as evidence of prompt response.
- ***Case Audit Framework*** - Structured review tool comparing performed procedures against documented standards; used for internal quality control and defense preparation.
- ***Chain of Custody*** - Verified transfer of biopsy or forensic specimens from clinic to lab, ensuring legal admissibility of reports.
- ***Clinical Photography Protocol*** - Series of standardized images capturing baseline, procedure, and outcome, authenticated by date stamp and consent.
- ***Consent (Informed)*** - Process of explaining diagnosis, procedure, risks, alternatives, and prognosis in language understood by the patient; signed by both parties.
- ***Consumer Protection Act (India, 2019)*** - Primary legal statute governing medical negligence and service accountability for dental practitioners.

- ***Defensible Documentation*** - Entries made contemporaneously, signed, legible, and specific. Forms backbone of every medicolegal defense.
- ***Disclosure Duty*** - Obligation to inform patient of complications, procedural errors, or adverse outcomes as soon as recognized.
- ***Emergency Readiness Record*** - Checklist confirming crash cart, drugs, and oxygen availability with expiry verification; critical in *Foundations and Clinical Setup*.
- ***Expert Testimony*** - Professional opinion presented in court by a qualified clinician, grounded in standard-of-care norms and documented reasoning.
- ***Failure to Diagnose*** - Most common cause of dental litigation. Prevented through comprehensive charting, radiographs, and written risk explanation.
- ***Failure to Refer*** - Omission to transfer a patient when complexity exceeds skill or equipment; treated as neglect if harm results.
- ***Forensic Odontology*** - Branch of dentistry involving identification, age estimation, and bite-mark analysis under legal mandate.
- ***Incident Register*** - Dedicated log for procedural deviations such as file fracture, perforation, or instrument breakage, with signature and date.
- ***Informed Refusal*** - Documentation that patient declined recommended treatment after being fully informed of risks and alternatives.
- ***Legal Chain of Evidence*** - Sequence of proof showing that all records, images, and samples remained untampered and properly stored.
- ***Litigation-Resistant Record*** - File that contains dated entries, consent forms, treatment notes, radiographs, and signed discharge instructions in one traceable folder.
- ***Material Safety Compliance*** - Maintaining sterilization certificates, graft sterility proof, and implant manufacturer data sheets.

- Negligence (Professional) - Breach of standard of care resulting in harm. Determined by deviation from accepted guidelines, not by poor outcome alone.
- Operative Note - Detailed intra-operative summary including anesthesia, incision type, instruments, complications, and closure; signed before discharge.
- ***Patient Communication Record*** - Log of discussions, calls, and advice given outside clinical hours, converted into dated entries.
- ***Referral Acknowledgment*** - Written confirmation from receiving specialist and patient noting referral reason and transfer of responsibility.
- ***Red Flags*** - Clinically significant signs demanding escalation or referral. Found throughout all procedural chapters.
- ***Risk Stratification*** - Assessment of systemic and procedural risks before treatment; foundation of consent and emergency planning.
- ***Standard of Care*** - Level of skill, knowledge, and diligence ordinarily exercised by peers under similar circumstances.
- ***Traceability Folder*** - Central repository of invoices, certificates, and batch details for all biological or implantable materials used.
- ***Vicarious Liability*** - Legal responsibility of employer or institution for acts of subordinates performed within scope of employment.
- ***Written Disclosure Statement*** - Signed explanation given to patient after adverse event, detailing occurrence, corrective action, and follow-up plan.

www.ingramcontent.com/pod-product-compliance
Lightning Source LLC
LaVergne TN
LVHW060543061126
851857LV00017B/1882